THE U.N.
In or Out?

THE U.N.
In or Out?

A DEBATE BETWEEN
Ernest van den Haag
AND
John P. Conrad

With a Foreword by Brian Urquhart

PLENUM PRESS • NEW YORK AND LONDON

Library of Congress Cataloging in Publication Data

Van den Haag, Ernest.
    The U.N.: in or out?

    Includes bibliographical references and index.
    1. United Nations. I. Conrad, John Phillips, 1913-   . II. Title.
JX1977.V276   1987   341.23   87-2552
ISBN 0-306-42524-6

© 1987 Ernest van den Haag and John P. Conrad
Plenum Press is a Division of
Plenum Publishing Corporation
233 Spring Street, New York, N.Y. 10013

Printed in the United States of America

Foreword

I should, at the outset, declare my own interest. After six years in the British Army during World War II, I worked for forty years for the United Nations. Those forty years contained many achievements as well as failures. While I probably know as much as anyone about the shortcomings and caprices of the world organization, I have no doubt whatsoever that it *has* to be made to work better and I believe that it *can* be made to work better. Considering the circumstances of our nuclear world, I am not prepared to accept the probable results of failure to make the United Nations work.

This book sets forth the conviction that we can, and must, shape our fate against a gloomy vision of historical inevitability. Mr. Conrad believes that the United Nations is the school in which the world is learning, and will continue to learn, a better way to manage its affairs. Professor van den Haag believes that war is inevitable—indeed a sovereign right; that there is no such thing as world opinion; and that international law is inconsistent with sovereignty. He believes that the United Nations hinders peace, creates new conflicts and magnifies existing ones, is impotent and useless, and in any case often opposes things which Professor van den Haag favors. His attitude to the United Nations is rather like the attitude of the feudal barons of the Middle Ages to the concept of central government.

Mr. Conrad may err, in company with the victorious World War II leaders, on the side of optimism, but if war is inevitable—if "war inheres in the existence of sovereign nations powerful and independent enough to go to war," as Professor van den Haag believes—presumably we have to accept that nuclear war is also inevitable, in which case the end of the human experiment is inevitable. This seems to me insane.

War among the feudal barons of Europe may have seemed inevitable in the Middle Ages, but when enough people came to the conclusion that it was unacceptable the central authority gained strength and brought a large measure of internal peace, justice, and representative government. In other words, political progress toward a more peaceful and equitable state of affairs was achieved. Why is a similar process inconceivable on the international level, especially with the new incentives of interdependence and the possibility of total disaster?

It is generally conceded that it is desirable, in the words of the United Nations Charter, "to save succeeding generations from the scourge of war." This was the primary purpose of the United Nations, and the organization certainly has a very long way to go to achieve it. If there were another form of international arrangement that could do the job better, obviously the United Nations should be declared obsolete. No such arrangement has so far been suggested, and governments continue to pin their hopes on the United Nations.

The United Nations does not work perfectly and sometimes fails, but surely the answer is not to abolish it. You do not abolish a city police force because the crime rate is going up. You make all possible efforts to make it work better.

Judged by absolute standards, few, if any, political organizations are a complete success. Judged by human problems and human needs, they are essential for present necessities and provide the possibility of a better future. Some people may, of course, wish to return to the haphazard arrangements of the often disastrous past, but in present circumstances this would seem, to put it mildly, unwise.

The United Nations is simply an instrument set up by governments to address great problems of war and peace. The problem is not so much whether a government should be "in or out" of the United Nations, but what is the best method of assuring human survival in reasonably decent conditions. Mr. Conrad believes that in an imperfect world the United Nations provides the best available approach to this objective. Professor van den Haag has no confidence in the United Nations and very little confidence that the objective can be reached at all. The reader of this stimulating book will be given ample basis on which to decide which position is to be preferred.

Brian Urquhart

Preface

Our first encounter, a debate on the value of capital punishment in the administration of justice,* was sufficiently well received to suggest to our publisher that another debate on a great issue would be useful for the clarification of public discourse. Well aware of our differences on the conduct of foreign affairs, we agreed to debate the future of the United Nations and whether the United States should continue its membership. We both are concerned about the state of the world. Yet we are far apart on the remedies we have in mind for the present epidemic of violence and for the danger of war. Conrad holds that the revitalization of the United Nations is essential to a new peace; van den Haag believes that the United Nations will be harmful to peace. A wide gap of principle and opinion—neither of us has managed to convince the other.

Our procedure has been roughly the same as in our first debate. We have exchanged position statements and rejoinders in transcontinental volleys between Manhattan and Davis, California, hoping that our presentations would be sufficiently well reasoned and provocative to catch the thoughtful attention of our readers. We have refrained from *ad hominem* abuse and have tried to keep to a proper level of civil discussion. That restraint did not rule out irony, skepticism, and vigorous denial of the validity of opposing arguments—but both of us are accustomed to verbal combat. We began as friendly adversaries and end with the same mutual respect with which we began.

Although we could not possibly read and digest the vast literature of the United Nations, to say nothing of the inexhaustible

---

*Ernest van den Haag and John P. Conrad, *The Death Penalty: A Debate* (New York: Plenum, 1983).

literature of international affairs and diplomatic history, we felt under some obligation to present a summary narrative of the origins and development of the idea of international organization. Part II contains the history of the idea and its implementation, which we kept neutral, and a descriptive account of the United Nations in operation, which occasioned some differences. The remainder of this book is the debate. As we proceeded, it became apparent that although we were covering a great deal of ground, an effort to deal with all the activities of the United Nations would be endless, exceeding the patience of our readers as well as our own resources for research. No one should conclude at the end of this book that we have swept up all the corners and washed all the windows. There are many issues that we haven't touched. International affairs are in an untidy condition at this stage of history, and it is beyond the capabilities of either of us to introduce order where so much disorder prevails.

A debate suggests a contest in which there is a winner and a loser. No judge makes an appearance in these pages to proclaim the victor in this skirmish. Readers must award the laurels in the privacy of their studies. We hope that some will let us know of their decision.

John P. Conrad
Ernest van den Haag

Acknowledgments

In preparing for this engagement I have incurred more indebtedness than I can settle in these short pages. I shall list some of the most generous creditors without meaning to slight the many who cannot be included here without using more space than I am allowed, but whose suggestions and information were invaluable.

My appreciation must begin with our editor at Plenum, Linda Regan, who proposed this debate. She has been patiently supportive throughout the peculiar processes of collaboration between two opinionated antagonists with inconvenient writing schedules. Her suggestions for the organization of this book have been especially helpful; I hope that we have at least partly fulfilled her expectations.

The United Nations staffs at New York and Geneva have been gracious and imaginative. Few of those whom my wife and I interviewed would allow us to leave them without recommending names of persons whom we should also see for a fuller understanding of some problem under discussion. To gain the perspective from the 38th floor of the Secretariat building, it was particularly useful to meet with Brian Urquhart and William Buffum, both of them undersecretaries-general at the time of our encounters. Robert Muller, now retired from his post as an assistant secretary-general, not only provided us with the benefit of his long and varied experience, as well as his contagious optimism, but also reviewed the historical and descriptive sections of my manuscript. Erskine Childers, of the United Nations Development Fund, and Michael Stopford, of the United Nations Office of Public Information, furnished documents for my reference promptly and relevantly; I don't know what I would have done without them. Paul Diamond, of the U.N. fiscal affairs section, helpfully read my final argument. Angela Gibbs, of the Secretariat staff, was an unfailing guide through the bureaucratic mazes of the U.N. both in New York and in Geneva.

We made a point of interviewing past and present permanent representatives from many nations. Justice Arthur Goldberg, a memorable American ambassador, and Lord Hugh Caradon, permanent representative from the United Kingdom during the dramatic events in the Middle East in 1967, both reflected at length on their experiences. Of the ambassadors now serving in New York, we recall with special gratitude the time given us by Stephen Lewis, the able and enthusiastic permanent representative of Canada, Kishore Mahubani of Singapore, and James Gbeho of Ghana. Gyula Szelei-Kiss, of the Hungarian mission, provided a crisp account of the foreign policies of the Eastern European bloc. Soud Mohamed Zedan of the Saudi Arabian mission discussed the point of view of the Arab nations in general and of the kingdom of Saudi Arabia in particular.

Outside the official orbits Edward Luck, president of the United Nations Association of the USA, and Malcolm Harper, of the United Nations Association of the United Kingdom, were both indispensable. James Olson, of the UNA-USA staff, was an informative guide. Through the good offices of Edith Segall, who serves as U.N. observer for the League of Women Voters, we had the benefit of the close scrutiny that the league has given the United Nations from the very beginning.

This account does not approach an exhaustive acknowledgment of all the help we have received from people who understood what we were trying to do and wanted to help us to do it better. While whatever merit may be found in my arguments must be largely attributed to others, I must reserve to myself the blame for errors of omission and commission.

It is customary in concluding a statement of this kind to proffer a perfunctory tribute to the author's wife, without whose patience, understanding, and good humor whatever was written could not have been written so well. I must go far beyond that convention. My wife, Charlotte Conrad, has been a full participant in the preparation of my side of this debate. She joined me in most of the interviews but found and interviewed some persons on her own. Upon the arrival of Dr. van den Haag's arguments, she reviewed them and suggested responses. Every word of my own manuscript was subjected to her critical review. I fear that she must share the blame for any deficiencies in my share of the debate, but that is the liability that a collaborator must assume.

John P. Conrad

Contents

Part IV: Concluding Statements

PART I

PROLOGUE

PROLOGUE

CHAPTER 1

What Kind of World Do We Want?

JOHN P. CONRAD

The whole world knew the answer to that question in 1945 when the nations allied against the Axis united to draft a charter to preserve the peace to come. In the euphoria at the end of a long and terrible war, good will and the best of intentions seemed to be universal. A world devastated by bombers and tanks would be reconstructed. Differences between peoples would be dissolved in friendship and understanding. The grievous mistakes made by the great powers in the years between Versailles and the Ribbentrop–Molotov treaty would be rectified and never repeated. The nations that had for so many years been locked in mortal conflict would unite to make certain that no such conflict could ever occur again. Delegations from all the allies met in San Francisco to draft a new charter for a new organization for peace, the United Nations. In the preamble to that charter the fundamental aspirations were eloquently set forth:

> WE THE PEOPLES OF THE UNITED NATIONS DETERMINED to save succeeding generations from the scourge of war, which twice in our lifetime has brought untold sorrow to mankind, and

> to reaffirm faith in fundamental human rights, in the dignity and worth of the human person, in the equal rights of men and women and of nations large and small, and

to establish conditions under which justice and respect for the obligations arising from treaties and other sources of international law can be maintained, and

to promote social progress and better standards of life in larger freedom,
AND FOR THESE ENDS
to practice tolerance and live together in peace with one another as good neighbors, and

to unite our strength to maintain international peace and security, and

to ensure by the acceptance of principles and the institution of methods, that armed force shall not be used, save in the common interest, and

to employ international machinery for the promotion of the economic and social advancement of all peoples,
HAVE RESOLVED TO COMBINE OUR EFFORTS TO ACCOMPLISH THESE AIMS

Forty years later. No worldwide warfare yet. There have been about 150 armed confrontations between nations of varying sizes. Some have been no more than skirmishes. Some have been deadly wars, like the Korean "police action" of 1950–1952, the long engagement of France and then the United States in Vietnam, and the callous slaughter of Moslem youth in the interminable war between Iran and Iraq. Did the nations mean what they said when the Preamble was drafted? If they did, do they still mean it? Does peace still matter? Is the idea of the United Nations really more than so much woolly-minded idealism?

I say that the answers to these questions are all affirmative. There are an increasing number of nostalgic politicians and political scientists who hanker after the old ways of diplomacy. Among them is my opponent. This debate is intended to expose and examine the nature of our differences.

No World War III yet. No one credits the United Nations for its prevention. Everyone knows that we have been spared that ultimate debacle—*so far*—by the reciprocal policies of mutual assured destruction that have been adopted and meticulously followed by the United States and the Soviet Union. Terror of the bomb has protected us. Must the world depend forever on terror for its survival?

Survival on such terms alone is not enough, nor is it tolerable for a future projected for the centuries. Peace and order in a context of freedom can be made a realistic prospect through a strategy aimed at the economic and political security of all nations—from the United States and the Soviet Union down to the newest and least advanced postcolonial member of the General Assembly.

That is the foundation of my stand in this debate. The United Nations is the school in which the world will learn a better way to secure the peace than the resumption of the archaic diplomacy of the nineteenth century. Americans and Russians as well as the nations of the Third and Fourth Worlds have much to learn in this school. It's open. Some of the students, among them our own government and its representatives, are strangely ambivalent. My adversary in this debate wishes to close down the school entirely—for reasons that he will doubtless try to make plain. He is certainly not alone. For some time now, we have had a "neo-conservative" movement in the United States that strives for a semianarchic goal. Government is a necessary evil, its spokesmen argue, but if we must have it, let it be minimal, the *least* government we can get along with.* For those who aspire to such a state of affairs, the United Nations does not fit the framework of minimalism in government. There is an abiding fear that the United Nations may become the maximum state—the world government. For the nervous neoconservative the logical course for the preservation of national autonomy is to abolish the United Nations.

A silly fear. In a world in which the ideas of sovereignty and nationalism reign, world government hasn't a chance—even if that were the objective of the United Nations movement, and even if

---

*For an intellectually impressive exposition of this principle, see Robert Nozick, *Anarchy, State and Utopia* (New York: Basic Books, 1974), pp. 297–334.

world government were a good idea—which it isn't. As with any bureaucracy, the United Nations must be watched for wastefulness, needless efforts for needless causes, and failures to proceed when its mission to promote peace calls for action. The fear that it may become too powerful is an absurdity born of ignorance.

For many others, apathy seems to be more becoming. Keep the United Nations alive, they say; attempts to demolish it will cause more trouble and harm than would be gained in diplomatic realism. Admit that it is irrelevant to serious negotiation of international issues. Perhaps most of these issues cannot be negotiated, anyway—the United States would be best off in splendid isolation from involvements of this kind. So speak the tough, neoconservative minds now flourishing in the American seats of power.

I wish to present an alternative to this defeatism. The world need not go up in flames. The best assurance of its safety is the kind of discourse that goes on in its East River headquarters, supported by the programs to improve the health, safety, and prosperity of all nations. In short, the United Nations must be *used*.

Returning to London after the final drafting of the Covenant of the League of Nations, of which he was an architect, Philip Noel-Baker was asked by reporters, "Will the League work?" He answered: "No—did you ever see a spade work?" A spade left idle in the weather will gather rust and eventually become useless—just as the League fell by stages into disuse and futility. The United Nations must be *used* skillfully and often or it will suffer the same fate as its predecessor. History shows that the alternative to the United Nations promises more conflicts, a prospect that humanity can no longer afford.

A plague on the pessimists, the cynics, the uncommitted, and the indifferent. Let them plan for the apocalypse while the rest of us shore up the hope for peace. That hope is fragile in this unruly world. If hope is to be married to reality, the long continuity that we ardently desire must be sustained by the ideals and fortified by the practice enjoined in the Charter of 1945.

The nostalgics long for the delicate balances of power, the tacit recognition of spheres of influence, the treaties that assured the subservience of buffer states, and best of all—they suppose—the quiet diplomacy that made understandings and ententes to keep military power balanced. The disintegration of the Concert of Europe in the nineteenth century led to the "Great Game" of diplomatic maneuver and with remorseless inevitability to the greater game of World War I.[1] No wiser for their experience, the statesmen of the 1920s picked'up the tools of their obsolete craft at Versailles in 1919. Their subtle and purblind maneuvers got the world into World War II.

Old habits die hard. The recent history of the United Nations is filled with examples of circumventions by politicians on all sides of the conflicts that fester in this unruly world. Statesmen on both sides of the Iron Curtain fancy the aggressive, "tough-minded" posturing that gets them credit among the simpleminded for "standing tall." Writing of Napoleon, Henry Kissinger observed that "a man who has been used to command finds it almost impossible to learn to negotiate, because negotiation is an admission of finite power."[2]

For different reasons than Napoleon's, the leaders of the Soviet Union and our own leaders have found it difficult to grant that the powers in their hands are subject to limits that they ignore at their own peril and the peril of the whole world. The Russian masters know that absolute power over their subjects is in their hands. They need not barnstorm the steppes to gain office or trade votes in the Politburo. As for us, the Americans, for the first two decades after World War II we became accustomed to unlimited power both in the United Nations and in all other international transactions. It has not been our way to adjust our demands to the requirements of others. We have always negotiated from strength; when we perceive that our strength is inadequate, we augment it.

Conflicts must be resolved by the arts of compromise and exchange of perceptions of realities. No better place for their resolution could be found than the forums of the United Nations. I turn now to the principal sources of these conflicts that infect the world's peace.

The Troubles We See

In an interview with us, Robert Muller, assistant secretary-general of the United Nations and a veteran officer of the Secretariat, remarked that of the 159 nations constituting the General Assembly, fewer than 20 are disposed to make trouble for their neighbors. Some of the troubles are lethal, as, for example, the foolish and bloody campaigns that Iraq and Iran have been waging against each other for the last six years, the consequences of which are impossible to calculate now but must surely contribute to future disorders, no matter which side is victorious. Other conflicts are studiously restricted to acts of terrorism, espionage, and the rhetoric of abuse. Most nations manage to negotiate their disagreements into settlements without calling out the troops or alerting the fleets and the air forces. Many negotiations are conducted under the auspices of the United Nations or through associated regional organizations such as the Organization of American States or the Council of Europe. Where the good offices of the United Nations Secretariat have been put to use in the resolution of crises, some credit must go to the availability of the United Nations. At least as much credit, sometimes more, must go to the governments of those nations that are willing to submit disputes to international mediation and arbitration. They *use* the United Nations.

The roots of most conflicts that threaten world security are old and familiar. As to some of these frictions, the United Nations should be a laboratory for their resolution. Others defy resolution, but the United Nations can provide the moral and diplomatic resources for their containment. I shall proceed here to some generalizations.

Territorial Conflicts. As old as the hunting tribes that preceded organized states, conflicts over territorial rights continue to oc-

cupy the time of diplomats and attract the attention of dema-
gogues. Such conflicts should be justiciable in the International
Court of Justice, but the more significant the real estate at issue,
the more likely a national leader is to decide that it would be un-
manly to submit the dispute to judicial review in The Hague rather
than to trust to the valor of the nation's fighting men.

Sometimes an arbiter outside of the United Nations can be
found—as when the Pope settled the dispute between Argentina
and Chile on the title to the Beagle Islands (a tiny archipelago
south of Tierra del Fuego), which, if alarmists are to be believed,
might have erupted into a war in which the very honor of both nations would be at stake. Cooler heads submitted the dispute to the
Vatican, and armed hostilities did not ensue. Who knows whether
shots might have been fired in fury over the possession of a group
of desolate islets in one of the world's least habitable climates?

No heads were cool enough to forestall the Argentine invasion
of the Falkland/Malvinas Islands in 1982. The dispute about
sovereignty over this remote and not particularly valuable property was of long standing, but their possession by the British for
well over a century seemed to be all the points of the law.
Nevertheless, the honor, such as it was, of the Argentine military
was at stake, and when the invasion turned into an occupation the
honor of the United Kingdom became at stake, too. The whole
world was fascinated at the spectacle of two such nations deciding
to settle their conflict by force of arms. The Security Council went
into full session for the duration. Although some concessions seem
to have been made by both sides, no settlement could be put together. The British regained possession of the islands at a considerable cost in blood and death. They continue in possession at
an enormous cost in pounds and pence. The Argentine generals
were turned out of their commands as well as the government of
their country. The Falklands/Malvinas tragedy leads to a generalization of obvious but vast importance to the world: *The good
offices of the United Nations are available for the settlement of international conflict, but the United Nations cannot impose a settlement on any nation or nations against their wills.*

From this self-evident truism there follows a lot of willful misunderstanding. Those who suppose that somehow the world would be better off without the United Nations rumble through a strained argument that because the United Nations cannot impose a resolution of such disputes it therefore follows that the organization is a futile waste of money and diplomatic talent.

Watch this line of superficial thought as we proceed in this debate. My opponent will have better arguments to present, but many of his fellow bashers of the United Nations believe that this is all that needs to be said. All of them would be shocked from head to toe if somehow a world government came into being, capable of dictating settlements to all international disputes. That prospect does not attract me, either. If a United Nations Army could be mobilized to mow down violators of the peace, not many Americans would wish to enlist in it, nor is it likely that any president would advocate its support or that any future Congress would authorize funds for its deployment.

We have to face the realities of a disorderly world. If world opinion, moral suasion, and negotiation by the East River cannot restrain generals and admirals in pursuit of military glory and credibility, the United Nations and the rest of the world must watch the cruel spectacle. We must hope that it will end without too much damage to the peoples whom these military men represent. We must do what is necessary after it's all over to restore and maintain the peace.

Anyone with a memory long enough to recall the events of the 1930s will retain indelible memories of the ineffectiveness and ultimately the disastrous futility of the attempts of France and Great Britain to negotiate a containment of the expansionist aspirations of Hitler, Mussolini, and the Japanese military. French and British statesmen were unwilling to use the League of Nations in the stages when Germany, Italy, and Japan were rearming but still weak enough to be restrained. Their depredations continued until neither the Anglo-French initiatives nor the League itself could contain the crazy defiance by the Axis powers. Without the moral force of world opinion mobilized in support of the sadly crippled

League, there was no way that these berserk governments could be prevented from starting the war that eventually ruined them and killed millions of their own innocent citizens, as well as millions more in the nations that allied themselves for defense. Too late it was discovered that the League's armory of sanctions had been stripped bare. The *Reichswehr* and the *Luftwaffe* were free to do as they pleased. World opinion was an irrelevance. The League was a dead duck.

Ideological Conflicts. The discovery that decades after their deaths the names of Karl Marx and Vladimir Ilyich Lenin could between them mobilize and command vast armies, fleets, and air power has corrupted the ideological purity of contemporary Marxism. No longer are the masters of the Kremlin much interested in the improvement of the lot of the toiling masses in their own country or elsewhere. Socialism has become an indispensable scaffolding for the organization of state power. Belief in Marx's ideology is even less than lip service, but socialism has the indisputable advantage of concentrating all power—political, economic, military, and social—in the hands of the central government. The power of the state cannot be allowed to wither, even though Marx predicted that outcome of socialism. It must be increased to remain vital, credible, and limitless.

In any strict sense, the confrontation between the United States and Russia is not ideological. It is a conflict about power, its increase in Russian hands and its maintenance in American hands. We are accustomed to referring to the polar opposition between Moscow and Washington as rooted in the rejection of capitalism by the one and the rejection of communism by the other. For the Russians, ideology is secondary to the contest for power. Americans have a commitment to freedom and a belief that freedom can survive only if our power is sufficient to protect us from the Russians.

Both positions have been set forth in language that is emphatic, uncompromising, and bitter. Both positions are supported by military power the like of which has never before been known.

Neither side is disposed to invite the United Nations to bring its good offices to bear on any of their essential disputes. The rest of the world can listen to the acrimonious representatives of these terrifyingly potent nations. Sides can be taken in the General Assembly and elsewhere, although neither Russia nor the United States seems to be particularly affected by the outcome of these deliberations. No action by the Security Council, no resolutions by the General Assembly will ease the hostile language or reduce the continued accumulation of arms.

The forums of the United Nations are still the best places to test world opinion and to mobilize it in support of a position. Neither the United States nor the Soviet Union has been very successful in attracting new support from the nonaligned nations. There are understandable reasons, to which our present representatives choose to be oblivious, and in later chapters I will deal with them. For the present, let it suffice to say that the usefulness of the United Nations in the confrontation of the superpowers is necessarily limited to providing a place for "jaw, jaw, jaw," which, as Winston Churchill once remarked, is a process that is infinitely preferable to "war, war, war." Rather boring, when the "jaw, jaw, jaw" is expressed in the stilted jargon of the United Nations discourse. Boring, but who wants the exciting alternatives of bombs and missiles?

I shall generalize again: *The United Nations cannot restrain the superpowers unless the superpowers choose to be restrained. It can only bring to bear the force of world opinion. Eventually both the Soviet Union and the United States will discover that it is to the advantage of both powers to accord a decent respect to the opinions of mankind.*

Religious Conflicts. Ever since the founding of the Zionist movement in the late nineteenth century, the Moslem world has been in a turmoil of hostility. Furious but unsuccessful resorts to arms responded to the culmination of Zionism in the founding of the state of Israel. There is no sign that the fury is abating, even though Egypt, the largest, the most populous, and the most powerful of the Arab nations, has made a sort of peace with Israel.

Beginning with the recognition of Israel as a state and a member of the United Nations in 1949, these tensions have been expressed annually in the General Assembly. The Arab tendency toward hyperbole has led to expressions of some ferocity that have not been well received by nations accustomed to more temperate language in diplomatic discourse. The Arabs have been able to induce some impoverished African nations to make common cause with them and against Israel. General Assembly resolutions declaring that Zionism is racism have particularly antagonized the nations that align themselves in general support of Israel.

On the four occasions when Israel and its neighbors have been engaged in armed conflict, the Security Council has been actively engaged in strategies to restore a semblance of peace to the Middle East. That peace has never been more than a semblance. The restraint that has been achieved is due partly to the efforts of the United Nations Secretariat, partly to the negotiations conducted by successive American governments independently of the United Nations, and partly to the maintenance of peace-keeping forces in the most dangerous areas. In a later chapter, I will discuss the formulas for peace that have been drafted by United Nations agencies but which have never received the support they deserve from the permanent members of the Security Council. For the present, the United Nations role in the Middle East is still crucial and could become the way out of the seemingly impenetrable jungle of hostilities that seal off that part of the world from ordinary international discourse.

South against North. Already the world's colonial past is so distant in time and concept that both the rationalizations for imperialism and the processes by which the nations that practiced it maintained their hold on subject territories are scarcely understandable or credible. The imperialist nations had tacitly accepted responsibility for civilized standards of government in their colonies. Once title to them was established they tended to refrain from interventions in each other's affairs. There were some exceptions, as in the case of the Belgian Congo, where exploitations of colonial authority exceeded the loose norms of nineteenth-century imperialism. That is not to say that exploitation by other powers in other places was not often almost as gross as that for which King Leopold II was responsible. Even where colonial administration was relatively benign, it was resented. There is no record of any colony resisting its liberation. It was to be expected that once set free, the new nations would press for economic as well as political autonomy.

Liberation was not enough. Nearly all these new nations were dependent in some way or another on their old masters or on the community of industrial states of the North. Some were fortunate enough to have natural resources such as petroleum or copper to keep themselves generally solvent. Others had cash crops, such as coffee or cocoa, to make a start in world trade. And others had practically nothing but a rapidly increasing population of desperate people. Their condition has not improved since the early 1950s. Desperate nations are especially vulnerable to brutal and cynical tyrants, and not only in Africa, as those who remember Europe of the years before 1939 know too well.

To the leaders of the new nations it was obvious that major changes in the world's economy had to be made. That led to the New International Economic Order, adopted by resolution of the General Assembly in 1974. It is a plan for economic redress to be administered by the United Nations, calling for transfer of some resources from the First to the Third World. It mentions, among other innovative ideas, the possible expropriation of multinational corporation properties.

The plan has caused paroxysms of contemptuous rage among American neoconservatives, who have not deigned to suggest an alternative route out of the desperate straits of these peoples other than reliance on the Invisible Hand of the Free Market. The Soviet bloc has indicated no interest in extricating the former colonies from the plight in which their masters left them. Clearly the United Nations must play a part in a coordinated program of accelerated development. For years such agencies as the United Nations Development Program, the International Labor Office, and the United Nations Conference of Trade and Development have done much with resources disproportionate to the tasks undertaken. But change is slow, and the generosity of the developed nations in hard times has been constricted.

It is difficult for the leaders of either the free world or the communist bloc to imagine themselves in the shoes of a president or prime minister of a Third World nation. One leader who tried to understand and may have succeeded is Willy Brandt, the former mayor of West Berlin when the Russians had to be fended off, and the former chancellor of the Federal Republic of Germany. As chairman of the Independent Commission on International Development Issues he is considered to be the principal author of *North–South: A Program for Survival.*[3] The problems confronting the Third and Fourth Worlds are described and analyzed. A program for their remedies is proposed. The massive nature of the actions required calls for international cooperation on a scale that rivals or exceeds the Marshall Plan of the 1950s. Later I shall discuss as fully as I can the Brandt proposals. For the present, I offer this generalization about the conflict between South and North: *Although economic equality of all nations is not to be expected, peace and order cannot be maintained indefinitely on a planet in which the hemispheres are divided by prosperity in the North and impoverishment in the South. The highest priority for the United Nations must be the creation of a plan to remedy the economic disparity of the hemispheres.*

I shall return to this theme. I hope that Dr. van den Haag will join me in a consideration of what is to be done about a condition that gets steadily worse, troubling the moral sense of the comfortable nations and, in the end, threatening their security.

South Africa against the World. The Republic of South Africa is deservedly the friendless nation. Its policy of apartheid is universally detested, at least in the stated policies of all national leaders who have expressed themselves on the subject. Even those politicians in other countries who privately favor this extremity of racism are cautious not to say so out loud—they merely vote when they must against measures taken to discourage the South Africans from their foolish and cruel policies.

The United Nations has two outstanding present problems and one momentous future problem with South Africa. Since the 1950s the General Assembly denounced with increasing vehemence the treatment of the black majority by the white regime. Since 1960 the Security Council has condemned apartheid and urged the South African government to abandon both policy and practice—with no apparent results. In 1963 the Security Council urged a voluntary arms embargo on South Africa. In 1974 the General Assembly rejected the credentials of the South African delegation and excluded it from its deliberations. All these and other measures have been adopted with little or no dissent, but South Africa persists in apartheid.

The second problem is Namibia, the former German colony that, after World War I, was assigned to South Africa as a League of Nations mandate. In 1966 the mandate was terminated by the General Assembly but South Africa continued to administer the territory anyway. To this day, no settlement acceptable to the United Nations or to the nations of Africa has been reached. South Africa has installed a regime of its own choosing for an autonomous government of the territory. The response of the United Nations to this flouting of its authority has yet to be made.

The anarchic behavior of the South African government has been continuous since 1946. No one can predict when or how it will end. The longer the present policies are maintained in the face of opposition that becomes progressively more fierce and violent, the more probable it is that the end will be a disaster for the sub-Saharan portion of the continent. The future problem for the United Nations will be the rescue of civilized values in a region where those values survive precariously.

My generalization: *The only power that the United Nations can exert over the South African outrage is the moral force of world opinion, supported by the willingness of the world to engage in the embargoes and boycotts called for by the agencies of the*

United Nations. So far, these appeals have not received the strict support that will be required for effectiveness.

Once again, the United Nations must be *used* to be effective. When actions do not match the words of the member nations, the perception of futility is to be expected.

The Case for Optimism

I have by no means discussed all the actual and potential conflicts that can be seen in a world that has never before been so troubled. In all the surrounding perplexities, it is difficult for anyone to think clearly, to plot a course toward relative tranquillity. I do not claim to be one of the few exceptions.

I begin with the conviction that despair cannot be a foundation for progress or even for survival. The self-interest of the peoples of the world will cause them to restrain their governments from plunging us all into extinction. The United Nations can keep our attention fixed on the dangers ahead; it can ease frictions and reduce the damage of conflicts. It cannot prevent folly, cure bigotry, or save the victims of unscrupulous governments. The annual turmoil in the General Assembly reflects the general turmoil of a desperate world. Unwise actions by American delegations have too often contributed to the disorder rather than to its remedy. In recent years we have not even tried to use the United Nations as a means to the goal of peace and general prosperity.

The General Assembly is not the whole of the United Nations. What is significant in the present state of the organization is the collection of specialized agencies designed to bring about health, prosperity, and understanding throughout the ailing world. In the brief observations I have been able to make in New York, Geneva, and elsewhere, I have been impressed with the success that very modest efforts have achieved in creating a foundation for peace in a world that has never before had such a foundation. Throughout the rest of this debate I intend to say much more about these achievements and how they can be increased to the benefit of all nations, including the United States.

Abolish the United Nations? I am glad that I do not have to defend such cynical defeatism.

Notes

1. I shall trace this disintegration in greater detail in Chapter 2.
2. Henry A. Kissinger, *A World Restored; Metternich, Castlereagh and the Problems of Peace 1812–22* (Boston: Houghton Mifflin, 1957), p. 43.
3. Cambridge, Massachusetts: M.I.T. Press, 1980.

ERNEST VAN DEN HAAG

When John Conrad and I decided to joust once more, this time about the U.N., we thought that an introductory historical chapter should start off the book. Instead, Conrad started with musings about the kind of world we (meaning Conrad but using a *plurale majestatis*) want. I think his instinct is right. It would not do to start a debate on the U.N. with a history of the organization. One has to start with its prehistory, found in the wishful thinking and the Utopian constructs shared at one time or other by most of us, and still championed by him, though, to be fair, in almost (but not quite) reasonable ways.

For centuries, people have lamented the futility of war. There hardly is a person who has not, at one time or other, bitterly complained about the loss of life, the maiming, the destruction of homes, industries, and whole towns. And we all have sometimes thought that "they" make war, using "us" as cannon fodder: Were it up to ordinary peace-loving citizens there would never be a war. Nor have people failed to notice that, after peace is made, new tensions build up, conflicts arise, and small wars are fought, until once more a world conflagration occurs. Not least, one of the "benefits" of the French Revolution was that wars are no longer fought by professionals (at the expense, always, of civilians). They are now fought by drafted civilians themselves. Each war is fought with more deadly weapons than the last, so that now, should there be a strategic nuclear war, civilization, even the human race itself, may be in jeopardy.

Why do governments fight wars or, rather, make their citizens fight? Each war has different causes. But theoreticians have looked for general causes. Thus, Marxists feel that the causes of war are economic, having to do with markets or raw materials. This sounds rational until one realizes that the costs of modern war are such that no economic benefit is likely to offset them. Perhaps, when the Israelites invaded and appropriated the promised land of milk and honey, war was profitable. In antiquity the defeated were literally sold as slaves and their land was taken from them. War could be profitable. It often was organized robbery. But modern wars are not profitable even to the winner. And the motives seldom are economic. A more primitive version of the Marxist fantasy used to attribute wars to the "merchants of death" who profit by producing armaments. That version is now discredited too. Wars are not avoided by nationalizing arms industries, and they occurred before there were defense industries.

V. I. Lenin in *Imperialism, the Highest Stage of Capitalism*,[1] wrote about the 1905 war between Czarist Rusia and Japan. He found that Czarist Russia had fought to protect major economic interests in Korea and Manchuria. Marxists thought he had demonstrated and exemplified the Marxist thesis. But in *The Economic Causes of War*[2] Lionel Robbins, after studying the now available archives, found that the Czarist foreign policy makers had induced Russian capitalists to invest in Manchuria and Korea so as to have an economic pretext to fight the Japanese, who were becoming too powerful to suit the Russian foreign office. In other words, there was an economic pretext for a political goal, not, as Lenin thought, a political pretext for an economic goal.

My friend John P. Conrad does not believe in economic causes. He is no Marxist (one can be wrong in other ways, as he will demonstrate anon). John believes, if I understand his first chapter, that wars are best avoided by talking with one another at the U.N. and by "world opinion." He seems to come perilously close to asserting that wars are due to misunderstandings that can be avoided by more talk or contact.

I don't believe so. Talking with Hitler would not have done much good—and indeed didn't. (Remember Munich and Prime Minister Chamberlain, who shared Conrad's faith in talk?) I don't think that talking with Stalin and his successors, or bringing to bear "world opinion" on them or on the Ayatollah Khomeini, or, indeed, on anyone not already on our side, is very promising.

Not that I am opposed to talk or negotiation. Misunderstandings can be removed sometimes, and wars may be avoided by compromises at other times. But talk does not have the magical properties that Conrad attributes to it. Most wars happen because either or both sides prefer war to compromise. Understanding (e.g., the Nazis) may lead to war as much as misunderstanding. Conflicts occur between governments that may understand one another all too well. Only some, usually minor, conflicts are due to misunderstandings. Most are not. When two people want the same thing and fight about it they do not "misunderstand" one another.

Further, there is no need, and no advantage, for talks to take place within, or under the auspices of, the U.N. Any coffee shop will do. The outcome does not depend on location or auspices. Nor does the willingness to talk seriously in the first place. The U.N. had nothing to do with averting war over the Cuban missile crisis, and did not contribute to settling the Korean or Vietnam conflict. It could do nothing about the Iran–Iraq conflict or the many other Middle Eastern conflicts—not to speak of embarrassments such as Afghanistan, Hungary, or Czechoslovakia.

As for "world opinion" as an independent force (which Conrad imagines it to be), it is but a wishful fantasy. Except in the democracies the organs of opinion are controlled by the government. There is no Soviet, Chinese, Vietnamese, Cuban, North Korean, East German, Rumanian, or Ghanian opinion (indeed, we can forget about Africa), other than the government's, that can be publicly manifested. Thus, there is at best the public opinion of the democratic world. It may influence democracies but has no impact on totalitarian countries such as the Soviet Union or Cuba.

What, then, are the causes of war? The answer is simple when we consider what makes war possible and in the long run probable. But the answer becomes more complicated when we consider particular wars.

Countries are sovereign. It is neither possible nor desirable to change this. Yet this is what makes war possible and ultimately likely.*

Sovereignty was defined by Jean Bodin in the sixteenth century as *potestas legibus absoluta*: power, not regulated or restrained by (independent of) laws. By definition, a sovereign government is not subjected to the will (law) of any other. It makes the laws to which it is subjected. It is the supreme lawgiver for itself—and, of course, it can change the laws it makes, which, therefore, restrain it only so long as it wishes to be restrained. Thus, the power of a sovereign government is inherently unlimited, except by the restraints it may choose to impose on itself (as is usually the case in a democracy) and which it can change or remove. The government may also choose not to restrain its power in the first place (as is the case in totalitarian systems).

Sovereign governments, then, have the right to go to war (*jus ad bellum*) when they feel they ought to do so. It is true that all kinds of international compacts have denied the right to wage unjust and aggressive war—but they have not denied the power to do so. Unenforceable rights do not protect anyone. Thus, the nations that deem themselves powerful enough to win may go to war when they find it in their interest to do so. Whether a war is, or was, just is operationally decided, *post facto*, by the winner, who usually will blame the defeated party for it. Thus, justice plays no independent role (I know that there are many books about just and unjust wars written by philosophers or law professors. But they affect mainly other professors, not governments.) We must conclude that the possibility and, in the long run, the probability of war in-

*"World government"—even if it were possible to get China, the United States, and the Soviet Union under one roof—would not solve anything. International wars would simply be labeled civil wars.

heres in the existence of sovereign nations powerful and independent enough to go to war.

Can we limit sovereignty so as to exclude war, so as to compel settlements of conflicts by means other than war?

We cannot. Of course, nations can negotiate about conflicts or volunteer to have a third party decide them. But they will not do so if they find it worthwhile to impose their will by war. If, on the other hand, they are ready to accept the decision of an impartial arbiter, such arbiters—the Pope, a group of law professors formed *ad hoc*—are not hard to find. The U.N. is probably least qualified as arbiter, for it rarely is impartial or trustworthy. (How can it be? It is only a name for all the governments assembled, each pursuing its own interests. Unlike a domestic court of law, it is not above the parties and independent of them.)

The relations among nations are very different from the relations of private citizens with one another in any country. If private citizens have a conflict, the party that feels wronged can appeal to a court of law, which can compel the defendant to appear and can impose and enforce its judgment on him and the plaintiff. Neither has the power to resist the court, or to impose his wishes on the other without the court's sanction. And the court is not a party to the conflict it decides. Not so with conflicts or violations of international laws or treaties among nations. What courts there are cannot compel the defendant nation to appear or to accept the court's jurisdiction, and the court has no means to enforce its judgment on plaintiff and defendant. (It would need an army bigger than that of either party. In the case of the United States and the Soviet Union that is a little hard to imagine. Even if Spain were the defendant found guilty, where would the police force needed to subdue it be stationed? Anyway, the imposition of the court's judgment could occur only through the war it was to avoid.)

The rule of law in international relations is a chimera then,* for it is inconsistent with sovereignty. War is inherent in sover-

---

*Except, as mentioned, where nations are willing to submit to arbitration: when they do not want to go to war. But the problem occurs when at least one government prefers to impose its will by means of war.

eignty as a possibility. What actualizes it? There is no single cause. Governments may feel their power threatened and go to war preemptively. Or, there may be a contest about territory, or about an ally or a neutral. There are as many possibilities for conflict as can exist in any relationship among independent groups. However, there is one general rule: War breaks out only if the initiator—the aggressor—rightly or wrongly thinks he can win at a tolerable cost. Put negatively: Nobody goes to war if he thinks he will be defeated.

Thus, Hitler thought he could win. Hitler was wrong.* The Soviet Union thought it would win in fighting Finland and later invading Afghanistan. The Soviet Union was right—though the cost of the war in Afghanistan may be higher than the Soviets thought. This calculation—can we win?—is also what prevents the surrounding nations from attacking South Africa: They realize they are going to lose (wherefore they pass U.N. resolutions condemning South Africa as an aggressor).

There is a simple rule to prevent war, well understood by a peaceful nation such as Switzerland—*Se vis pacem para bellum*†: Be so well prepared for attack as to discourage attackers with the prospect of defeat or, at least, of high cost. It doesn't always work. Often the forces of the would-be attacker and those of the would-be defenders are nearly even. Peaceful nations too often are reluctant to arm enough to discourage aggressors. They often place their hopes on appeasement. And perceptions differ. But the rule, when followed, works better than anything else has.

If I have not mentioned the U.N. so far the reason is simple: It has no place whatever in a serious discussion of war and peace. John Conrad thinks otherwise, although, to be fair, he seems to see but a modest role for the U.N. He does not think, as some of

---

*Hitler at the time was confronted with a disarmed Great Britain, an unprepared France, a Soviet Union and a United States that promised not to intervene. Thus, his perception that he could win was not unreasonable, though it turned out to be wrong.
†Literally, if you want peace be prepared for war.

the more foolish supporters do, that it can prevent war. But he thinks it can help.

This is where we differ. The U.N. not only does not help peace but, in my opinion, hinders it, and itself creates conflicts and magnifies existing ones beyond what would be the case without it. It is not only helpless about major wars but useless even about totally foolish and, as it were, transparently avoidable ones, such as the war between Iraq and Iran. Iraq, you remember, wanted to profit from Iran's postrevolutionary weakness to snip off some territory. Iran mobilized and prevented it. Whereupon Iraq shrugged and offered to restore the *status quo ante* and peace. Nothing doing, said Iran, you have to get rid of your government first and pay us an indemnity (a totally unrealistic figure was mentioned). Ever since, Iraq has successfully defended itself against Iranian (counter) invasion. This has cost both, but particularly Iran, untold dead. There is no end in sight. Syria supports Iran (mildly), mainly because it hates the government of Iraq (as ruthless as its own). Most of the other Arabs root for Iraq, fearing that a victorious Iran would destabilize the area. Now, where is the U.N. in all this? I don't know. Perhaps Conrad can find it. Even if it were to pronounce itself—perhaps it has—on the matter, what difference would it make?

While we are in the Middle East, note that the U.N. has been unhelpful in establishing peaceful relations among Israel, Egypt, the Sudan, Libya, Jordan, Lebanon, and what not. The U.N. is useless; it tries to hide the obvious by protesting what it does not like (a useless gesture) and blessing what is occasionally accomplished by diplomatic efforts independent of the organization (an equally useless gesture). But the U.N. is worse than useless, as I shall demonstrate as we go on.

There are a few things now in John Conrad's opening argument that I want to pick up or question him about.

He asks (p. 5), "Must the world depend forever on terror for its survival? [This] is not enough, nor is it tolerable for a future projected for the centuries." This rhetorical gambit seems overambitious and unrealistic to me. John Conrad wants certainty and is dissatisfied with mutual deterrence. But certainty is not of this world. Deterrence in some form or other has postponed, if not avoided, wars in the past. Nothing else has and, I'm afraid, nothing else can.

It seems to me that it is foolish to ask for more. When I go to see my physician I am not upset to learn that death ultimately is unavoidable. I knew it all along. I'm not out to picket the hospital. I'm satisfied if he helps me postpone death, if he helps me overcome the current difficulty. Can we ask more of governments with respect to war?

Unlike John Conrad, I think the U.N. can be of no help. It is no substitute for, or help to, diplomacy and armament. It certainly is not, to quote his words (p. 5), "the school in which the world will learn a better way to secure the peace than the resumption of the archaic diplomacy of the nineteenth century. Americans and Russians as well as the nations of the Third and Fourth Worlds have much to learn in this school."

What have we to learn from the U.N.? How to confuse Zionism with racism? How to violate one's own rules, as the U.N. has done for years with respect to Israel, South Africa, *et al.*? Who does the teaching? What is being taught? Anything we don't know? What is being learned by Iran? or Lebanon? or Uganda? Cuba, China (remember Tibet), Vietnam (remember Cambodia)? What is being taught to the Soviet Union? to Syria?

Conrad goes on (p. 6): "The world need not go up in flames. The best assurance of its safety is the kind of discourse that goes on in its East River headquarters, supported by the programs to improve health, safety, and prosperity of all nations."

I'm all for health, safety, and prosperity. I have not noticed that the U.N. fosters any of these. American capitalism has been rather successful in doing so, but it is constantly attacked in the U.N. Further, however worthwhile prosperity and health are, I fail to see the connection with war and peace. Do healthy or prosperous people not go to war? On the contrary; the weak and poor don't.

With reference to the last world war Conrad writes (p. 1) "French and British statesmen were unwilling to use the League of Nations in the stages when Germany, Italy, and Japan were rearming but still weak enough to be restrained. Their depredations continued until neither the Anglo-French initiatives nor the League itself could contain the crazy defiance by the Axis powers. Without the moral force of world opinion mobilized in support of the sadly crippled League, there was no way that these berserk governments could be prevented from starting the war. . . .''

Stuff and nonsense. France and England were quite willing to use the League, but the League was of no use, just as the U.N. is of no use. France and England could have prevented the war if instead of relying on the League and other ineffective devices, they had rearmed in time and used their power to prevent Germany from rearming. It was their failure to rearm that made them an inviting target, which Hitler did not resist. The League? A bad joke at best.

Conrad also writes (p. 12), ''The United Nations cannot restrain the superpowers unless the superpowers choose to be restrained.'' Right. And one may add that if the superpowers ''choose to be restrained'' they have to restrain themselves. No one else could do it—certainly not the U.N., which consists of the superpowers, their allies, and some neutrals. But if the superpowers choose to restrain themselves (as they have done in fear of one another), what need is there for the U.N., which cannot do anything that they cannot do for themselves?

Further on, Conrad writes, ''[The U.N.] can only bring to bear the force of world opinion. Eventually both the Soviet Union and the United States will discover that it is to the advantage of both powers to accord a decent respect to the opinions of mankind.''

World opinion does not exist and has no force—as France and England discovered when confronted by Hitler. The Soviet Union has never been interested in ''the opinions of mankind,'' which, moreover, can be fairly easily manipulated—as the General Assembly of the U.N. demonstrates every day.

Similarly, Conrad tells us (p. 15) that ''peace and order cannot be maintained indefinitely on a planet in which the hemispheres are divided by prosperity in the North and impoverishment in the South. The highest priority for the United Nations must be the creation of a plan to remedy the economic disparity of the hemispheres.''

He does not bother to tell us why a prosperous part of the world cannot live in peace with a poor one. It always has. And the threat to peace does not come from impoverished parts of the world—it is rather the Soviet Union that threatens peace, not, say, Bangladesh. If one considers Iran and Iraq, differences in poverty or wealth played no role in their war. Or in the invasion of Afghanistan. Or in the last world war. Conrad's idea needs some sort of evidence. He has not bothered to present any. He dislikes poverty and war. (Who doesn't?) And Conrad seems to conclude illogically that they must be related. But they have only our dislike in common. Poor nations rarely can afford war. (Iran and Iraq could afford it only because of their oil revenue.) Libya could afford to invade Chad because it is oil-rich. Chad could not afford a defense without French help.

As for the Brandt proposal, which Conrad eulogizes, it simply says that the wealthy nations ought to ''redistribute'' (actually, give away) part of their wealth to the poor nations. Not only has this nothing to do with peace, I can find nothing to recommend it. It has been justly forgotten except by John Conrad and his friends.

The poverty of the poor nations is not due to the wealth of the rich ones—although they like to think so. On the contrary, the colonial powers, as long as they held power, helped the colonies (now called the Third World) by providing stability and by investing, thus providing industrialization. The present independent governments of the ex-colonies are so unstable, arbitrary, corrupt, and inefficient as to discourage investment. Moreover, they have a peculiar tendency to steal the investor's money, which also does not encourage investment. Nonetheless, they have received unprecedented help from the developed nations. It has been mostly wasted. There is no reason to believe that ''redistribution'' would help them.*

---

*On these matters the works of Peter Bauer (now Lord Bauer) are very instructive.

A few *obiter scripta*—Namibia, the former German colony, was conquered by South Africa in the First World War, as Conrad neglects to mention, and the "mandate" of the League of Nations merely blessed that conquest. The U.N. could not (and did not) prevent South Africa from keeping that possession. Conrad writes (p. 16): "The only power that the United Nations can exert over the South African outrage is the moral force of world opinion, supported by the willingness of the world to engage in the embargoes and boycotts called for by the agencies of the United Nations. So far, these appeals have not received the strict support that will be required for effectiveness."

Now, Conrad is right, that is all the U.N. can do. But I can't see why the U.N. chooses South Africa as a target rather than any of the much worse dictatorships on the continent. Surely in terms of living standards, civil rights, or democratic rights South Africa is better than most other African states. Not to speak of such monstrosities as the Soviet Union. So why pick on South Africa? Because, despite the oppression of blacks, they are better treated than in most black-run countries and have more liberties, more education, and a higher living standard than in, say, Uganda, Burundi, Tanzania, Mozambique, or Angola.

Indeed, it is in the Third World that the U.N. does the most mischief by giving a platform to misgovernment and non-democratic Third World nations to attack the civilized world, usually with the help of the Soviet Union, and by insisting that the Western nations ought to punish South Africa for its domestic arrangements (far from ideal, but not as bad as those of, say, Burundi or Uganda) as though an aggressor. The same tactics are used against Israel. The U.N. has indeed denied credentials to the South African government (surely more legitimate than that of the Soviet Union) and desisted from doing so with regard to Israel only when the United States threatened to leave. Should we? We shall discuss this in the chapters to come.

Notes

1. V.I. Lenin, *Imperialism, the Highest Stage of Capitalism* (New York: International, 1939).

2. Lionel Robbins, *The Economic Causes of War* (London: Jonathan Cape, 1939).

JOHN P. CONRAD

This is a chapter for laying out the foundations of our arguments, to be built on in chapters to come. Some of Dr. van den Haag's propositions are too sweeping and too bold for me to leave unchallenged at this early stage of our proceedings. Before going on to the discussion of more complex matters, I must defuse the most obvious oversimplifications that my adversary has introduced into this discourse. One by one:

1. *Conflicts occur between governments that understand one another all too well.* Perhaps this is true, but political conflicts between well-informed antagonists do not lead to war. We have to go back to the age of Louis XIV, give or take a few decades, to find wars occurring between governments that knew approximately which option an adversary would choose and what his capabilities were for carrying it out.

Even in the crazy condition of diplomacy that preceded World War I, none of the governments that became belligerents had a clear idea of what the lineup would be. Italy was a party with Germany and Austro-Hungary to the Triple Alliance. The Kaiser had some reason to believe that the British would be neutral, or at least nonbelligerent. The French, the British, and the Russians believed that Germany could not win a two-front war. There is a large literature in many languages that tries to account for World War I. Misunderstanding of the intentions and capabilities of allies and adversaries certainly leads any list of the causes.

At the outset of World War II, Hitler's intuitions told him that the British would not support Poland and France. Although an accomplished deceiver himself, Stalin assumed to the last that the Ribbentrop–Molotov treaty meant what it said and that Russia was safe from the Reichswehr. The Japanese attack on Pearl Harbor was based on a wildly improbable scenario, assuming that it was not necessary to conquer the United States; it was sufficient to neutralize us.[1] The Korean "police action" would not have hap-

pened had Stalin correctly apprehended President Truman's commitment to the containment of Russian expansion.

And so on, down to the wretched General Galtieri's misunderstanding of Mrs. Thatcher's willingness to assume great risks and
immense costs to defend a group of islands that had no crucial
economic or strategic significance for British interests, and his
professional incompetence in assessing British naval and military
capabilities. Or down to Iraqi President Hussein's grievous mis-
calculation of Iranian solidarity under the Ayatollah Khomeini.
Vain politicians are given to attributing magical powers to their intuitions. They claim an insight into what their adversaries intend
while disregarding the relative capabilities of the two sides.

From such muddles wars ensue. Such encouragement as we
can find in the enduring confrontation between Russia and the
United States must be based on each nation's detailed knowledge
of the capabilities of the other. Neither side may be sure what the
other side *intends*, but each knows that the balance of terror is
truly a balance.

Can the United Nations be an instrument for the increase of
understanding? Neither the Ayatollah Khomeini nor Colonel Qaddafi will avail himself of the General Assembly as a forum for
listening. Their interest in the United Nations is primarily in the
platform it provides for broadsides to denounce the rest of the
world. It is tragic that so few of the more experienced nations
have produced leaders and diplomats who can listen for the purpose of understanding better the international environment and to
speak so as to increase the understanding of others.

During my preparation for this debate I talked with a good
many diplomats working in the United Nations apparatus. All of
them, even Eastern Europeans, believe that the constant interchange of opinions and ideas in the great United Nations centers in
New York, Geneva, and Vienna do increase understanding and
could increase it more as more diplomats come to appreciate the
potentiality of discourse in this new kind of environment. Unfortunately, there are many who are unwilling to understand, and
they are to be found on both sides of that miserable Iron Curtain
that splits the world so needlessly.

"Any coffee shop" will not do, as my opponent flippantly suggests. Serious discourse about serious affairs calls for continuities of discussion and personal contacts. In turn, those continuities require an organization and the support that an organization provides for the collection of information. To use such an organization wisely and well leads to collective security in which each nation knows not only its own interest but also the interests of other nations. To refuse to use such an organization is to embark on a road back to international anarchy, the kind of world we had in the *belle époque* before World War I and the even worse world that preceded World War II, when everyone knew in his bones what would happen but did nothing to forestall the terrible events of 1939.

2. *World opinion is irrelevant to the political and strategic decisions of the Communist powers.* As a force to be reckoned with in international diplomacy, "world opinion" is a newcomer and less effective in national policy making than it will be as the years go on. The princes whom Machiavelli and Bodin advised could ignore world opinion with impunity. So could Louis XIV and Napoleon, and, in our own times, Hitler, Mussolini, Tojo, and Stalin. After World War II, Stalin could disregard it entirely, and did. Khrushchev moved into Hungary at a time when Western opinion was preoccupied with the Suez episode. (Like ordinary mortals, statesmen have great difficulty attending to more than one crisis at the same time.) Whether Brezhnev expected the outrage that arose from the Russian termination of the Prague Spring will not be known for many years to come, if ever. But instead of marching the Red Army into Warsaw to correct the Polish deviations from the true Marxist-Leninist gospel—much more serious from the Russian point of view than the revisionism of either Imre Nagy in Hungary or Alexander Dubček in Czechoslovakia—Brezhnev dithered. Alternative policies were tried, different leadership approaches were offered before General Wojciech Jaruzelski's regime was installed. That dismal caretaker of Polish communism evidently satisfies his sponsors in Moscow, but his effectiveness in reviving the Marxist faith has been negligible. One of the main reasons for his marginal performance is that world opinion takes a

poor view of the general's economic and social policies and fails to cooperate in their fulfillment.[2]

So what about Afghanistan, about which a sense of chronic but impotent outrage is general? I cannot penetrate the Kremlin enigma any better than Winston Churchill, but it is a hypothesis as good as any that the Russian invasion of that unhappy country was Brezhnev's folly, the error of a doddering old man whose judgment in such matters had never been very good. It is impossible to verify the Moscow gossip that the Red Army would dearly like to get out of its Afghan adventures but has yet to find a way of doing so without a disastrous loss of face. The fact that the Western nations cannot bring themselves to back up their magnificent rhetoric in support of the Afghans with more substantial measures certainly gives the Politburo reason to suppose that their persistence in this wicked cause will ultimately be rewarded with the success of Russian arms.[3]

3. *Sovereignty makes war "ultimately likely."* In the course of this confrontation, I expect to have a lot to say about sovereignty, and I reserve the right to expand at some length on this subject in a later chapter. Here I want to give fair warning. The sixteenth-century notion of sovereignty advanced by Jean Bodin does not represent the concept we know in the twentieth-century international community. Bodin himself was well aware of the limits that the realities of power would impose on the Renaissance state. "A prince," he said, "will demand neither war nor peace if necessity...does not force him to do so; and will never wage battle, provided there is no more apparent profit in victory than in loss if the enemies were victorious."[4] About two centuries later, Montesquieu recognized the constraint that self-interest would place on the rulers of the republic: "The law of nations is naturally founded on this principle, that different nations ought in time of peace to do one another all the good they can, and in time of war as little harm as possible, without prejudicing their real interests."[5]

The necessities of international life have eroded the traditional idea of sovereignty. For a long time the nations of the world have engaged in various international regulatory activities, as, for example, the International Postal Union (1875), in which a narrow supranational authority is established to make possible the free movement of mails from country to country. The Postal Union acts by majority decision, with no veto right allowed to any state, however rich and powerful. Similar rules govern other international agencies. The member states of the European Common Market have ceded some sovereign rights to that supranational body. What we see in the evolution of the concept is a distinction between the idea of sovereignty as it applies within a state, where the rulers are not in principle limited by any outside influence,[6] and a concept of interstate sovereignty, in which many real limits apply to a nation's freedom of action.[7]

How far and how fast this evolution will proceed is a matter for futile conjecture. We can be sure that necessity, as Bodin saw, will work changes in the concept, and self-interest, as Montesquieu observed, will require other limits, as, for example, the European Common Market.

One thing is certain. Sovereignty is not an immutable concept, like a mathematical term, as Dr. van den Haag would have me concede. It has changed since the day of Bodin and Machiavelli, and since the publication of Montesquieu's *Spirit of the Laws*, that cornerstone of Western political science. It will continue to change, whether or not my opponent believes that change is desirable.

It is a variable in space as well as in time. The sovereignty enjoyed by the Republic of Chad is far different from that which is enjoyed by the United States—the same term hardly applies to both nations. When the nations of the Common Market agree to various restrictions on the prices of commodities, very important abridgments of sovereignty have occurred, and of a nature that would have been inconceivable 50 years ago. We can expect that necessity and self-interest will continue to modify the essentials of sovereignty as we know them now. Even the Russians may come to accept foreign interference in their internal affairs.

4. *"The colonial powers, as long as they held power, helped the colonies...by providing stability and by investing, thus*

providing industrialization.'' At best, the record of the colonial powers is mixed—a great deal of exploitation from which the indigenous peoples got precious little industrialization and the stability of heavy-handed oppression. The legacy of European systems of governance was not accompanied by cadres of trained native personnel to man the systems. Natives could be allowed the menial tasks of government but were seldom thought capable of carrying out the duties of the administration or the judiciary. Professor van den Haag's apparent nostalgia for the good old colonial days is not shared by either the old colonial powers or the peoples that were colonized.

The record of the Third World is sad but not hopeless. New regimes took over new countries. Some of them were countries defined by ethnically meaningless geographical boundaries within which religious, ethnic, and tribal hostilities had smoldered for centuries—suppressed but not resolved by colonial power. Personnel had to be trained and placed into service on complex technical tasks essential to modern government, even in darkest Africa. That money was wasted, that violence got frequently out of control, that policies were ill-conceived is all true enough. But if my censorious adversary thinks that money is not wasted in advanced and developed societies, that violence is not a significant problem, or that policies are always wise, he is not in touch with the real world around him in metropolitan America.

Later, I shall have a lot more to say about the Brandt report and its implications. It certainly is not the only way out of the economic morass in which most of the Third World is floundering. But it is a more promising and more magnanimous plan than the sanctimonious preachiness of American conservatives who have nothing more to offer than the Invisible Hand of Adam Smith.[8] Indolence and greed never had more dedicated defenders.

5. *Why Pick on South Africa?* Professor van den Haag thinks that the condition of the blacks in South Africa is better than what the people of Burundi and Uganda enjoy. Maybe so, although as I write the South African government has adopted repressive measures to control the black population that shock most of the rest of

the world, though not the American conservative battalions, marching under the banner of Senator Jesse Helms. The notion that the government of South Africa is more "legitimate" than that of, say, the Soviet Union displays a naive misunderstanding of the concept of legitimacy. As the term is used by Western jurists and political scientists, the *legitimacy* of any government is dependent on the consent of those governed. In the United States, that is an idea enjoying the respectability of the two centuries since the drafting of our Declaration of Independence. When about two-thirds of the inhabitants of South Africa are denied any part in the political process, it is humbug to attribute legitimacy to the regime that oppresses them. I hold no brief for the Politburo of the Soviet Union, but it is not credible that two-thirds of the population of the USSR are oppressed in the way that we now see in South Africa. With all its faults, which I can recite as well as anyone else who believes the Communist regime to be an anachronistic distortion of the socialist ideal, the Politburo is careful to coddle the Russian masses as best it can, which, so far, is sadly less coddling than the masses in even the poorest Western European countries enjoy. The same cannot be said for the policies of the Botha government and its long line of intransigent predecessors.

None of the above is intended to get to the bottom of Dr. van den Haag's bald assertion, "The United Nations is good for nothing." I had to scrape away some of the misapprehensions that abound in his response. In chapters to come, he will tell us exactly why he thinks the United Nations is not only useless but harmful. I do not expect that he will convince many of our readers or that his arguments will be irrefutable.

Two Visions of the Future

Dr. van den Haag has spoken for himself and I want to underline our basic differences. Like the good conservative that he is, my opponent does not believe that the world can change or that efforts should be made to bring about change. War is inherent in the nature of things and will inevitably recur. As we all must die so must we all face the certainty of future wars. The balance of terror, the mutual assured destruction, that our thermonuclear theorists have tried to achieve is the best we can do. As a pessimistic conservative, van den Haag believes that we must all reconcile ourselves to the inevitability of death. We all must die, but it does not follow that we must all die in a thermonuclear blast, or that nothing can be done to relieve the miseries of those who were born in the wrong country at the wrong time.

As an optimist, I view human history as a record of survival, too often by the skin of our teeth. Some of us have examined the lessons of the increasingly catastrophic crises that have destroyed millions and terrified their children and grandchildren. I think we can do better than our ancestors did, simply because we can study their mistakes. I have to infer from my gloomy adversary's first contribution to this debate that he is resigned to an ugly fate for all of us. He has read the prophets and the philosophers and has concluded that nothing can be learned from history except the inevitability of doom.

The United Nations as a concept cannot stave off the apocalypse that van den Haag seems to foresee. The nations it comprises can use the structure to divert the forces leading to the horrible end to which the doom-sayers are resigned. I an not willing to bequeath terror to my grandchildren. I look to the United Nations as an instrument for easing hostilities to the point where terror is no longer a daily concern. The United Nations has a long way to go. Its start may have been shaky, but it is going. To stop now would be a cross between tragedy and folly.

Notes

1. See Raymond Aron, *Peace and War*, trans. Richard Howard and Annette Baker Fox (Garden City, New York: Doubleday, 1966), pp. 31–32, for a succinct account of the Japanese plan.
2. Before my opponent makes the point himself, I must add that another reason for General Jaruzelski's failures is that even in the best of times Communists have never achieved a successful economy by any criterion of success.
3. Recent studies of the Russian economy suggest that if the United States had persisted with the grain embargo imposed by President Carter, the conse-

quences for the Soviet Union's ability to feed its people would have been very grave. But a business-minded Republican administration impetuously decided that the embargo was ineffective as well as damaging to its political standing with the Farm Belt. See Mikhail S. Bernstam and Seymour Martin Lipset, "Punishing Russia," *The New Republic*, 5 August 1985 (Vol. 193, No. 6). In this case, words and exalted intentions could not be matched for long with effective deeds.

4. Jean Bodin, *De la Republique* (1576), quoted by Raymond Aron, note 1, p. 247.

5. Charles Louis de Secondat, Baron de Montesquieu, *The Spirit of the Laws* (1746), trans. Thomas Nugent, ed. David Wallace Carruthers (Berkeley: University of California Press, 1977), p. 103 (Book I, Chap. 3, Para. 4).

6. How often have we heard from supersensitive Russian oligarchs that it is impermissible for one nation to interfere in the internal affairs of another. This precept is, of course, sauce for the gander but not for the goose.

7. Aron, note 1, pp. 743–749, presents a close analysis of the trends toward change in interstate sovereignty, particularly with reference to the European Common Market, and other European organs for economic cooperation.

8. Incidentally, I must doubt that Adam Smith would be pleased with the credit that neoconservatives give him for the Invisible Hand as a justification for greed and selfishness. From all accounts, he was a generous man, much concerned with the problems of poverty and convinced that the free market was not the whole solution. See Gertrude Himmelfarb, *The Idea of Poverty* (New York: Knopf, 1984), pp. 42–63.

ERNEST VAN DEN HAAG

In John Conrad's response I find many statements crying out for correction. Before turning to them, though, let me stress one simple matter. Despite all the noise he makes in "laying out the foundations to be built on," Conrad does not even come near to doing what he intended: He does not establish the relevance of the U.N. to its main purpose, avoidance of war among the major powers. The U.N. was not and is not relevant even to avoiding war between such minor powers such as Iran and Iraq or Chad and Libya. Or, to turn to more civilized powers, Great Britain and Argentina. Conrad did not offer a plausible explanation of how the U.N. could play a role in a serious conflict among the superpowers. It cannot, for the U.N. *is* the superpowers, plus some comparatively powerless allies, neutrals, and ministates. There is also an overpaid, busily paper-shuffling, but fortunately powerless bureaucracy calling itself the "U.N." It has nothing whatever to do with war and peace or international relations. It keeps itself busy organizing endless and useless meetings.

Conrad misunderstood my view that wars as often arise from understanding as from misunderstanding. He says that if the antagonists had known each other's moves, their own moves would have been different, and in some cases they might not have attacked. Certainly. But by "understanding" I did not mean "predicting." Wars would be altogether unnecessary if all the moves determining the outcome could be predicted with certainty. Wars are based on uncertainty: The party that ultimately is defeated certainly did not foresee its defeat—else it would not have engaged in war. No, when I wrote that understanding does not always prevent war, and sometimes causes it, I meant (and it still seems obvious to me) that Great Britain declared war on Hitler, not because it was all that interested in Poland, which Hitler had invaded, but because the understanding that Hitler wouldn't stop there dawned even on the silly government of appeasers Britain had at the time. The United States entered the war because we understood that Hitler would not rest with the conquest of Europe and that we could not afford to let him conquer Europe. It is understanding the ultimate intentions and the purposes of actual policies, as distinguished from accurately predicting the opponent's moves, that may lead to peace or war. Misunderstandings do not play much of a role. It was Churchill's (and France's) understanding of Hitler's ultimate intentions (and our intervention) that finally saved Europe. Had we not understood Hitler, Europe would have lost its freedom. Had the understanding come earlier to France and England, there might have been a minor preventive war, instead of the gigantic world war. But our understanding of Hitler hardly was fostered by the diplomatic contacts Conrad thinks so highly of. On the contrary, Hitler's diplomacy served to foster misunderstanding of his true intentions. It was meant to do no less. So is most of the current Soviet diplomacy.

Let me use a homey illustration. People get married, usually because they like each other, and divorced, usually because they have come to dislike one another. Perhaps they understood each other when they got married, although, when they get divorced, they often contend that they did not. At any rate, by the time they get divorced they have come to know each other much better; they certainly have had more extensive contacts than diplomats have in the U.N. Does the intimate and prolonged contact produce peace and understanding? Or do they divorce due to misunderstandings? Only in the movies. In reality they often understand each other and their intentions better than they did when they got married, well enough to become hostile to one another or, at least, to find it impossible to live with one another. Each may feel misunderstood by the other, but "misunderstood" here may simply mean "disapproved of."

The law prevents physical warfare when couples separate, having come to understand one another all too well. But there is no law preventing warfare among nations who have come to understand one another's intentions. The war between Finland and the Soviet Union was caused by Stalin's desire to annex the former and the failure of Finland to indulge it. There was no misunderstanding. Stalin simply did not foresee how willing the Finns were to resist, and how capable. If he had, he might have attacked anyway, but with more preparation. Again, Libya attacked Chad, not foreseeing how much resistance it would meet, but there was no misunderstanding of intentions. Nor was there between Iraq and Iran, although neither foresaw and accurately estimated the strength of the other. Nor were the several wars by means of which the Arabs hoped to annihilate Israel caused by any misunderstanding. The Arabs simply had not foreseen their own defeat. But both parties well understood one another. I am all in favor of avoiding misunderstandings. That is what diplomacy is for. But anyone who believes that conflicts and wars could be avoided if only "people understood each other" lives in a fool's paradise.

Small military conflicts, such as the Argentine–British one about the Falklands, may be due to miscalculations by at least one party of the other's will to resist. To avoid them, and bigger wars as well, one must credibly convince the prospective attacker that he will be resisted. One must convince the prospective attacker not only of one's resolution to resist but also of one's ability to win. He won't attack if convinced of the victim's will and ability to beat him back. This is why unilateral disarmament invites aggression and a strong defense force deters it.

Contrary to Conrad's assertion, the Japanese attack on the United States and Hitler's attack on his ally, Stalin, were due to the basic understanding, not misunderstanding, the attacking government had of the obstacle to its ambitions represented by the target of the attack. Hitler wanted to dominate the world, starting with Europe, and knew he couldn't as long as the Soviet power remained. His calculations of relative strength were wrong, as the result showed. His basic understanding of the situation was not. Stalin's was. He had not understood Hitler's basic ambition. But if he had, he would still not have avoided the attack, although he might have been better prepared for it. As for Japan, its government knew full well that it would never be allowed to dominate China and Southeast Asia as long as America was not defeated. We did not foresee Pearl Harbor. But the administration did expect war with Japan. Miscalculations of relative strength, yes, and of timing and points of attack. But there was no misunderstanding of intentions.

Conrad tells us that he spoke with "a good many diplomats working in the [U.N.]" and (surprise!) "All of them, even Eastern Europeans, believe that constant interchange of opinions and ideas...do increase understanding...." It did not occur to him that the Eastern Europeans like the opportunities for spying and deluding the Western powers. Further, all these diplomats do have some interest in not depicting their activity as futile. They are clearly self-serving in what they told him. But even if their beliefs were sincerely held, they would be as wrong as Conrad's are. Shared delusions do not generate truth and do not amount to evidence.

At any rate, the Eastern European diplomats at the U.N. are not there to foster understanding, as Conrad so naively believes.

Rather, they try to promote misunderstanding of the true intentions of their governments and the power that dominates them, the Soviet Union, so as to induce suckers to disarm and to make loans to them. They have been reasonably successful. The jocular definition "A diplomat is a man sent abroad to lie for his country" is no joke at all at the U.N. It is a description.

Conrad himself intimates how hopelessly he misunderstands the situation when he writes of "that miserable Iron Curtain that splits the world so needlessly." I deplore it as much as he does, but, unlike Conrad, I am not befuddled by U.N. equivocations. Therefore, I understand that the Iron Curtain, or the Berlin Wall, is not needless from the Soviet viewpoint. A ruthless, oppressive dictatorship, which exploits its population to increase its military might and to prepare for expansion, cannot allow people to leave or to find out that life in the Western capitalist democracies is better. To let people find out that prosperity is achieved elsewhere without oppression, while oppression behind the Iron Curtain only achieves poverty, would risk the collapse of the Soviet regime. And to let naive persons (I shall not name names) find out the Soviet's constant preparation for aggression would weaken their efforts to persuade the West to disarm and to rely for defense on U.N. incantations, contacts, or resolutions. No, the Iron Curtain is not "needless," any more than the KGB is. Both are indispensable to the Soviet dictatorship, which cannot afford freedom of information, opinion, or movement.

Conrad thinks me flippant when I write that "any coffee shop will do" for a discussion if people are ready for it. Yet the Cuban missile crisis was settled in a coffee shop. The U.N. had nothing whatever to do with settling it.

To refuse "to use [the U.N.]" would lead to "international anarchy," according to Conrad. He has not realized that we have never had anything else, and the U.N. has never been useful in doing anything about it. By "anarchy" we usually mean a society without law and government. Does Conrad really believe that the U.N. provides either? It is not a supernational organization but, at best, an international meeting place, in which opinions are expressed and resolutions passed. There is no decision-making legislative, judicial, or enforcement power. Relations among independent governments are determined by power, not by law. This is what is meant by anarchy.

Conrad thinks that world opinion is important and will influence the actions of the Soviet Union. His evidence is that the Soviet Union did not invade Poland when its communist government seemed to sway under the impact of the Solidarity movement, although the Soviets had invaded Czechoslovakia, Hungary, and Afghanistan, and before that the Baltic states. As Conrad sees it, the influence of "world opinion" has somehow grown since Afghanistan. He even notes "Moscow gossip" that "the Red Army would dearly like to get out" of Afghanistan. Unlike Conrad, I am not tuned in to "Moscow gossip." But if some people in Moscow are displeased by the invasion of Afghanistan, I believe it has nothing to do with world opinion, but rather with the costly resistance of the Afghans, which does not compare with the token resistance the Soviet army easily did overcome in Hungary, let alone Czechoslovakia. Again, the reason for not invading Poland has nothing to do with world opinion. Poland might have seriously resisted, leading to a long-drawn-out battle. And a pro-Soviet army general took over the government and was effective in keeping Poland in line. What would have been the purpose of an invasion? The threat achieved more cheaply what an invasion would have: a pro-Soviet government. What does all this have to do with the U.N. or world opinion?

About sovereignty Professor Conrad is—well, odd. He quotes Bodin to the effect that princes are rational as though this were inconsistent with sovereignty, or Bodin's description thereof. He does the same by quoting Montesquieu about the constraint of self-interest on rulers. Of course. My point was that sovereigns follow their self-interest as they see it, without being constrained by any superior power or law, by anything but self-interest, exactly as Bodin's definition of sovereignty, "power unfettered by law," so succinctly puts it. Of course, there is a Postal Union and the other international treaties Conrad mentions. They function and are enforced as long as sovereign governments find it in their interest to have them function. None of these conventions or, for that matter, none of the customs and rules of "international law" can be enforced against the wishes of even a small sovereign government, such as Albania—unless the enforcers are willing to go to war, which defeats the major purpose of enforcement.

Surely sovereigns can voluntarily submit to regulations by an entity they create, such as the European Common Market; they can even delegate some of their power to regulate international commerce. They will do so if they find it to be in their interest. But as long as they are sovereign they can stop adhering to, or enforcing, agreements whenever they find it in their interest. They can stop making effective whatever they don't like. When I make a contract with John Conrad I can be compelled to act accordingly, or to pay for the harm I cause by not doing so. A sovereign nation cannot be compelled to do either. Moreover, much of my relationship to John Conrad is limited and regulated by the superior power of government, apart from any contract we may make. Thus, I can argue with him, but I cannot use violence. Not so with relations among sovereign nations. The treaties among sovereign nations are as temporarily useful and as permanent and valuable as Hitler's nonaggression pact with Stalin was—or the U.N. promises of peace.

I have not noted that major nations, such as China, the Soviet Union, the United States, or Japan, are inclined to give up any sovereignty. How could they? What nation would want to be governed, even in part, by an alien government or committee of governments pursuing its own interests? At any rate the logical concept of sovereignty, as formulated by Bodin, contrary to Conrad's notion, is as "immutable" as $2 + 2 = 4$. Either a nation is sovereign, the supreme lawgiver independently deciding on its own actions, or it is subjected to compulsory superior legislation and thus it is not sovereign. The state of New York is not sovereign. The United States is. So is Canada. That they both may voluntarily submit to regulations, treaties, and arbitration does not mean they can be compelled to. They can refuse because, unlike the state of Nevada, they are sovereign.

There always have been gradations of the practical extent of sovereignty. Finland, though sovereign, knows better than to use its sovereignty to engage in foreign policies disapproved by its powerful neighbor the Soviet Union. I doubt that we would tolerate a Soviet allied Canada, although we do tolerate a Soviet allied Cuba. In practice, sovereignty always depends on power distributions. But the concept has not changed.

I disagree with John Conrad on the effects of decolonization. It has increased the power and prosperity of native elites (though not their security: They tend to kill one another) but decreased the prosperity and influence of the native peoples. Those countries, such as India, that have done slightly better have achieved this through the injection of huge funds, usually from the United States, and through agricultural advances made in the West (the green revolution). Still, millions of people died because the withdrawal of England led to the subcontinent's being split into two hostile and occasionally warring states, Hindustan and Pakistan.

I am not defending the South African government, but, unlike John Conrad, I hold no brief for its would-be successors. They are certain to be worse—at least for those of us who open their eyes to experience instead of dreaming. I regret the measures the South African government took in self-defense and the hundreds of deaths caused by racial rioting. But I'd rather see hundreds of deaths in South Africa than tens of thousands, as in Burundi or Uganda. One can hope for reform and greater participation of all races in the government of South Africa. But a switch from government by the present white elite to government by a black elite, whether it occurs peacefully or by violence, would be a disaster for all concerned, including the black masses whose leaders advocate it.

If one accepts Conrad's view of legitimacy—government by consent of the governed—the governments of East Germany, Hungary, Poland, and the Soviet Union are less legitimate than that of South Africa. Anyway, he confuses legitimacy with desirability. Consensual government is desirable, but normally governments are regarded as legitimate if they hold effective power, seem sta-

ble, and are willing to act in such a way as to make relations with
them worth having. Thus, the Soviet government is recognized as
legitimate, although it does not have the consent—and never asked
for it (under reasonable conditions)—of the governed, and so is the
East German government; so was Hitler's and Mussolini's; so are
the governments of Syria or Iraq, Pakistan, Rumania, Burma, or
Vietnam.

"Two-thirds of the inhabitants of South Africa are denied any
part in the political process," as Conrad says. Nobody informed
him that in the Soviet Union more than three-fourths of the population are. He thinks "it is not credible that two-thirds of the
population of the USSR are oppressed [as in] South Africa." Why
not? By definition a dictatorship uses organized force and its monopoly of means of communication to oppress, i.e., to do without
the consent of those it governs. How can this be news to Conrad?
Surely he does not confuse the Soviet Union with a democracy?
Even the most dedicated fellow travelers have long since stopped
doing so. Actually, oppression in South Africa is far less than in
the Soviet Union. South Africa never had any Gulag. Opposition
is vocal. South Africa did compel some parts of its black population to move to designated areas—but not whole populations, as
the Soviet Union did. South Africans can freely leave; actually,
blacks from Mozambique and other neighboring states move in because they are better off. Soviet people cannot—and nobody
moves in. Conrad presents no evidence indicating that the "Politburo is careful to coddle the Russian masses." Perhaps he should
not trust his sources of "Moscow gossip" as much as he seems to.
I think the Politburo at most is careful to try to make people
believe—and it seems successful with Conrad—that it cares for
"the masses." I don't think the masses feel coddled—and the
Politburo must have some reason for not allowing them any freedom to express their views.

"As a conservative" I do believe indeed that "we must
reconcile ourselves to the inevitability of death." I had not realized that liberals do not. However, I do not believe any more than
Conrad does that "we must all die in a thermonuclear blast." It is

possible. But it is not probable, as long as we rely on deterrence and not on either world opinion or the U.N. to prevent ward. Deterrence so far has worked, and it is the only thing likely to work in the future. We must rely on making it clear to any aggressor that he will not be able to win anything. Nobody attacks unless he feels that he can win, and that the advantage of victory will exceed the cost. Nobody will think so if we stay sufficiently armed. However, even Albania will think it can attack us with impunity if we rely on world opinion for protection, as John Conrad recommends, or on the U.N.

JOHN P. CONRAD

On the basis of some idiosyncratic interpretations of my argument, Dr. van den Haag has constructed an impressive position. I hope that our readers will defer judgment on the relative merits of our positions until they have been exposed in more detail.

Meanwhile, I protest that my sources of Moscow gossip are no more than a reading of our better informed journals of opinion, which Dr. van den Haag probably also reads. Perhaps the Red Army really enjoys its predicament in Afghanistan. I doubt it, but all military regimes know that face must be saved, no matter what the cost.

Regardless of the value of the Afghan exercise for training, General Secretary Gorbachev wants to bring it to an end. In his address to the 27th Congress of the Communist Party, he referred to the Afghan war as a "bleeding wound." His statement went on to say:

> We should like, in the nearest future, to withdraw the Soviet troops stationed in Afghanistan at the request of its government. Moreover, we have agreed with the Afghan side on the schedule for their phased withdrawal as soon as a political settlement is reached that will ensure an actual cessation and dependably guarantee the non-resumption of foreign armed interference in the internal affairs of the Democratic Republic of Afghanistan. It is in our vital national

interest that the USSR should always have good and peaceful relations with all its neighbours. This is a vitally important objective of our foreign policy.[1]

Professor van den Haag will be quick to note that this is a carefully phrased statement that commits the Soviet Union to nothing at all. That it is included in the address is significant; the Soviet establishment has been rather chary of such discussions. My opponent may think what he likes, but I infer that the General Secretary would like to find a way out of Afghanistan as soon as he can without losing too much face.

Note

1. Mikhail Gorbachev, *Political Report of the CPSU Central Committee to the 27th Congress of the Communist Party of the Soviet Union* (Moscow: Novosti Press Agency Publishing House, 1986), p. 86.

PART II

THE FACTS

CHAPTER 2

The Undebatable Facts and Events

JOHN P. CONRAD

The Background

Before we can proceed with this debate we must establish the facts. Here is a brief and nonjudgmental history and description of the United Nations and its predecessor, the League of Nations. No clash of opinion here; the pyrotechnics will be found elsewhere.

The idea of an international organization is old. In a sense, it is at least as old as the Roman Empire and the memory of the *Pax Romana*. Over the centuries, history and folk memories deceive in proportion to the hopes of men and women for peace. The Roman peace was oppressive and enforced by the emperors' legions, but for a few centuries order and stability prevailed, contrasting with the incessant petty warfare of the centuries that followed the fall of Rome. The Holy Roman Emperors and Napoleon justified their conquests with the pious claim that through their domination of Europe they could bring about a new imperial peace by achieving the unity of mankind. Their failure demonstrated that in a world of nation-states, armed coercion cannot keep the peace for long.

The peace following the fall of Bonaparte depended partly on the Concert of Europe, a sort of tacit agreement among the Great Powers to consult each other when the peace of the continent was threatened,[1] and partly on the Royal Navy of Great Britain, which policed the world's trade routes. It was a peace that stood up well until the time of Bismarck and the succession of Prussian wars that established the German Reich as the principal power on the Continent. Few statesmen foresaw that the collapse of this system in 1914 would lead to the unprecedented tragedy of World War I.[2] No one anticipated the long and unprecedented slaughter that took the lives of millions of young men in that pointless conflict.

The worldwide desire to avoid a repetition of the horrors of mechanized war led to the creation of the League of Nations, a voluntary organization of national states committed to the objective of collective security. Means and ends were set forth in the Covenant, the League's constitution. That document was produced by the peace conference at Versailles that brought World War I to a bitter formal end. It was unanimously adopted on April 28, 1919, by the participants of the conference—the victorious "Big Four": the United States, France, Great Britain, and Italy.

President Woodrow Wilson had made the formation of the League the 14th of the 14 points that he proposed as the basis for a peace. He had not always been in favor of international organizations. Wilson's Republican predecessor, William Howard Taft, had organized a "League to Enforce the Peace" as an American initiative toward international organization. It is a political irony that Theodore Roosevelt and Senator Henry Cabot Lodge were also members of this league.[3] As the war in Europe continued in an apparently interminable stalemate, Wilson gradually became a strenuous advocate of the League, believing that the obvious faults of the Treaty of Versailles would be corrected in due course through the influence of the League in allaying hostilities and fostering international cooperation.

He reckoned without the United States Senate. Ratification of the Covenant collided with the isolationist traditions of American foreign policy and the open personal enmity of Senator Lodge toward Wilson and all his works—although in principle Lodge was in favor of international organization. There was a majority of the Senate favoring American membership in the League, but that majority fell seven votes short of the two-thirds required by the Constitution for the ratification of a treaty. A group of "irreconcilable" Republican senators, led by Lodge,[4] the majority leader and chairman of the Foreign Relations Committee, effectively prevented the United States from taking a seat in the League that President Wilson had done so much to bring into being.[5]

The failure of the United States to join the League did not prevent its formation. The other great powers proceeded in the expectation, never fulfilled, that the Senate would eventually reverse itself. It became a league organized to create a collective security against war, but the richest and most powerful nation of all, the nation that had done the most to create it, had refused to participate.

In the minds of the statesmen who organized the League, the absence of the United States had a practical significance even more serious than the symbolic effect of the Senate's rejection. The heart of the Covenant was contained in Articles 10–17, which followed the sections prescribing the administrative structure and the general principles to which member states were expected to adhere. Articles 10–17 dealt with the procedures for settling disputes and the sanctions to be applied against nations that violated the Covenant. These sanctions were to be economic and they were to be applied collectively by all member nations. Without unanimity on the application of sanctions, collective security would be meaningless. The absence of the United States from the League cast doubt on the effectiveness of any action that might be taken against an aggressor.

As we shall see, the League could not effectively apply sanctions against Japan for its invasion of China or against Italy for its invasion of Ethiopia—mainly because of the unwillingness of its two most powerful members, Great Britain and France, to proceed with the stringent economic sanctions the Covenant required.

Despite this inauspicious beginning, forty-one nations were represented at the first meeting of the Assembly on November 15, 1920. As time went on, twenty-one additional member states joined, making a total of sixty-two delegations in September 1934, when the last recruit, the Soviet Union, took its place. Seventeen nations withdrew before World War II, most notably Japan, Germany, and Italy, and the Soviet Union was expelled in December 1939 because of its invasion of Finland.

The Structure of the League of Nations. The Covenant
provided for an Assembly, the parliament of the League, comprising representatives of all the member nations. The Assembly was
originally intended to meet every three or four years, but at the
first session the delegates decided that the meetings should be annual. Because the Assembly was composed of the representatives
of sovereign nations, all decisions had to be by the unanimous vote
of all representatives, thereby effectively providing each nation
with a veto. The Assembly sessions began with wide-ranging discourse about the problems of the world with a view to setting the
Assembly's agenda. It then broke into committees, in which each
member nation could be and usually was represented, to study
problems and to recommend solutions to the Assembly as a whole.
After all the committee deliberations had been completed, the Assembly would reconvene to act on the recommendations, almost
always positively. Differences were supposedly reconciled in committees. When a committee member dissented from the majority,
his delegation would normally abstain from voting in the Assembly, thereby refraining from the veto in any Assembly vote that
each member possessed in principle.

The second organ of the League was the Council, composed
of the Great Powers and a rotating membership of smaller powers.
The Council, comprising the nations with the most economic and
military strength, was empowered by Article 4 of the Covenant to
"deal at its meetings with any matter within the sphere of action
of the League or affecting the peace of the world." In effect, it
was a board of directors with the League's authority at its disposal, and responsible to the Assembly for its use.

Originally the Council of the League was to consist of
representatives of the United States, Great Britain, France, Italy,
and Japan, as the permanent membership, and six members
selected by the Assembly. The American seat was never occupied.[6] It was obvious that eventually, when Germany became a
member of the League, it would have to have a permanent seat in
the Council. The nature of the Council and the concept of permanent membership identified the powers that held permanent seats

as "Great Powers." This provision of the Covenant led to considerable trouble.

Germany applied for admission to the League in February 1926, an event that brought about the League's first constitutional crisis. In the preceding years there had been much uncertainty on both sides about whether Germany should join and, if it did, what its role in the League's affairs should be. Some French politicians found it advantageous to argue that Germany should remain an outcast nation, whereas most of the other member states regarded Germany's membership as both inevitable and desirable. This issue was settled in the Locarno treaties of 1925, which bound the signatories, Germany, Belgium, France, Great Britain, and Italy, to respect each other's borders as inviolable, and under no circumstances to resort to war against any other signatory. The pacific intentions of Germany being thus established—or so it was believed, even by the French, the most intransigent of the belligerent nations—all the Great Powers agreed that these treaties opened the door for the admission of Germany as another Great Power in good standing.

Unfortunately for the League, there were a number of other member nations with aspirations to be counted as Great Powers. Brazil,[7] Spain, and Poland considered themselves as also entitled to permanent membership in the Council. Brazil withdrew from the League when the Assembly refused to amend the Covenant to accommodate more permanent members. Germany's status as a permanent Council member was formalized. To assuage the disappointment of the smaller nations about their prospects for Council participation, the nonpermanent membership of the Council was expanded from six to nine.[8]

The Collapse of the League. In 1931, the Japanese government was taken over by the military, and that country's invasion of Manchuria began. This was clearly a Covenant violation requiring action by the Council. Obviously, economic sanctions against Japan would have to be universal to be effective. It was by no means certain that both the United States and the Soviet Union would join

with the nations of the League in imposing the severe penalties required by the Covenant.

It was decided that since the imposition of sanctions was so
doubtful of success, the League should investigate the invasion on
the spot, a decision characteristic of any legislature in a quandary.
A commission headed by Lord Lytton, an English diplomat, was
appointed and sent to the Far East to find the facts and recommend
appropriate action to the Assembly. By the time the Lytton Commission's ship arrived in China, months after its formation, Japanese control of Manchuria was an accomplished fact, about which
the League could do nothing that would affect the course of events
in the Orient. The upshot was a declaration by the Assembly calling on Japan to withdraw from Chinese territory and establishing
that no member of the League would recognize the puppet state of
Manchukuo, which Japan had installed in Manchuria. Japan refused to accept any part of this action by the Assembly and withdrew from the League in March 1933 amid eloquent expressions
of general regret at the loss of the skillful collaboration of the Japanese diplomats accredited to the Council.[9]

Later in 1933, the overthrow of the Weimar regime in Germany by the Nazis brought about the next crisis in the League's
affairs. The advent of an aggressive and militaristic leadership in
that nation was almost immediately followed by the withdrawal of
Germany from the League. Reacting to the ominous implications
of the Nazis' rise to power, Josef Stalin decided that the USSR
must reverse its previous hostility toward the League and take
steps to participate in whatever collective security membership
might provide. In 1934, the USSR formally joined the League and
took a permanent seat in the Council.

The withdrawal of Italy from the League in 1937 vacated another Council seat. The tortuous series of events that led to the
Italian invasion of Ethiopia, to the annexation of that nation by the
Italian crown, and, finally, to Mussolini's contemptuous withdrawal from the League is a long, tragic tale reflecting shame on
the prewar practice of diplomacy. It foretold the evasions of

responsibility for the peace that led up to World War II. The tale has been often told, and I do not propose to encapsulate it here.[10]

This episode, coming so soon after the Japanese invasion of China and Germany's abrupt exit, was a humiliation from which the Council and the Assembly never recovered. The deliberations of these bodies over the invasion of its neighbors by Nazi Germany and, later, the Russian assault on Finland were painfully irrelevant. The magnificent Palais des Nations built to house the League in Geneva was opened in 1936 and for a few years more the League survived as the organizer of international technical and social services. After the outbreak of World War II, a skeleton staff huddled in the Geneva headquarters, while the economic and financial staff moved in 1940 to the campus of Princeton University in the United States. The final action of the Assembly took place on April 19, 1946, when that body voted to dissolve the League and to transfer its records, assets, and functions to the newly organized United Nations.

The Secretariat of the League of Nations. The whole structure of the League of Nations was an innovation brought into being by the weary statesmen who botched the Treaty of Versailles. There were no precedents to guide them, the objectives were unclear, and the practical means to the uncertain ends were hopefully left to future experience. That the League's administrative services worked as well as they did was largely due to the vision and skill of its first secretary-general, Sir Eric Drummond. He has been praised for many accomplishments. Probably his most significant contribution to the League's achievements was the concept of an international civil service composed of administrators and professional staff whose primary commitment was to the League and not to their own nationality.[11] It was considered by many to be an impractical organizing principle, a guarantee of conflicts and intrigue, but the record does not reveal that the expected difficulties arose. The idea of the international civil service was carried over to the United Nations, with much less success.[12]

Drummond organized the Secretariat into a number of sections, each charged with the administrative and staff work required by the Covenant. Special sections were established for the administration of the former German and Turkish possessions that were mandated under the peace treaties to the control of the League. Other sections were organized for international economic and financial studies, studies of the international narcotics and white slave traffic, staff work for the Council in dealing with disputes that the Council was to settle, and the protection of minorities in central and eastern Europe. The basic design of the League Secretariat was adopted by the United Nations, with considerable expansion.

Throughout the life of the League, its enemies complained of its extravagance and high costs. To a present-day observer it is sobering to note that its annual budget for the entire period of its life, including the considerable cost of building the Palais des Nations in Geneva, averaged about $5,500,000—a modest outlay, even allowing for vast inflation of the dollar's value.

The record of the Council and the Assembly in dealing with the world's political affairs is mixed. There were some early achievements, followed by a succession of failures, and collapse in the face of the war that the League was designed to prevent. Perhaps the most positive accomplishment of the League was its creation of a Secretariat manned by an international civil service of unquestioned competence and skill. That example is still a substantial asset for the conduct of transnational services.

History and Structure

The Formation of the United Nations. Beginning with the Declaration of London on June 12, 1941, at the nadir of allied fortunes, the nations at war with Germany and Italy stated their intention to establish "a world in which, relieved of the menace of aggression, all may enjoy economic and social security." Seven months later, on January 1, 1942, the phrase "United Nations" was first used in the United Nations Declaration, to express the unity of the allies in a desperate war against common enemies. This sense of unity came to inclue the USSR. Throughout the war, after the Nazi invasion of Russia, Western statesmen generally assumed that the common interests of the powers at war with Germany would lead to a firm alliance that would surely survive the defeat of the Nazi regime. Diplomatic conversations took place among the major powers about the form the peace would take. There was general agreement that the mistakes that were made at Versailles should not be repeated, and that the international organization replacing the League of Nations should be stronger in the interest of collective security. Just how this strength should be achieved was never clear. It is still unclear.

There was, however, a general understanding of a basic difference from the League of Nations that would have to be established if the United Nations was to succeed. The League hoped to achieve by its existence a *collective security*. Aggression by any nation was to be officially established by the Council of the League, and the Covenant provided that all member nations should participate in an economic boycott of the offending nation. There was nothing mandatory about the boycott; it was assumed that in the interest of collective security aggression would be deterred by the Covenant's provisions and, if it occurred, it would be terminated by the collective action of the member states.[13]

The Charter of the United Nations returns to the fundamental concept of the Concert of Europe in accepting the principle of the hegemony of the Great Powers. The architects of the Charter accepted the reality that only the Great Powers are strong enough to enforce the peace when it is broken and have sufficient authority to make binding decisions for the organization.[14]

By August 1944 confidence in the ultimate victory of the Allied cause had reached a point at which serious consideration of the peace to come was appropriate. A conference at the foreign minister level of the "big four powers"—the United States, the USSR, Great Britain, and China—was convened at Dumbarton Oaks, an estate in the District of Columbia, to draft plans for an international organization. Because at that time the Soviet Union was neutral in the war with Japan, the conference had to be held in two stages; the Soviet Union and China could not participate in the planning process together. First, the United States, the USSR, and Great Britain hammered out a document entitled "Proposals for the Establishment of a General International Organization." Once the three powers had arrived at an agreement on the content of these proposals, the USSR representatives bowed out and China was brought in to consider and ultimately to endorse the proposals.

It was agreed that there should be a United Nations organizations, and most of its structure was outlined at that time. There were two serious hitches. The USSR insisted that the permanent members of the Security Council should each possess a veto power over proposed actions by the Council. It was clear to the Soviet delegates that the interests of the USSR would be jeopardized unless the Security Council was prevented from adopting any resolution that interfered with Soviet concerns. Various compromises were proposed, including a suggestion that when a power's interests were at stake in Security Council deliberations that power should abstain from voting. The USSR rejected all compromises of the principle of the veto, thereby creating a structural obstacle to the Security Council's action in any situation involving a permanent member. As Brian Urquhart, long an under-secretary-general, comments, this unanimity rule "guaranteed that the Security Council would not take enforcement action against one of the five great powers."[15]

The second dangling issue concerned the representation of the USSR in the United Nations. Stalin proposed that each of the 16 republics constituting the Soviet Union should be represented separately with a delegation of its own. This was an understandable, if preposterous, proposal, even though the autonomy of the Soviet republics as to foreign policy or anything else was less than that enjoyed by the states in the United States. After all, Stalin reasoned, with only one vote, the USSR would be at a hopeless disadvantage in any General Assembly decision making. He took it for granted that the United States could count on the supporting votes of the Latin American countries and that the United Kingdom would be joined by the Commonwealth nations in a solid bloc.

Decisions on these issues were deferred to the summit meeting at Yalta in February 1945. Roosevelt and Churchill consented to the veto on which Stalin had insisted. The question of representation was compromised; Stalin agreed that the augmented Soviet representation would be limited to the republics of Byelorussia and the Ukraine in addition to the USSR. To this day, Byelorussia and the Ukraine maintain permanent missions to the United Nations, although nothing has occurred to establish the autonomy, let alone the sovereignty, of these republics. Naturally, their missions to the United Nations share the same address as the Permanent Mission of the USSR.

The Charter. The compromises at Yalta resolved the critical problems in organizing the United Nations. The next step was to draft a charter. For this purpose the United Nations Conference on International Organization was convened in San Francisco on April 25, 1945, remaining in session until June 26, when the Charter was signed by the representatives of the nations attending. Forty-six states participated in the conference from the beginning; five others were admitted before its adjournment. Ratification by a majority of the 51 nations thus united speedily followed, and the Charter went into effect on October 24, 1945, as the constitutional scaffolding of the new organization.[16]

No powerful senator opposed American membership in the United Nations. Sentiment in the Congress overwhelmingly favored the Charter as a treaty to which the United States would adhere. There was a widespread determination that nothing should stand in the way of American membership. No "irreconcilables" could be mobilized to obstruct the United Nations Charter as Senator Lodge and his "small band of wilful men" had prevented ratification of the Covenant of the League of Nations in 1920. Statesmen, publicists, political scientists, and other prominent citizens extolled in the most extravagant terms the wisdom and foresight of the participants of the San Francisco conference who created the Charter. Opposition to United States membership was limited to two votes in the Senate and two major newspapers, the New York *Daily News* and the Chicago *Tribune*, both owned by Colonel Robert McCormick, an uncompromising isolationist.[17] The Charter was duly ratified by the Senate, and the United States was admitted as an original member state on October 24, 1945.

The Structure of the United Nations

The Security Council. The Charter had many structural similarities to the Covenant of the League. The Security Council, with its array of five permanent members[18] and a rotation of non-permanent members, is roughly similar to the League's Council in organization and functions. However, the League's Council operated on a unanimity rule—all decisions had to have the affirmative support of all Council members. The Security Council's decisions can be blocked only by the veto of a permanent member, a negative vote by a nonpermanent member being without the force of preventing the proposed action.

The veto power exercised by the permanent member states has had the effect of paralyzing decisions by the Security Council. Because most international disputes impinge on the interests of the major powers and almost always affect the real or presumed interests of the two superpowers, any resolution proposed for the settlement of such disputes will find at least one permanent member in disagreement and exercising the veto prerogative. In principle, the Security Council alone has the power to make decisions for the United Nations, which all members are obliged under the Charter to accept. In practice, the Security Council has often been unable to make such decisions for the prevention or resolution of major armed conflicts or for the imposition of sanctions against an aggressor state.

The most significant exception to the Security Council's inability to act occurred when, on June 25, 1950, the Democratic People's Republic of North Korea invaded South Korea. The Security Council met immediately and passed a resolution denouncing this invasion as an act of aggression by the North Koreans. This action was made possible by the Soviet Union's boycott of the Security Council, which began in January 1950 as a protest against the exclusion of the People's Republic of China from the United Nations. That was a blunder that the Soviet Union did not repeat. It rejoined the Security Council, but too late to prevent the military campaigns that followed.[19]

The General Assembly. The General Assembly of the United Nations allows one vote for each member nation, however great or small. Much frustration and annoyance has been addressed to this seeming anomaly, mostly by American observers compelled to listen to denunciations of American foreign policy by delegates from impoverished, inconsequential, but sovereign member states that were all too recently colonial possessions. Various corrective measures have been proposed, usually in the form of amendments to the Charter providing that votes in the General Assembly should be weighted by population, gross national product, contributions to the United Nations budget, or some other differentiating parameter. None of these proposals is likely to find favor with a majority of the General Assembly members, who are well satisfied with the present egalitarian voting rights.

The Charter is clear on the powers of the General Assembly. It has the right to discuss questions and matters within the scope of the Charter and to recommend action to the Security Council. It also has the power to expel a member nation upon the recommendation of the Security Council. It is responsible for approval of the annual budget of the organization.[20] Finally, it elects the nonpermanent members of the Security Council, the Economic and Social Council, and the Trusteeship Council when vacancies in those bodies occur.[21] It was never intended to be a decision-making body with powers to require member nations to take specific actions.

Although the powers of the General Assembly appear to be specifically limited to the matters indicated here, the superpower paralysis by Russian veto in the Security Council required a liberal reinterpretation of the Charter's language early in the life of the

United Nations. At the initiative of the United States during the early phases of the Korean war, the General Assembly adopted in November 1950 a "Uniting for Peace" resolution.[22] This resolution provided for several innovations:

1. Convening the General Assembly in emergency session on 24 hours' notice upon request by the Security Council or a majority of the member states.
2. Establishment of a Peace Observation Commission to report on conditions in any area in which international peace and security is endangered.
3. Invitation to member states to survey resources and inform the United Nations of the nature and scope of the assistance that could be placed at the disposal of the United Nations military command for the restoration of peace and security.
4. Appointment of a Collective Measures Committee to coordinate contributions of troops and to plan concerted action.

The legality of this resolution was plausibly contested by the USSR. In 1962 the International Court of Justice ruled that the resolution was based on a lawful interpretation of the Charter.

The original purpose of the Uniting for Peace resolution was to provide such legitimacy for the military operations in Korea as the United Nations could confer. At the time of its passage the Uniting for Peace resolution looked like an ingenious circumvention of the Soviet veto, and for the occasion for which it was drafted it certainly served that purpose. Diplomats with a longer view into the future noted that just as the Soviet veto was weakened, in other conflicts at other times the United States would find its veto weakened in exactly the same way.[23] In spite of the original Russian objections, the Warsaw Pact nations had no compunctions about invoking the Uniting for Peace resolution to circumvent French and British vetoes in the Security Council at the time of the Suez crisis in order to bring the General Assembly into an emergency session.[24] In effect, as experience with the Uniting for Peace resolution has accumulated, the General Assembly has become a major instrument of the United Nations' authority.

Decolonization of the old European empires was a declared objective of the United Nations from the first. Articles 73 and 74 of the Charter are unambiguous about the organization's commitment to the self-government of colonized peoples. That goal was reached sooner than anyone expected, with the consequence that the General Assembly expanded from its original membership of 51 in 1945 to 100 in 1960 and 159 in 1985. This expansion was inevitable, but it caused special strains on the Assembly. The 51 original member states were mostly European or American, all of them with well-established diplomatic traditions and experience in the conduct of foreign affairs. Most of them were in reasonably secure economic circumstances. Very few had been subjected to colonial rule. Discourse in the General Assembly was usually temperate and reasoned, even when the vast differences between Western republicanism and Eastern Marxism led to confrontations.

All that changed with the admission of over a hundred new states in the course of 40 years. Some had almost no educated classes.[25] Very serious economic and social problems faced these new nations after the euphoria of liberation was dissipated. One by-product of these perplexities was the rancor of the accusations and complaints against the former colonial powers, in particular, and the prosperous north, in general, that surfaced in the General Assembly. Positions to which the northern powers held tenaciously as matters of principle were questioned by the impoverished south as matters of opposing principle.

An outstanding example of this unbalanced confrontation between the new and weak nations (with the USSR usually making common cause with them for its own purposes) and the old and powerful was the General Assembly resolution condemning Zionism as racism.[26] This resolution had been under subterranean discussion for several years and finally surfaced in 1975 for debate and a vote on the floor of the Assembly. It was passed by a vote of 72 to 35 with 32 abstentions. The roll call of the majority included all the Communist nations (14), all the Muslim nations (28), most of the non-Muslim African nations, and a scattering of Asian and Latin-American nations.

The General Assembly has been likened to an international debating society, one in which anyone may say anything so long as the traditional courtesies of diplomatic discourse are observed.[27] It can be more than that, and will certainly evolve with experience, changing conditions, and changing personnel. Whether this evolution will lead to an improvement over the present state of affairs remains to be seen.

The Economic and Social Council. The political activities carried on in the Security Council and the General Assembly attract the attention of the general public. Judgments about the usefulness of the United Nations have largely drawn on the content and quality of discourse in these bodies. However, the United Nations has from the first been committed to a large variety of nonpolitical activities coming under the general coordination of the Economic and Social Council, informally known to connoisseurs of U.N. acronyms as ECOSOC. Some of the programs under the economic and social headings have been conceded to be effective by the severest critics of the U.N.

The original planning that led to ECOSOC began under the League of Nations in 1938, when, as we have seen, the League had suffered several disasters in the political fields over which it was intended to maintain the peace. A commission was appointed to consider new initiatives that the League might undertake to restore its reputation. The commission's report was submitted in 1939, days before the outbreak of World War II, recommending the expansion of the League's economic and social programs under a new council created to coordinate them.[28] Obviously nothing could be done to put these recommendations into effect. The whole world was preoccupied with a deadly conflict generated by critical economic and social strains that had not responded to the measures that individual states had applied.

These ideas were revived in 1945 during the preparation of the Charter in San Francisco. At a time when the urgency of international cooperation to rehabilitate shattered continents was obvious, the United Nations was the appropriate vehicle to bring it about. It was understood that in taking on such tasks, the United Nations would sometimes be acting in matters that would ordinarily be under the exclusive "domestic jurisdiction" of some of the sovereign member states.[29] This was a term that defied precise definition, but John Foster Dulles, a delegate to the conference and later the secretary of state under President Eisenhower, explained that the principle of domestic jurisdiction was "now broadened to include functions that would enable the Organization to eradicate the underlying causes of war as well as to deal with economic and social problems."[30]

With its legitimacy thus proclaimed by a subtle and conservative legal authority, Articles 61-72 of the Charter were drafted to provide for ECOSOC and a virtually unlimited scope of activity defined in Article 62 to include "international economic, social, cultural, educational, health and related matters...." The first order of business was the creation of services to provide for the care and resettlement of refugees and displaced persons. This immense task was carried out by the United Nations Relief and Rehabilitation Administration, which was set up in 1945 and dissolved in 1946 so as to distribute its immense responsibilities to agencies with specialized charges for the accomplishment of specific goals. The United Nations Children's Fund (UNICEF) was created in 1946, followed by the United Nations Relief and Works Agency for Palestinian Refugees (UNRWA) in 1949 and the United Nations High Commissioner for Refugees (UNHCR) in 1950.

Over the four decades following its creation, ECOSOC has taken on many tasks, some of them indispensable in an interdependent world economy, and some of them of marginal utility at best. By the mid-1980s ECOSOC was coordinating the work of 8 standing committees, 9 functional commissions, 5 regional commissions, and 15 "specialized agencies." The specialized agencies are listed here to show the wide scope of United Nations interests:

> The International Labor Organization (ILO)
> Food and Agricultural Organization (FAO)
> United Nations Educational, Scientific and Cultural Organization (UNESCO)
> World Health Organization (WHO)

International Bank for Reconstruction and Development
(World Bank, IBRD)
International Finance Corporation (IFC)
International Development Association (IDA)
International Monetary Fund (IMF)
International Civil Aviation Organization (ICAO)
Universal Postal Union (UPU)
International Telecommunication Union (ITU)
World Meteorological Organization (WMO)
Inter-Governmental Maritime Consultative Organization
(IMCO)
World Intellectual Property Organization (WIPO)
International Fund for Agricultural Development (IFAD)

In addition, the International Atomic Energy Agency,
(IAEA), which was established in 1957 under the auspices of the
United Nations, reports annually to the General Assembly but is
not included as a specialized agency under the Charter definition
of the term.

Some of these agencies had a life long before the United Nations came on the world scene. The Universal Postal Union and the
International Telecommunication Union go back to the nineteenth
century, and the International Labor Organization was formerly an
agency of the League of Nations. Membership in these agencies is
open to U.N. member states making voluntary contributions to the
budgets. Each has its own administrative and rule-making structure. Autonomy is virtually complete except for the provision that
annual reports must be made to ECOSOC.

In addition to the specialized agencies under the aegis of
ECOSOC, several other development organizations have been
created by ECOSOC in conjunction with the General Assembly.
These include the United Nations Development Program (UNDP),
the United Nations Conference on Trade and Development (UNC-
TAD), the United Nations Industrial Development Organization
(UNIDO), and the United Nations Environment Program (UNEP).
There has been since the inception of ECOSOC a succession of in-

ternational conferences on a bewildering variety of subjects, ranging from the control of crime to the development of new and
renewable sources of energy. The number and sometimes the
agenda of these conferences have given rise to the acid criticism
that much more of the United Nations' effort in the economic and
social fields has gone into talking rather than doing. Whether and
to what extent this derogation is justified will, of course, be a
topic for further debate in these pages.

ECOSOC began with 18 member states, elected by the
General Assembly. It has twice been expanded, first to 27 states in
1965 and then to 54 states in 1973. Terms in the Council are for
three years and are renewable by the General Assembly. The
Council holds month-long sessions twice a year, alternately in
New York and Geneva.

The Trusteeship Council and the road to decolonization. The
Trusteeship Council is almost out of business to transact. When it
was first established there were 11 trust territories, all of them
former colonial possessions of nations defeated in World Wars I
and II. The Trusteeship Council was set up to administer them
through a system whereby authority would be delegated to a member state taking responsibility for the government of a trust territory, periodically reporting on progress toward self-government.

All but one of these trust territories have found their way to
independence or a merger with a neighbor that was acceptable to
both populations. Even Nauru (population 4,000), once a German
possession, then a Japanese mandate under the League of Nations,
achieved affluent sovereignty in 1968 through the good offices of
the United Nations and the good fortune of vast deposits of phosphate on this remote little island. As yet, it has not been admitted
to the United Nations.

The one remaining trust territory is Micronesia, or the Pacific
Islands, formerly a Japanese mandate under the League and now
administered by the United States. It has been designated a ''stra-
tegic'' trust territory under an agreement approved by the Security
Council in 1947, meaning that formal control is assigned to the
Security Council.

The record of the Trusteeship Council is one of some success in that independence has been achieved for ten populations of limited resources and no previous experience as nation-states. There is one vexing problem where the United Nations claims to responsibility are disputed by a tenacious claimant on the ground. This is the former German possession, Southwest Africa (now generally known as Namibia), which had been mandated by the League to South Africa. After World War II and the demise of the League, South Africa proposed that this territory should be annexed as an integral part of that nation. That suggestion got nowhere with the General Assembly. South Africa then agreed to administer the territory under the terms of the League mandate and to submit reports to the United Nations but outside the trust territory system. One report was actually submitted in 1947, but thereafter no further accounting was made.

At the request of the General Assembly, the International Court of Justice issued an advisory opinion that the United Nations should exercise the supervisory functions of the League over the administration of the territory. South Africa firmly rejected this decision. To this day it continues to occupy the territory in spite of world opinion in general and the virtually unanimous resolutions of the General Assembly and the Security Council.

The South African government refused to allow a United Nations inspection commission to visit the mandated area. The committee did go to South Africa, and returned with the report that the territory was being administered in complete disregard of the League's mandate, the United Nations Charter, and the Universal Declaration of Human Rights.[31]

In 1969 the Security Council declared that the continued presence of South Africa in Namibia was illegal, and in 1971 the International Court of Justice decreed in an advisory opinion that South Africa was under an obligation to withdraw from Namibia. To no one's surprise, South Africa refused to comply. Throughout the 1970s the Security Council and the General Assembly annually condemned the continued occupation of Namibia by South Africa. In 1978 the Security Council approved a plan for a settlement of the Namibian confrontation. In Resolution 435, the Council created a United Nations Transition Assistance Group (UNTAG) to provide for the independence of Namibia after the conduct of free elections under U.N. supervision. There were three elements to the plan: [1] the cessation of hostile acts by all parties; [2] the repeal of discriminatory laws, the release of political prisoners, and the return of exiles and refugees; and [3] the elections to be held after a seven-month period followed by the adoption of a constitution and the proclamation of independence. There has been a vague acceptance of this plan in principle by South Africa, but action has been deferred because of the presence of Cuban troops in Angola, whose departure is specified as a precondition for proceeding with Namibian independence. Although the General Assembly has rejected this condition nothing further has been accomplished as of the time of this writing.[32]

Articles 73 and 74 of the Charter required members of the United Nations with colonial possessions to secure the well-being of the inhabitants of these territories and to plan for their self-government, security, and economic stability. This was a program of decolonization. This goal has been largely achieved, with the result already noted—the expansion of the U.N. from 51 members in 1946 to 159 at present. For most of these new states U.N. membership has been the seal of independence. One Third World ambassador frankly states that the United Nations is "the custodian of our sovereignty."

The U.N. commitment to decolonization has not been the sole cause of the emancipation of the colonized territories.[33] For the United Kingdom, France, and the Netherlands, the prestige of empire was an increasingly costly and precariously maintained ornament. As to most colonies, the relinquishment of imperial pretensions was an economic necessity, sometimes too hastily carried out. The Portuguese empire in Africa was tenaciously maintained much longer until a revolution in 1974 in Portugal itself ousted the regime that had squandered blood and meager national resources to suppress the movement to independence in its overseas possessions.

The history of the United Nations coincides with the remaking of the map of the world. That has been an often untidy and sometimes bloody course of events. Unrealistic expectations by newly sovereign nations, the maintenance of the arbitrary boundaries of the old colonies, and the inadequately prepared elites of the new nations have combined to make decolonization a painful disappointment for many. Through its specialized agencies and the mobilization of resources from the wealthy nations, the United Nations has tried to ease these difficult transitions, sometimes with outstanding success, as in the case of the Republic of Singapore, and sometimes with frustrated hopes, as in the case of Tanzania and Chad.

The International Court of Justice. The International Court of Justice had a predecessor, the Permanent Court of International Justice, established in 1920 and associated with the League of Nations without being an organ of the League. The International Court of Justice, however, is the principal judicial organ of the United Nations, and its authority and existence are legitimated in Articles 92–96 of the Charter. Its organization, competence, and procedures are prescribed in the Statute of the International Court of Justice, which is almost identical with the Statute of the old Permanent Court of International Justice.[34]

The court consists of 15 judges, no two of whom may be of the same nationality. They are elected by the General Assembly and the Security Council for six-year terms. The Statute specifically requires that they should be selected for their qualifications in jurisprudence and as representatives "of the main forms of civilization and of the principal legal systems of the world." These terms are admittedly vague—what is a "main form of civilization" and what is a "principal legal system"?[35] The seat of the court is in The Hague, but it may conduct its proceedings anywhere it finds convenient.

As of 1984, the court had received over 50 cases and 17 advisory opinions had been requested by various international organizations. Fifteen of the cases submitted by member states were withdrawn, and in 10 other cases the court decided that it lacked jurisdiction to intervene.

Article 36 of the Statute of the Court prescribes that only states may be parties in cases before the court. In becoming parties to the Statute, the states

> may at any time declare that they recognize as compulsory the jurisdiction of the Court in all legal disputes concerning,
>
> a. the interpretation of a treaty;
> b. any question of international law;
> c. the existence of any fact which, if established, would constitute a breach of an international obligation;
> d. the nature or extent of the reparation to be made for the breach of an international obligation.

The Statute goes on to call for states to file declarations of agreement to these conditions of jurisdiction. In 1979 only 45 of the 150 states that were then members of the United Nations had filed such declarations. Some of the declarations that have been made are hedged to the point that they are almost meaningless. The United States, for example, has provided that the court has no jurisdiction over matters in which the United States might be a party if, in the opinion of the United States, they fall within the "domestic jurisdiction of the United States." This is the language of the "Connally Amendment" of 1946, and an example that has been followed by several other countries.

Under the Charter (Article 94, §2), failure of a losing party to comply with a judgment of the court may be presented by the other party to the Security Council, which may "make recommendations or decide upon measures to be taken to give effect to the judgment." This provision has never been invoked.

By any criterion, the record of the International Court of Justice is disappointing. Nevertheless, as with all the organs of the United Nations, original expectations have far exceeded reasonable goals. Idealistic optimists have hoped that somehow the rule of law would replace the rule of force through the establishment of the court. The Danish commentator Alf Ross remarks that this hope rests on a gross misunderstanding of the role of a court in any society. A court, he argues, is limited to the interpretation of a law in deciding a conflict. Where there is no law applicable to a matter in conflict, the court must yield to the legislature. In short, a court should limit itself to the interpretation of an existing law, whereas it is only for a legislature to decide what the law *ought* to be.[36]

States are understandably reluctant to risk an adverse decision by the International Court of Justice. Unlike disputes among ordinary citizens, the rule of law is not compulsory in international affairs. It is very doubtful that greater acceptance of the role of the court would introduce more order to the chaotic state of international relations. Until more states agree to use the court, its role will continue to be peripheral to the great international issues of the times.

The Secretary-General. With the founding of the United Nations a significant new actor arrived on the international stage, the secretary-general. The League of Nations used the same title for its principal administrative officer, but the Covenant was vague about his duties other than the management of the Secretariat in Geneva. Sir Eric Drummond, the League's first secretary-general, was a typical specimen of the British administrative civil servant, an excellent manager, trained to administer public affairs as an anonymous subordinate to political chieftains. We are told by those who observed him at first hand that his advice to members of the League's Council was valued in political as well as in administrative matters, but as I have mentioned above, he is remembered mainly for his organization of the League's international civil service.

The intentions of the statesmen who planned the Charter were to create a new kind of executive. President Roosevelt had in mind a "World's Moderator," an official who would take initiatives for the mediation of international conflicts before they could threaten the peace.[37] Everyone engaged in the original thinking about the United Nations agreed that he should be authorized to be much more of an activist than the secretary-general of the League.

The Charter reflects these intentions. Articles 97–101 set forth the powers and duties of this new actor on the world scene. Not only was he to manage the affairs of the organization as its chief administrative officer, but he was also to "bring to the attention of the Security Council any matter which in his opinion may threaten the maintenance of international peace and security.''[38] This provision has been interpreted by all five of the successive occupants of the office as a license for political initiative, although each has used stratagems of his own to play the part.

The first secretary-general was Trygve Lie, a Norwegian labor lawyer who was foreign minister of the government-in-exile throughout World War II. His term of office as secretary-general was exceptionally stressful. He presided over the organization of the Secretariat and the arrangements for headquartering the organization. Inevitably he was deeply involved in the role played by the United Nations in the founding of the State of Israel and the beginning of the endless conflicts generated by that momentous event. He played a fateful role during the Korean War, which brought about his demise as secretary-general. Because he cooperated with the American government in mobilizing an international force to support the South Korean government against the North Korean invasion, he incurred the implacable hostility of the Soviet Union and the rest of the Eastern bloc. He was blamed for not preventing the United States from passing the Uniting for Peace resolution, which the Soviet Union pronounced illegal. Thereafter, the USSR boycotted the United Nations and went out of its way to insult Lie as a creature of the West.

Ironically, he was pilloried by some American politicians as ''soft'' on the Communists, and accused of tolerating American Communists on the staff of the Secretariat. To relieve this suspicion he allowed the Federal Bureau of Investigation to take up offices in the United Nations Secretariat to interview and otherwise monitor the American members of the staff, thereby raising serious questions as to the international control of the U.N. personnel.[39] When his first term expired, the Soviet government vetoed his reelection in 1951, and the General Assembly took the evasive expedient of voting to continue him in office for three years without reelection. That turned out to be an impossible arrangement; the Russian barrage of criticism was so heavy that Lie resigned in 1952.

He was replaced by Dag Hammarskjöld, at the time director-general of the Swedish Foreign Ministry. Virtually unknown in the international diplomatic community at the time,[40] he became an admired celebrity in the West and a despised antagonist in the Kremlin during his tenure of office, which ended in 1961 with his death in an airplane crash in the Congo. Many observers of the United Nations suppose that if another Hammarskjöld could be found to preside over the Secretariat, all would be well, or at least much better.

That opinion is almost certainly wrong. At the time of his death, Hammarskjöld had engaged in aggressive and remarkably efficient activism that infuriated the Russians and often irritated Western governments, which found him more of a high-minded internationalist than they were ready to accept. In 1960, when Nikita Khrushchev invited him to "muster up enough courage to resign in, let us say, a chivalrous way," Hammarskjöld at once turned to the small nations. "The Organization is first of all *their* Organization," he said. "I shall remain in my post...as long as they wish me to do so."[41]

What were the reasons for Khrushchev's hostility to Hammarskjöld? In his memoir, Shevchenko provides a colorful account of his master's perception of the situation:

> Khrushchev was enraged that "the Congo is slipping through our fingers.
>
> "I spit on the UN," he raged after Oleg Troyanovsky read him some particularly bad piece of news from Africa. "It's not *our* organization. That good-for-nothing Ham [the Russian word for "boor" applied as a nickname to the U.N. chief] is sticking his nose in important affairs which are none of his business. He has seized authority that doesn't belong to him. He must pay for that. We have to get rid of him by any means. We'll really make it hot for him."[42]

The United Nations intervention in the civil disturbances that followed the Belgian proclamation of that African colony's independence had provoked Khrushchev's fury. The story is too complex for a full account here.[43] Patrice Lumumba, the elected president of the new nation, was unable to establish control over the rich province of Katanga. At the same time he was thought to be under the control of Soviet interests. Under these circumstances, the Congo situation was deteriorating into anarchy, and the United Nations was called in to stabilize this dangerous and chaotic situation.

The Security Council maneuvered to find a formula for intervention that would be satisfactory to both Washington and Moscow, with the consequence that, as passed, the charge to the secretary-general and the participating nations was vague to the point of allowing the secretary-general *carte blanche*. At the same time Hammarskjöld had mobilized almost overnight a peacekeeping force of about 20,000 troops drawn from the armies of small and middle-sized powers, including contingents from several African states, to take charge of law and order in that disordered new nation.

It soon became apparent that Soviet interests were not being served by the United Nations Operation in the Congo (ONUC),[44] and indeed, any aspirations that the USSR might have entertained for dominance in Africa were likely to be frustrated by Hammarskjöld's efficient execution of the Security Council's purposely vague resolution.[45]

While he was on a mission of inspection, Hammarskjöld's airplane crashed in Rhodesia (now Zimbabwe) on September 17, 1961. The event was mourned as an immense tragedy throughout the Western nations. That Hammarskjöld's achievements were brilliant in most of the numerous crises that occurred during his tenure is not to be doubted. However, many observers have commented that his role could not be duplicated by a successor in this post. It is improbable that Hammarskjöld would have survived as secretary-general for long if he had not been killed.

Despite Soviet obstruction, despite the unfavorable situation presenting itself in the Congo—now Zaire—ONUC was more of a success than could have been expected at the outset of the operation. With the troops maintaining a semblance of stability and U.N. experts providing technical assistance of many kinds to the inexperienced and untrained Zairean personnel, there emerged, in the grudging words of one of ONUC's severest critics, "the relatively cohesive and governable nation of Zaire."[46]

Hammarskjöld was succeeded by U Thant, a Burmese diplomat who had been his country's permanent representative to the United Nations. He was appointed to serve out Hammarskjöld's term as acting secretary-general. In 1962 he was elected to serve a full term, which expired in November 1966. He was reelected for a second term, and retired at its expiration in 1971.

Like Hammarskjöld, U Thant was committed to an active role. He made it clear that his assignment was not merely administrative—"a glorified clerk"—but that it must be seen as requiring of him initiatives in the interest of maintaining the peace. In 1965 he articulated his perception of his responsibilities:

> Two simple considerations are inescapable. First, the Secretary-General must always be prepared to take an initiative, no matter what the consequences to him or his office may be, if he sincerely believes that it might mean the difference between peace and war. In such a situation the personal prestige of a Secretary-General—and even the position of his office—must be considered to be expendable. The second cardinal consideration must be the maintenance of the Secretary-General's independent position, which alone can give him the freedom to act, without fear or favour in the interests of world peace.[47]

U Thant came to office with the Congo conflicts still unsettled. It fell to him to preside over a protracted United Nations military campaign to prevent the secession of the province of Katanga, richly endowed with copper and other minerals that the Belgian company mining them, the Union Minière, did not wish to be controlled by the new Zairean government. It was a long struggle, in the course of which U Thant got little sympathy from the major European powers, including, for different reasons, the United Kingdom and the USSR. By 1963 the struggle came to an exhausted end because of dwindling financial support for the Katangan secession.[48]

U Thant's tribulations had only begun. The long American intervention in Vietnam was soon to begin. U Thant thought that his responsibility was to facilitate the peaceful reconciliation of the two sides. This position did not endear him to the Johnson administration, and he became an unpopular figure in those American circles pressing for vigorous prosecution of the war. Believing that mediation of the conflict was feasible and frustrated only by the blind resistance of President Johnson and the American military, U Thant maintained a vigorously articulate barrage of demands for negotiation. His proposals certainly had a powerful effect on the American antiwar movement and succeeded in infuriating the president and Dean Rusk, the secretary of state. Thomas Franck comments that this episode demonstrated that the secretary-general could be, if he chose, a dynamic force in American politics, even if he had seriously misinterpreted the facts available to him.[49]

U Thant's successor was Kurt Waldheim, an Austrian diplomat who was believed to have sought the post as a stepping-stone to the presidency of his country. That opportunity did not come to him, and he remained as secretary-general until 1981. His long tenure was studded with no great successes, but he managed to make no angry enemies as each of his predecessors had done. Enemies surfaced much later when, in 1986, he successfully resumed his pursuit of the Austrian presidency. Accusations that during World War II he participated in war crimes against Balkan Jews were not resolved in his favor, but it is fair to say that no evidence of anti-Semitic decision making marred his undistinguished career as secretary-general.

The present secretary-general, Javier Perez de Cuellar, a Peruvian and formerly the under-secretary-general for special political affairs, assumed office in January 1982. He came to his office deeply dissatisfied with the way in which the organization's effectiveness had been diminished over the years and determined to make a change in its course. He presented his conception of the secretary-general's role in his annual report for 1985:

> ...I am sometimes concerned that the delegation of responsibility to the Secretary-General may, in certain instances, have the effect of diminishing the effort that is expected of the Member States under the Charter. This will not serve the development of the United Nations as a political institution.

That being said, I nevertheless believe that it would be in the interests of the Organization as a whole if the Secretary-General's capacity to serve as an objective third party were to be further developed. There is much, of course to be said for quiet diplomacy, but sometimes more is required. I am thinking in particular of a wider and earlier use of fact-finding and observation. I am also thinking of the need to survey more regularly and systematically the world-wide state of international peace and security—a task in which the Security Council and the Secretary-General should be jointly involved. The best radar in the world is not reliable or effective unless it makes systematic surveys of the surrounding space. The same applied, it seems to me, to the task of maintaining international peace.[50]

When Trygve Lie turned over his office to Dag Hammarskjöld, he referred to it as "the most impossible job on earth." Hammarskjöld's perception of the secretary-general's responsibilities as he took over was less gloomy:

In my new official capacity, the private man should disappear and the international public servant take his place. The public servant is there in order to assist, so to say, from the inside, those who make decisions which frame history. He should—as I see it—listen, analyze, and learn to understand fully the forces at work and the interests at stake, so that he will be able to give the right advice when the situation calls for it. Don't think that he—in following this line of personal policy—takes but a passive part in the development. It is a most active one. But he is active as an instrument, a catalyst, perhaps an inspirer—he serves.[51]

Lie may have been right. As Luard, the historian of the United Nations, observed,

By the nature of his office the Secretary-General must be a solitary figure. It is almost impossible for him to appear right in the eyes of all UN members. Either excessive activity or inactivity will be equally criticised. He must be politician, diplomatist, and civil servant all in one. It is thus an office that is impossible to fill to the satisfaction of all.[52]

The objectives of all the secretaries-general have been identical, even though their theoretical statements have differed in particulars. In the long run, it is indeed an impossible job, one that will lead to vituperative hostility from powerful enemies and ambiguous support, at best, from fair-weather friends. This is the condition within which the United Nations itself must function, and as long as the divisions within it are sharp and bitter the secretary-general cannot escape excoriation from one side or look for certain and staunch support from the other.

The Secretariat of the United Nations. The secretary-general is responsible for the United Nations' civil service, its budget, and the general administration of the organization. The service consists of 16,000 employees stationed in New York, Geneva, and Vienna, the principal centers of business, and in various smaller offices throughout the world. The United Nations staff is an international civil service, members of which are under oath not to seek or accept instructions from any government or authority outside the United Nations, including the government of their own countries. Under Article 100 of the Charter, each member state must respect the international responsibilities of the secretary-general and his staff and not attempt to influence them in the discharge of their duties. The extent to which these undertakings are observed is open to question. Arkady Shevchenko, the former Russian under-secretary-general, has described in some detail and with specific examples the extent to which he, as a ranking United Nations staff member, and other Russian employees of the organization were and undoubtedly still are required to subject themselves to instructions from the home government in Moscow, regardless of their own oaths and the terms of the Charter.[53] Shevchenko asserts that the Soviet Union is not alone in its disregard of these undertakings, but it is "alone in one respect. . .its mendacity and cynicism are fully institutionalized." According to him, many Soviet citizens assigned to work as international civil servants are mainly occupied with KGB assignments. Beyond doubt, this abuse of the international civil service creates special difficulties for the organization within the host nations—the United States, Switzerland, and Austria. Probably more difficult to resolve are the frequent charges that United Nations employees are overpaid and politically selected according to nationality quotas and pressures from influential states. Persons making these charges dismiss without consideration the problems facing administrators who must contend with the need for excellent specialists and at the same time must satisfy each member state that its representation on the staff is somehow proportionate. As to the overpayment of staff, the difficulties of relocation to three of the world's most expensive cities receive little sympathy from United Nations' critics.

We come now to the fiscal affairs of the United Nations, always a topic for some rancor, although the total expenditure is a relatively small amount when compared to the outlays of the major industrial nations.

The budget of the United Nations organization, exclusive of the specialized agencies that are funded by separate and voluntary contributions, totaled $1,611,551,000 for the 1984–1985 biennium. This sum was distributed among the following categories as follows:

I	Overall policy making, direction, and coordination	$40,173,400
II	Political and Security Council affairs, peacekeeping activities; Department for Disarmament Affairs	91,584,400
III	Political affairs, trusteeship, and decolonization	28,696,500
IV	Economic, social, and humanitarian activities	503,404,800
V	International justice and law	24,090,400
VI	Public information	70,170,600
VII	Common support services (administration and management; conference and library services)	570,060,200
VIII	United Nations bond issue	16,769,100
IX	Staff assessment	224,735,600
X	Capital expenditures (construction, alteration, improvement, and major maintenance of premises)	20,366,200

XI Special grant to UNITAR (United Na-
tions Institute for Training and
Research)   1,500,000
TOTAL $1,611,551,200

Income other than the assessed contributions of member states
totaled $301,439,100, of which $246,895,300 consisted of staff assessments, and $54,542,800 was expected from various revenue-
producing activities.

Contributions from member states are in principle assessed
according to ability to pay but cannot exceed 25% of the U.N.
budget, the proportion paid by the United States. The minimum
assessment is 0.01%.

Outside the regular budget, assessments are imposed for the
costs of UNIFIL and the United Nations Disengagement Observer
Force in the Middle East. Other programs, such as the United Nations Development Program, the United Nations High Commissioner for Refugees, UNESCO, and many others, are funded by
voluntary contributions from participating nations.[54]

Achievements and Disappointments

It is the business of the United Nations to damp down international turbulence. We turn now to some of the situations in which
the organization has tried to intervene on behalf of peace, sometimes successfully, sometimes not.

The United Nations and the Middle East. The political and
peacekeeping activities of the United Nations have extended to all
parts of the world. Nowhere have they been as difficult and protracted as the effort to bring about a state of peace and constructive relations among the nations of that relatively small part of the
Mediterranean littoral we know as the Middle East. The crisis in
Palestine was the first in which the good offices of the United Nations were used. Forty years later the crisis persists, having taken
many different forms over the years and having spread far beyond
the borders of Palestine. Because both the strengths and weak-

nesses of the United Nations have been tested in this long history of violence, misunderstanding, and bitter hostility, I shall review the principal events in a separate section of this chapter.

Palestine was a Turkish possession before World War I. The dominant population was Arab, but the Zionist movement initiated by Theodor Herzl in the last years of the nineteenth century had commenced a steady flow of immigration, mostly from Russia, into the area. By 1914 there were about 90,000 Jews in Palestine, still a small minority of the population.

During World War I, the British Army drove Turkey out of Palestine and occupied that former Turkish province. In the peace settlement that followed, Turkey was divested of its empire, and Palestine, along with other possessions, was placed under a League of Nations mandate. Since Great Britain was the occupying power, it was awarded the mandate.[55]

The mandating document included in its preamble the famous Balfour Declaration, a letter to Lord Rothschild, a leading early patron of Zionism, written by Arthur Balfour, the British foreign secretary. The declaration stated that the British government viewed with favor "the establishment in Palestine of a national home for the Jewish people, and will use their best endeavours to facilitate the achievement of this object, it being clearly understood that nothing shall be done to prejudice the civil and religious rights of existing non-Jewish communities in Palestine. . . ."

Between World War I and World War II the Jewish population rose to about 450,000, the majority arriving after 1933, the year of Hitler's accession to power. The increasing numbers of immigrants caused great unrest among the Arab population, and a number of incidents of armed violence.[56]

After World War II the influx of Jews from Europe increased. British attempts to contain it within limits failed, and the government turned the problem over to the United Nations. A Commission of Inquiry was appointed and in August 1947 recommended the partition of Palestine into Arab and Jewish states, politically separate but merged into an economic union. There was a specific requirement for an international zone for Jerusalem. The General Assembly approved this recommendation in the following November, with the United States and Russia jointly supporting it against the vigorous opposition of all the Islamic states.

Civil war then broke out in which the Zionists were victorious, and thousands of Palestinian Arabs poured out of the country, creating a refugee problem that continues to the present time. On May 14, 1948, the Zionist Council proclaimed the establishment of the State of Israel. The government was immediately recognized by the United States and the USSR. A hastily assembled alliance of neighboring Arab states initiated hostilities that did not come to an end until July 1949, when an armistice agreement was negotiated by Ralph Bunche, then the director of the U.N. division of trusteeship and assigned by the secretary-general as mediator for this conflict.[57] Israel had already been admitted to the United Nations.

Although there was an armistice, that did not end the hostilities between Israel and its Arab neighbors, between whom there continues to be a technical state of war to the present time.[58] In 1956 the seething hostilities between Israel and Islam boiled up again with an operation conducted jointly with Britain and France to defeat the Egyptian take-over of the Suez Canal. The Israeli forces were brilliantly successful in obtaining the surrender of the Egyptian forces in a brief campaign.

The General Assembly, nearly unanimous, called on Israel to withdraw. Obviously the situation continued to be dangerous for both sides. At the initiative of Canada, the Assembly then voted to station an emergency force, composed of troops from 10 nations, and acronymized as UNEF, to keep the peace between Israel and Egypt. UNEF remained on Egyptian soil from 1956 to 1967. It was a protracted emergency, but with the force stationed at the boundary between Israel and Egypt, the borders were secure to both nations and a kind of détente was achieved.

In June 1967 President Nasser of Egypt demanded the withdrawal of UNEF from Egypt. U Thant, as secretary-general, immediately ordered the UNEF positions to be dismantled and the troops returned to their home countries. Three weeks later the Six-Day War began.

U Thant was severely criticized for his precipitate compliance with the Egyptian demand. He did not submit the transaction to the General Assembly, which had authorized UNEF in the first place. Defending himself against the abusive criticisms in the United States Congress and the press, U Thant claimed, first, that the legal basis for UNEF's presence in Egyptian territory depended on Egyptian consent. Second, UNEF was greatly outnumbered by the mobilized Egyptian army that surrounded it, making its continued task of peacekeeping impossible.[59]

In the event, the war ended with stunning speed. Israel occupied the Sinai area of Egypt and took temporary control of the Suez canal, from which it soon withdrew. It captured the Golan Heights in Syria, and the West Bank of the Jordan, comprising the ancient lands of Judea and Samaria, and reunited the entire city of Jerusalem, which had been divided between Israel and Jordan. Except for the Sinai, which was returned to Egypt in the peace process initiated at Camp David, Israel continues to retain these territories.

The General Assembly and the Security Council were concerned about the gains that Israel had made through military conquest. It called on Israel to desist from any action that would alter the status of Jerusalem, an appeal with which Israel did not comply.

More important was the passage of Resolution 242 by a unanimous vote of the Security Council in November 1967. This resolution was intended to define the elements of a Mideast settlement. It provides for two basic requirements for the peace: (1) the withdrawal of Israeli armed forces from occupied territories, and (2) the termination of all claims of belligerency and respect for the sovereignty and territorial integrity of all states in the area and their right to live in peace within secure and recognized boundaries.[60]

Resolution 242 remains the U.N. framework for Mideast peace, but efforts to implement it have been unavailing. Syria rejected it out of hand, and negotiations with the other Arab countries were protracted and without result when the "Yom Kippur War" of 1973 broke out.

The Egyptian forces capitalized on a surprise attack and inflicted heavy losses on Israel. The Security Council was called into session but was unable to agree on a formula for a cease-fire. While the Egyptians and their allies were doing well they could not agree to a halt, nor could Israel concede them their gains. Eventually, the Israeli army broke through the Egyptian lines. At this point, the United States and the USSR arrived at an agreement on the elements of a cease-fire, which was presented to the Security Council and endorsed by all members except for the Chinese delegate, who abstained from voting.

The fighting continued; the Israeli army crossed the Suez Canal, encircled the Egyptian Third Army, and moved toward Cairo. At this point, eight members of the Council, all representing nonaligned states, proposed a resolution a create a new UNEF to be stationed between the Israeli and Egyptian forces. This resolution was adopted and UNEF II was mobilized and put into place, where it remained until the Camp David accords were consummated in 1979 and a sort of peace was established between Egypt and Israel.

To stabilize the border between Israel and Lebanon, across which guerrilla operations had been conducted by the Palestine Liberation Organization (PLO), with retaliatory actions by Israeli forces, the Security Council interposed another peacekeeping force, acronymized as UNIFIL (United Nations Interim Force In Lebanon), in 1978, where it remains to the present time in spite of an Israeli invasion of Lebanon in 1982.[61]

Throughout most of recorded history the Middle East has been one of the most troubled regions of the world, and Palestine has been the epicenter of its storms. Romans, Saracens, Crusaders, Turks, Britons, Americans, and now the United Nations have tried to create conditions of peace. There have been occasional successes throughout the centuries of conflict, lapsing into armed struggles and sometimes almost anarchic conditions. The experience of the United Nations demonstrates that more than

Security Council resolutions are required, but no formula for enduring peace has yet been found.

The United Nations and Cyprus. Sovereignty over the island of Cyprus has passed from empire to empire throughout its history; until 1960 it had never enjoyed an episode of independence. Even now its autonomy is precarious, subject to agreements and guarantees among three powers with special interests, each of them with treaty rights that limit Cypriot freedom of action. Since 1964, the United Nations has maintained a peacekeeping force to minimize armed conflict between two communities whose mistrust of each other is abetted by outside powers, Greece and Turkey, with centuries of hostility that have yet to wane.

Until 1878, when the British assumed its administration, Cyprus had been a Turkish possession for 300 years. Technically, sovereignty remained in the hands of the sultan, but because of concern over the security of the nearby Suez Canal, *de facto* control of the island was transferred to the British. In return, the British promised support for Turkey in the event of Russian aggression.

This peculiar arrangement came to an end with the outbreak of World War I, in which Turkey was allied with the Central Powers. Cyprus was then annexed by the British as a crown colony, in which status it remained until 1960, when it became an independent nation.

It was an independence that the Greek majority accepted only as a lesser goal; the aspiration for union (*enosis*) with Greece seems to have been the ardent preference of most Cypriots. That objective was just as ardently opposed by the Turkish minority. The outcome was thus an unstable compromise leading to conflicts that have defied resolution.

The troubles preceding independence were severe, and they continue to the present time. The difficulties are basic and intractable. The Greek majority constitutes over 80% of the population; the Turkish minority makes up the rest. It would be difficult to find two ethnic groups that distrust each other more. To accent the hostility between the two, both Greece and Turkey take an intense interest in the welfare and safety of their ethnically related Cypriots, and both have treaty rights to maintain small armed forces on the island—950 Greeks and 650 Turks. In addition, the United Kingdom retained two large military bases.

In late 1963, little more than three years after independence, fighting broke out between the two communities, The Cyprus government appealed to the Security Council for support in its effort to pacify the disturbed areas, and accused the Turkish government of supporting the insurgency by the Cypriot Turks. There followed several months of conferences and negotiations among the four parties directly involved (the governments of Cyprus, Greece, Turkey, and the United Kingdom); the situation continued to deteriorate. In March 1964 the Security Council in an unusual unanimous resolution recommended the mobilization and dispatch of a peacekeeping force (the United Nations Peacekeeping Force in Cyprus, or UNFICYP), with a charge to prevent further fighting and to foster the restoration of law and order. It was expected that its goals could be accomplished in three months. It has remained on the island ever since, with a strength varying between 2100 and 6200, composed of troops from Austria, Canada, Denmark, Finland, Sweden, and the United Kingdom. There have been repeated episodes of fighting, and there was an invasion in 1974 by Turkish air and naval forces, which have remained in the northern, Turkish sector of the island ever since, despite continued unanimous resolutions by the Security Council calling on Turkey to remove all forces except the small contingent allowed under the basic treaty.

In February 1975 the Turkish Cypriots proclaimed the Turkish Federated State of Cyprus, to stand in a federation with the Greek community. This arrangement was rejected by the Greek Cypriots, and in June 1983 the Turkish community proclaimed itself an independent nation, an action that has not been recognized by the United Nations or by any nation other than Turkey.[62]

There the stalemate rests. UNFICYP, originally sent for a three-month stay in 1964, remains on the island, a guarantor of a cease-fire. Its mandate to remain was renewed in June 1985 by the Security Council. There is no sign of progress toward a resolution of the conflict between the Greek and Turkish communities. The Turkish Republic of Northern Cyprus has elected and reelected a president and a parliament, even though its existence has been denounced not only by the Security Council and the General Assembly but also by all the powers concerned. Franck, a former United Nations official and now a critical observer, crisply sums up the situation as unsatisfactory but better than any plausible alternative:

> ...neither the Turkish nor the Greek Cypriot community wishes to see [UNFICYP] removed. To each side, while the *status quo* is highly unsatisfactory, all but one of the alternatives is worse. That alternative, outright victory over the other side, would be extremely costly and is probably beyond the military capability of either side. The respective governments in Athens, Ankara and in the two Cypriot communities are realistic enough to know this, but are also politically aware that were the U.N. not in the way, they would come under irresistible pressure from their own supporters to attempt a military solution. Thus UNFICYP and other U.N. peace-keepers, also serve as a convenient excuse for governments not to pursue popularity by courting disaster.[63]

The achievement of UNFICYP is modest indeed, measured by the exuberant expectations of the founders of the United Nations. For a world riven with hate-based hostility, the accomplishment of a stalemate on a small and bloody island may be a model for the first steps toward stability and eventual peace.

Summary

Finally, in galloping through the history of the United Nations and touring its structure I have scamped many important events and many significant activities. Every major library contains many shelves of books dealing with the history and political science of international organizations. Many of those shelves are filled with publications recounting the triumphs, reporting the work, and, sometimes, denouncing the shortcomings of the United Nations. Passing on to another section, volumes of treaties, resolutions, reports, minutes, and debates published by the United Nations are to be found in intimidating profusion. Who can enter the U.N. library in the Secretariat building without a sense of awed impotence at the sight of all that paper? And how can the sense of all that paper be compressed into a few pages?

All that I have tried to do in this chapter is to rough out the broad outlines of the United Nations, choosing a few emphases that seem important to me, and bearing in mind that any institution on earth, regardless of its aims, must be staffed by fallible men and women. It is for Professor van den Haag and me to consider whether this institution, whose aims are the most lofty of all worldly enterprises, can achieve them with the human and material resources it can summon.

Notes

1. In the introduction to his *The Concert of Europe*, Rene Albrecht-Carrie summarizes the salient events of the "Concert" as the prelude to the League of Nations and the United Nations (New York: Walker, 1968), pp. 1–24. Immediately after the Congress of Vienna, which made the first post-Napoleonic settlement, the tsar of Russia, Alexander I, proposed that the great powers should meet regularly to assure that breaches of the peace should be prevented or, if necessary, be subjected to joint military intervention by the Great Powers. This proposal was rejected by the British cabinet on the ground that British arms should not be mobilized for causes in which British interests were not at stake. See F. H. Hinsley, *Power and the Pursuit of Peace* (Cambridge: Cambridge University Press, 1963), pp. 213–237.

2. One of the few who did was Sir Edward Grey, the British foreign secretary, who gave voice to his apprehension in a memorable lament: "The lamps are going out all over Europe; we shall not see them lit again in our lifetime."

3. The positions of Wilson, Roosevelt, Taft, and Lodge, the principal actors in a momentous conflict, are outlined in John Milton Cooper, Jr., *The Warrior and the Priest* (Cambridge: Belknap Press, 1985), pp. 301–302, *et seq.*, *passim.*

4. By an ironical train of events, the father of Henry Cabot Lodge, Jr., a distinguished permanent representative of the United States to the United Nations

throughout the Eisenhower administration (1953–1960). For a thorough account of the historic conflict in the Senate, told from the standpoint of Senator Lodge, himself a historian, see Henry Cabot Lodge, *The Senate and the League of Nations* (New York: Scribner's, 1925). See also Ralph Stone, *The Irreconcilables; The Fight against the League of Nations* (Lexington, Kentucky: University of Kentucky Press, 1970).

5. For the history of the drafting of the Covenant and its fate in the Senate, see F. P. Walters, *A History of the League of Nations* (London: Oxford University Press, 1960), pp. 25–74.

6. But throughout the life of the League there was much American cooperation with the League's social and economic projects, and many prominent Americans served as League officials. See Walters, note 5, pp. 348–354.

7. Brazil's insistence on membership in the Council as a Great Power was based on the argument that in the absence of the United States, Brazil was the largest and strongest member nation in the western hemisphere. It contended that the New World was entitled to at least one permanent representative on the Council.

8. For a full account of this complex episode, see Walters, note 5, pp. 316–327.

9. Walters, note 5, pp. 477–495.

10. Walters, note 5, pp. 623–691, has as good a brief account as a general reader will need. However, the course of these shabby events is an instructive case study in the problems of maintaining collective security through an international organization. For a relentless presentation of the details of the Italian aggression and the failure of the League to apply the provisions of the Covenant, see George W. Baer, *The Coming of the Italian–Ethiopian War* (Cambridge: Harvard University Press, 1967), pp. 304–350.

11. Walters, note 5, pp. 75–79. See also *The New Cambridge Modern History* (Cambridge: Cambridge University Press, 1960), p. 477.

12. For an account of national interference in the personnel selection of the international civil service in the early days of the United Nations, particularly by the United States Federal Bureau of Investigation and the McCarthy Committee on Investigations, see Shirley Hazzard, *Defeat of an Ideal* (Boston: Little, Brown, 1973), pp. 3–69. The memoir of Arkady N. Shevchenko, *Breaking With Moscow* (New York: Knopf, 1984), recounts many instances of Soviet abuse of the concept of an international civil service. While Shevchenko's veracity as to other matters has been vigorously challenged, there is no reason to doubt his account of the assignment of Soviet intelligence personnel to United Nations civil service duties.

13. See Article 16 of the Covenant.

14. This distinction is elaborated in Alf Ross, *The United Nations: Peace and Progress* (Totowa, New Jersey: Bedminster Press, 1966), pp. 194–198. Ross thought that the distinction was of more theoretical than practical significance.

15. Brian Urquhart, *Hammarskjöld* (New York: Knopf, 1972, reissued by Harper & Row, 1984), p. 4.

16. To maintain an orderly succession, the Assembly of the League of Nations met for the last time on April 18–19, 1946, for the purpose of dissolving the League and transferring the Palais des Nations, and all its other possessions and archives, to the United Nations.

17. See Thomas M. Franck, *Nation Against Nation* (New York and Oxford: Oxford University Press, 1985), pp. 6–24. Franck impressively documents the naive and unreflective comments of some celebrated political figures of the 1940s in support of American membership and in ill-considered praise of the Charter. It is interesting to observe that no political figures of other nations exhibited such overweening certainty of the prospects for the United Nations' success in preventing war forever.

18. The United States, China, France, the United Kingdom, and the USSR.

19. For a brief but instructive account of the diplomatic antecedents of the Korean War and the United Nations' part in its origin and prosecution, see Franck, note 17, pp. 33–39.

20. Not including the specialized agencies, whose budgets depend on the voluntary contributions of those nations desiring to participate.

21. See the Charter, Articles 9–22.

22. General Assembly Resolution No, 377 A(V), November 3, 1950.

23. The Uniting for Peace Resolution has received much scholarly attention. I have found the discussion by Alf Ross and Thomas Franck particularly useful. Ross, note 14, pp. 44–45, 176–177; Franck, note 17, pp. 39–41, *passim*. See also Linda M. Fasulo, *Representing America; Experiences of U. S. Diplomats at the UN* (New York: Praeger, 1984), interview with Ambassador Ernest A. Gross, pp. 41–45. Dean Acheson, our secretary of state at the time, recounts his intentions in drafting this resolution in *Present at the Creation* (New York: W. W. Norton, 1969), pp. 450–451. Conceding that the American veto would be weakened in the long range, he argued that "present difficulties outweighed future ones, and we pressed on."

24. Urquhart, note 15, pp. 179–183.

25. It is said that in the republic of Zaire, when it was admitted to the United Nations in 1960, there were fewer than 10 citizens who were university graduates. That was an extreme case, but there were other African nations that were not much better provided with elites of administrative competence upon attaining their independence.

26. General Assembly Resolution 3379 (XXX), November 10, 1975. For two discussions of the antecedents of this resolution, see Fasulo, note 23, pp. 165–167 (interview with Rita A. Hauser, former U. S. delegate to the General Assembly) and pp. 205–206 (interview with former Ambassador Daniel Patrick Moynihan). See also Franck, note 17.

27. That is, all delegates are "distinguished," and all chairmen of any sessions are to be complimented on their wisdom, learning, and discretion.

28. For a fairly comprehensive account of the Economic and Social Council, with a reasoned appraisal of most of the activities it coordinates, see Evan Luard, *The United Nations: How It Works and What It Does* (New York: St. Martin's Press, 1979), pp. 55–71.

29. Article 2, § 7 of the Charter: "Nothing contained in the present Charter shall authorize the United Nations to intervene in matters which are essentially within the domestic jurisdiction of any state or shall require the Members to submit such settlement under the present Charter.... "

30. Ernest A. Gross, *The United Nations: Structure for Peace* (New York: Harper & Brothers, 1962), pp. 86–89.

31. For an account of the Namibian episode and its antecedents up to 1965, see Ross, note 14, pp. 381–384.

32. In November 1985, the United Kingdom and the United States vetoed a proposed resolution calling for mandatory sanctions to be imposed by all member states against South Africa because of its refusal to terminate its occupation of Namibia. See *The New York Times*, 16 November 1985.

33. The comments of Alf Ross, the Danish jurist, are on the mark: "Even though the forces that during the past 20 years have led to the collapse of the colonial system were not conjured up by the United Nations, there can scarcely be any doubt that the Organization has precipitated this process.... The more the former colonial territories...crowded into the General Assembly...the more one-sided and insistent the Assembly became in its demand for the unconditional and immediate ending of all colonial rule. The Eastern bloc states have...supported this demand as a move in the cold war and the competition to gain friends and win sympathy among the young states." Ross, note 14, p. 406.

34. See Appendix B for the full text of the Statute.

35. Ross, note 14, p. 143, cites six principal legal systems as qualified under the statute—common law, Roman law, Marxist law, Islamic law, Indian law, and Chinese law—but concedes that there is no consensus about these six. He cannot "connect any idea with the phrase 'main forms of civilization.' "

36. Ibid., pp. 145–146.

37. Luard, note 28, p. 96.

38. Article 99.

39. See Hazzard, note 12, for an account of this episode, for which she vigorously criticizes Lie as responsible for the demoralization of the U.N. civil service.

40. Brian Urquhart, his biographer, noted that "he had been proposed originally by the Western permanent members of the Security Council on the mistaken assumption that as Secretary-General he would be a safe, rather colorless, non-political technocrat." Brian Urquhart, "International Peace and Security: Thoughts on the Twentieth Anniversary of Dag Hammarskjöld's Death," *Foreign Affairs* 60(1) (Fall 1981), pp. 1–16.

41. Hammarskjöld's moving response to Khrushchev in a speech before the General Assembly is reproduced in full in Urquhart, note 15, pp. 463–464. Urquhart records that the Assembly responded with a protracted ovation while Khrushchev and Gromyko pounded the table with their fists.

42. Shevchenko, note 12, p. 102. Shevchenko adds that "friends working on African affairs once told me that they had seen a top-secret KGB report indicating that the aircraft [on which Hammarskjöld had been traveling] had been shot down by pro-Soviet Congolese forces penetrated and guided by operatives from the USSR (p. 103). Urquhart is skeptical; "so far none of [the conspiracy theories] is backed by anything other than rumor, speculation, and fantasy." Urquhart, note 15, p. 593.

43. For details of this ultimately tragic episode, see Urquhart, note 15, pp. 389–456, 499–529, 545–589.

44. Opération des Nations Unies au Congo.

45. For a good brief account of Hammarskjöld and ONUC, see Franck, note 17, pp. 174–177. Much more detail will be found in Urquhart, note 15, pp. 389–456, and 565–589.

46. Franck, note 17, p. 176. It was at this time that Khrushchev proposed that the office of the secretary-general should be abolished and its administrative functions carried out by a "troika" consisting of three officers representing the West, the socialist states, and the nonaligned states. Shevchenko, note 12, p. 102, characterizes the idea as "zany," an opinion that was widely shared in the General Assembly. The idea was never put to a vote in either the Security Council or the General Assembly, although the Russians attempted various stratagems to bring about a veto power on the actions of the secretary-general.

47. Quoted by Franck, note 17, p. 121.

48. Andrew Boyd, *United Nations: Piety, Myth, and Truth* (Harmondsworth, England: Penguin, 1964), pp. 121–159.

49. Franck, note 17, pp. 152–158. Franck holds that negotiation could not have succeeded because as early as 1964 the North Vietnamese knew that they could win and would have accepted no settlement other than complete capitulation. In view of the final outcome of this war, an early attempt at negotiation could hardly have been a harmful exercise and might have saved lives and treasure.

50. *Report of the Secretary-General on the Work of the Organization* (United Nations General Assembly, *Official Records of the General Assembly, Fortieth Session, Supplement No. 1 (A/40/1)*, September 1985.

51. Urquhart, note 15, p. 15.

52. Luard, note 28, p. 101.

53. Shevchenko, note 12, pp. 220-229.

54. United Nations Department of Public Information, *Basic Facts About the United Nations* (New York: United Nations, 1984), p. I.12.

55. France received the mandate for Syria and Lebanon, the other Mediterranean Turkish provinces, which it retained until the end of World War II.

56. For a vivid account of conditions in Palestine immediately before World War II, see Hugh Foot, *A Start in Freedom* (London: Hodder and Stoughton, 1964), pp. 35–57. Foot was later to become the permanent representative of the United Kingdom to the United Nations and served as such during the aftermath of the Six-Day War in 1967.

57. The negotiation of the armistice was regarded as so significant a contribution to peace in the Middle East that Bunche was awarded the Nobel Peace Prize.

58. Except, of course, for Egypt, which signed a peace accord with Israel at Camp David under the auspices of President Carter in 1979.

59. Franck, note 17, pp. 87–93. Franck makes the cogent point that this episode demonstrates a serious weakness in the concept of a U.N. peacekeeping force. A national contingent can be expected to remain in place only so long as the interests of the nation are seen to coincide with the purpose of the emergency force. In the case of UNEF, the Yugoslavian and Indian contingents represented nations with serious reservations about their interests in an Israeli–Egyptian conflict.

60. For an account of the negotiations preceding the passage of Resolution 242, see Lord Caradon's article. "The Security Council as an Instrument of Peace," in *Multilateral Negotiation and Mediation; Instruments and Methods,* Arthur S. Lall, (New York: Pergamon Press, 1985), pp. 9–13. See also Fasulo's interview with Ambassador Goldberg in Fasulo, note 23, pp. 103–104, and her interview with William Buffum, pp. 116–120.

61. Franck, note 17, has a summary account of the Yom Kippur War and the diplomatic maneuvers that accompanied and followed it, pp. 170–177. See also Shevchenko, note 12, pp. 253–261.

62. For a factual account of the present situation and its antecedents, see Frederica M. Bunge, ed., *Cyprus: A Country Study* (Washington, D.C.: Department of the Army, 1980), pp. 37–52, 155–204. A more recent account is contained in Christopher Hitchens, *Cyprus* (London: Quartet Books, 1984), Hitchens's book is written "in sorrow but more—much more—in anger." Well documented, full of villains to excoriate, sympathetic to the Cypriot people, but devoid of suggestions for the eventual resolution of the persisting conflict, the book is a pessimistic case study. For the Turkish case, see Rauf R. Denktash, *The Cyprus Triangle* (London: George Allen & Unwin, 1984). See also Kurt Waldheim, *In the Eye of the Storm* (London: Weidenfeld and Nicolson, 1985), pp. 78–92, for a compelling account of the difficulties of moderating negotiations between two intransigent parties.

63. Franck, note 17, p. 179.

Talking, Studying, Planning, and Doing

The Service Agencies of the United Nations

JOHN P. CONRAD

It is beyond the requirements of this debate to describe all the specialized and otherwise affiliated agencies clustered around the United Nations. Some are inconspicuous, some perform routine services in the international arena that would have to be provided for whether or not the United Nations were in existence. Some, however, need discussion because their programs are poorly understood and others because their activities have brought them into intense controversy. By these criteria, here are brief accounts of a few of the many agencies affiliated with the United Nations.

The Food and Agricultural Organization (FAO). Founded in the immediate aftermath of World War II, when the relief of famine was a worldwide concern, the FAO has the continuing mission of bringing the developing world as far as possible to self-sufficiency in food from agriculture and fisheries. Its program consists of technical assistance, the training of local experts in Third World nations, and, probably most important of all, the negotiation of investments by the World Bank, the United Nations Development Fund, and the International Fund for Agricultural Development.

Famine in East Africa has shocked the world into recalling that it is a widespread curse that threatens the survival of millions. The FAO is engaged in a campaign to combat drought, soil erosion, and declining water tables, and to create distribution systems capable of maintaining food supplies for populations that have been growing more rapidly than local harvests can feed them. Four-fifths of the funds available to FAO—about $200,000,000 a year at the present rate of contributions—are allocated to field projects. The victories that have been won in India and Mexico with the Green Revolution encourage confidence that the campaign can succeed. The obstacles are formidable and the tasks in areas where food shortages have persisted for decades will not be accomplished soon. But if famine at catastrophic levels is to be eliminated from the prospects for mankind in years to come, the FAO's technical and funding resources must be expanded.

The International Atomic Energy Agency (IAEA). Convinced that international consultation and controls were essential to the peaceful application of atomic energy, President Eisenhower proposed the creation of the International Atomic Energy Agency in December 1953. The General Assembly endorsed the proposal and work began on a statute to set forth the purposes, organization, and operations of the IAEA. Three years later the statute was drafted and was signed by 80 nations, and the agency became a functioning entity on July 29, 1957. There are now 112 member states.

The purposes of the agency are twofold. First, the statute calls for it to "seek to accelerate and enlarge the contribution of atomic energy to peace, health, and prosperity throughout the world." Second, it is "to ensure, so far as it is able, that assistance provided by it or at its request or under its supervision or control, is not used in such a way as to further any military purposes."[1]

With the signing of the Treaty on the Non-Proliferation of Nuclear Weapons in 1970, the IAEA assumed critical responsibilities for assuring that fissionable materials are not diverted for military uses. A system of material accounting was developed for this purpose, and IAEA inspectors verify the compliance of cooperating nations with the safeguards required by the treaty.

As important as preventing the diversion of plutonium and other weapons-grade radioactive substances from peaceful to martial uses is the general assistance afforded by IAEA to countries wishing to develop atomic capabilities for peaceful purposes. Research, training, technical assistance, and the formulation and dissemination of safety standards make possible the development of nuclear technology in countries without such capabilities of their own.

The prevailing cliché in discourse about atomic technology dwells on the release of a genie from a bottle. The genie has indeed been released, and history will tell whether for good or ill. No one can be sure where the genie will go or what its possibly favorable impact on civilization or on the very survival of the human race will be. The IAEA represents the collective international concern that the mortal dangers be averted and that the gains for humanity be pressed as far as safety will allow.

The International Fund for Agricultural Development (IFAD). During the early 1970s, the world food situation worsened into one of the periodic crises that have converted conditions that are marginal at best into desperation. In 1973, at the annual meeting of the nonaligned nations, many if not most of them grievously affected by the famine, a recommendation was drafted and forwarded to the secretary-general of the United Nations urging that a world food conference be convened. This was done, and representatives of 133 nations met in Rome to consider measures that might be collectively undertaken to meet the chronic world food shortage. The conference settled on three measures: the establishment of the International Fund for Agricultural Development as the newest specialized agency, the creation of a standing Committee on World Food Security in the Council of the FAO, and a Universal Declaration on the Eradication of Hunger and Malnutrition committing the United Nations to the protection of the right of all persons everywhere to be free from hunger and malnutrition.

IFAD has a special and narrow charge. It is to receive funds voluntarily contributed by member nations for providing grants and low-interest loans to developing countries to support projects to increase food production, especially from small farms, and to improve the transportation and distribution of food. Most of its projects are closely coordinated with the FAO, whose technical expertise assists in the selection and execution of IFAD projects.

IFAD's receipts from member nations in 1984—the latest year for which figures are available—totaled $192,464,000. Loans to 26 recipient nations totaled $194,691,000. These loans ranged in size from $1,450,000 to the Solomon Islands for agricultural development to $23,600,000, by far the largest loan, to Bangladesh for the establishment of the Grameen Bank scheme, a bank for rural development. The Grameen Bank is as good an example as any of the IFAD strategy for bringing about economic self-sufficiency in Third World countries. The IFAD loan represented only a part of the capital of the Bangladesh banking project. Sweden and Norway jointly contributed $13,800,000, the Ford Foundation contributed $1,800,000, and the government of Bangladesh invested $11,300,000, making a total capital investment of $50,500,000. With this capital, the Grameen Bank can make loans to peasant farmers who have no collateral for the purchase of cattle and simple farm equipment, or to set up as peddlers, tailors, or small shopkeepers. Loans are usually in amounts of about $50 and are payable over a period of 50 weeks at interest rates of about 10%. So far the bank has been able to report a repayment rate of 99%, and it appears that many borrowers have been able to double their previous incomes.

IFAD is a collective act of faith by the prosperous nations in the process of helping the poorest nations to help themselves toward agricultural self-sufficiency. For a country like Bangladesh, the process may not even approach completion within decades to come. To begin the process may relieve nations with money to spare from the wasteful alternative, repeated disaster relief campaigns.

The International Labor Organization (ILO). The ILO was formed in 1919 as an agency of the League of Nations, in the wake of the Treaty of Versailles. Although its later functions were primarily addressed to the improvement of working conditions through the drafting of standards, one of its most significant achievements was its early work with refugees during the 1920s. After the Russian Revolution, hundreds of thousands of refugees streamed into the western European countries. The League's high commissioner for refugees, Dr. Fridtjof Nansen, turned over the administrative work of resettlement to the ILO, which arranged emigration, work, and new homes for thousands of refugee families.[2]

Although American labor leaders were active in drafting the plans for the new organization, it was not until 1934, during the administration of President Roosevelt and on the initiative of Frances Perkins, then secretary of labor, that the United States was formally affiliated. During this interval, opposition from employer groups and continuing hostility in Congress to the League of Nations (with which the ILO was tied) outweighed the strong advocacy of the ILO by the American Federation of Labor.

The United States did not play a significant role in the ILO until after World War II. The organization's influence was most notable in Europe, where its promotion of labor standards and social legislation made some important gains.

World War II reduced the ILO to a small group of caretaker officials in Montreal. Late in the war, President Roosevelt convened a conference in Philadelphia to consider the organization's future. This conference produced the Declaration of Philadelphia, its continuing statement of purpose.

The original constitutional goals of the ILO, established in 1919, called for standards for maximum working hours, miminum wages, protection of workers from occupational disease and injury, pensions for the old and disabled, equal pay for equal work, and vocational education.[3] To these familiar goals, the Declaration of Philadelphia added the following objectives:

1. Full employment and increased living standards.
2. Provision for migration and training so that workers could be employed at their full skills.

3. Effective recognition of the right of collective bargaining, and labor–management cooperation in improving productivity.
4. Extension of social security to provide for basic income support and medical care.
5. Provision of adequate nutrition and housing.
6. Equality of educational and vocational opportunity.

To promote the worldwide achievement of these goals, the ILO has a unique constitutional structure. Each country affiliated with the ILO must send a delegation with representatives from employer associations and unions as well as from the governments themselves. This "tripartite" representation is intended to assure that the work of the ILO will have the broad support of employers and workers as well as politicians. While this arrangement has worked fairly well in most Western countries, there has been considerable dissatisfaction with the representation of the Communist nations, in which neither the employer groups nor the unions can be seriously regarded as entities independent of their governments.

Although the ILO worked effectively enough toward its goals to receive the Nobel Peace Prize in 1969, its deliberations have been increasingly occupied by polemics. The Arab nations and their primarily Eastern European sympathizers have kept denunciations of Israel high on the ILO conference agenda. Similarly, the African members have insisted on discourse on the evils of apartheid and measures to isolate South Africa. The American position has been consistent on the introduction of political matters in ILO meetings, insisting that regardless of the merits of these or other political issues, the ILO is not competent to pass resolutions on these topics or to monitor their compliance. In 1975, President Ford notified the director-general of the ILO of the American intention to withdraw, on which President Carter acted in 1977.

The reasons assigned for the withdrawal of the United States are significant. In the notice presented in 1975, four complaints were advanced. First, the "tripartite system" of representation allowed the Communist nations to claim that their delegations included representatives of employers and labor unions who were in fact Communist party officials or officers of government. Second, the legitimate concern of the ILO for human rights was selective in its application; some states, especially South Africa and Israel, were vigorously cited for violations, whereas the Communist nations were exempt from denunciatory resolutions. Third, ILO procedures to assure due process before resolutions were adopted condemning human rights violations were disregarded. Fourth, "the ILO [had] become increasingly and excessively involved in political issues which [were] quite beyond the competence and mandate of the Organization.... International politics is not the main business of the ILO. Questions involving relations between the states and proclamations of economic principles should be left to the United Nations and other international agencies where their consideration is more relevant to those organizations' responsibilities."[4]

In 1980 the United States rejoined the ILO. President Carter issued a statement asserting that "a majority of ILO members...have successfully joined together to return the ILO to its original purposes. Through their efforts, steps have been taken to strengthen the independence of employer and worker delegates, undertake investigation of human rights violations in a number of countries including the Soviet Union, reinforce the principle of due process, and generally reduce the level of politicization in the ILO."[5]

These conclusions were not wholly borne out in the 1980 conference. Nevertheless, in spite of the serious problems that still disfigure ILO deliberations, the ongoing work of the organization toward the improvement of worldwide working conditions and living standards continues to have some impact in the less developed countries. Its statistical reports reflect the extent of compliance of all members to the standards agreed upon in the conventions that they have adopted.

The United Nations Conference on Trade and Development (UNCTAD).[6] Formed in 1964, primarily on the initiative of the developing nations, UNCTAD is designed to promote the economic interests of all countries, but especially the developing ones, by increasing and diversifying foreign trade opportunities. For most of these countries the dependence on the export of one or at most a few commodities such as tin, natural rubber, cocoa, or phosphate, to name only a few, is both an obstacle to development and a cause of social and economic instability. Fluctuations in world prices are often extreme, and investment policy becomes difficult, if not impossible, to maintain.

To remedy this obstacle to prosperity, UNCTAD has worked toward the formulation and adoption of world commodity agreements. The model that developing countries hoped to create was aimed at cooperation between producing and consuming nations. It was reasoned that if international agreements could stabilize commodity prices such as tin, then rubber, cocoa, coffee, sugar, and other commodities might benefit from the same approach. At least, the feast-and-famine cycle might be transformed into a system of some income stability.

These aspirations have not yet been fulfilled. In April 1982 an international rubber agreement was put into force. Agreements on tin, cocoa, and sugar were to have been concluded. As to tin, however, Bolivia, the fourth largest producer, refused to join up. The Ivory Coast, the largest producer of cocoa, preferred to go it alone. As for sugar, the precipitous decline in prices since 1982 made it impossible to continue the agreement for their stabilization.[7]

It is a matter for debate as to whether price stabilization is a realistic objective for the commodities on which the developing countries depend for revenue. It is likely that many of them would settle for guaranteed minimum prices rather than the control of the gross fluctuations with which they have had to contend in the past. Some understandings of this kind would probably be acceptable to the consumer nations.

Although the plight of the developing countries is difficult, and not responding as well as hoped to the measures that UNCTAD and other United Nations agencies have introduced, there are among them 37 countries whose difficulties are so serious that special plans have had to be made for them as least developed countries (LDCs). These are countries whose resources are so meager that there are not even raw materials to be exported. They range in size from populous Bangladesh to small island states like Western Samoa and Comoros. In such countries, annual per capita gross domestic product is often less than $100. Literacy rates are less than 20%. Economic growth rates are stagnant, transport facilities are inadequate, and manufacturing facilities are negligible or nonexistent. Fifteen are landlocked, and 5 are situated in small and remote island groups. Birth and death rates in most of these states are the highest in the world.

UNCTAD's program for remedying the desperate condition of the LDCs was formulated in 1981 under the title Substantial New Program of Action (SNPA). The program is explicitly grounded on the concept of reciprocity of rights and obligations. It assumes that the developed countries have an obligation to provide systematic and appropriate assistance to the LDCs, and that the LDCs' right to assistance has both historical and moral foundations. In return for assistance, the donor international community has a right to assure that funds and resources are put to their intended use for the good of the whole people of each LDC and therefore has the right to monitor their use. The objective of the SNPA is the achievement of self-reliance in each LDC. As the UNCTAD *Bulletin* puts it:

> The SNPA is not a blue print for a gigantic relief operation, although relief measures have their place in it. It is a long term program for deep-rooted structural change intended to transform the economies of the LDCs toward sustainable growth and self-reliant development. Its vision is a participatory development process and its prescriptions address all strata of the LDC populations as both contributors to and beneficiaries of that process.[8]

Anyone who has visited a least developed country, as I have done, will have a perspective of the long haul ahead for UNCTAD. It is a task that has never before been attempted, and the difficulties are enormous. The final accomplishment is impossible to visualize at this early stage. What will be the final level of development for each of the nations assisted by UNCTAD? At what point will self-reliance be sufficiently assured so that the present LDC can be considered "developed" and dispense with further assistance? What level of affluence can be expected in a country with few natural resources and a constantly growing population—even with sympathetic and adequate assistance from UNCTAD and other specialized United Nations agencies?[9] No one knows the answers to these questions or to many others that SNPA poses to the international community. But a beginning has to be made, even if the end is too remote to comprehend.

The central question confronting the nations supposedly working together in UNCTAD is practical. It is almost an article of faith among the developing nations that there is a mutual interest between them and the developed nations to strengthen the economies of the former. If a country like India or China, for the two largest examples, can achieve consistently growing economies, the exporting nations like the United States and Japan will benefit from the ability of Indians and Chinese to import more. The same would go for the much less populous nations in lesser degree. This set of contentions has never reached a consensus in which the developed nations have wholeheartedly joined.[10]

As in most United Nations forums, the UNCTAD conferences have included a good deal of ideological debate. The American response has been one of impatience leading to a demand for "reform." At the September 1984 meeting of the UNCTAD board, the United States representative urged that UNCTAD return to its main purpose, "to allow member states to discuss their concerns and share their views with others...and *then* to seek agreements on issues or parts of issues where agreement is possible or likely.... Agenda items which ought to be opportunities for exchanges of views have become opportunities...to introduce prejudged and poorly conceived resolutions. Too often these resolutions represent politically motivated attempts for rhetorical victory rather than an occasion to thoroughly discuss concrete economic problems.... True dialogue is sacrificed to score debating points."[11] Whether this orderly process can soon replace the culture of confrontation remains to be seen, particularly in an organization in which intellectual commitments have been made to global and "statist" solutions to problems presented by countries in a hurry for results.

The United Nations Development Program (UNDP). In 1965 the General Assembly created the United Nations Develop_ ment Program to serve as the principal channel for the movement of technical assistance funds, expert personnel, and needed equipment through the United Nations system to the developing countries. In the 20 years of its existence, UNDP has become the largest program administering multilateral technical assistance grants. It currently supports over 4500 projects in 154 nations and self-governing territories in the Third World with funds voluntarily contributed by member states. In addition, it administers another 1600 projects funded by other United Nations agencies, as, for example, the World Bank. The total cost of UNDP projects now under way will be about $7,500,000,000 when they are completed, of which the UNDP share is about $3,260,000,000, the remainder being provided by the countries receiving assistance.

The assistance provided depends on the needs of the country and its ability to make use of UNDP services. Two examples will indicate the great diversity of problems with which the agency has assisted.

In Kuwait, for several years a nation with one of the world's highest per capita incomes, there was concern about the quality of food inspection services. It was decided that about 150 inspectors should be trained. UNDP made the arrangements for training Kuwaiti personnel in the United Kingdom and the United States at no cost to the United Nations. The project allowed not only for the training of the inspectors but also for training supervisory personnel to train additional inspectors in Kuwait.

A vastly different situation was presented by the kingdom of Tonga, an island nation in the South Pacific that has so far not applied for membership in the United Nations. Although Tonga is situated in an ocean area with an abundance of fish far exceeding the needs of its people, the fishermen were not well enough equipped with boats and modern equipment to supply the local demand. A UNDP-funded project was carried out by the FAO to create a small boat-building facility so that an adequate supply of fish could be caught and distributed. UNDP organized the project at the request of the Tonga government. Support came from the United Nations Capital Development Fund, the governments of Japan and Australia, and the Foundation for the Friends of the Peoples of the South Pacific. As of 1984, the total cost of the project was $2,868,242, of which UNDP funds amounted to $621,272, and the government of Tonga contributed $230,702. For this investment, Tonga got two new boatyards and the training of Tongan personnel in modern boat-building methods and the use of new techniques of fishing and preserving the catch. The kingdom now has 40 new fishing boats capable of long-distance and all-season fishing, and the capability of building more when needed.

These examples are two randomly selected projects from thousands undertaken by UNDP. Neither of them is especially dramatic; no UNDP projects will revolutionize the economy of any nation overnight or over a period of years. Some projects fail to produce the expected results, and some have to be redesigned or written off as failures. It is fair to note that all of the advanced industrial economies have experienced failures to meet objectives. The experiment in international cooperation that is the essence of the UNDP is a new thing on earth, an enterprise that has never been attempted before. It would be a supernatural accomplishment if within 20 years of effort the UNDP had replaced the poverty of the Third World with Utopias in every desert, jungle, and swamp. That the effort is being made is a foundation for hope in nations where hope has hitherto been an unknown virtue.

The United Nations Educational, Scientific and Cultural Organization (UNESCO). In 1945 the British Hellenist Gilbert Murray proposed that the Conference of Allied Ministers of Education, which had been organized by the United Kingdom, should be expanded into an international organization. An international preparatory commission was assembled, the distinguished biologist Julian

Huxley was appointed as its executive secretary, and a plan was devised that became UNESCO. The organization came into being in November 1946 with 20 member states, a complement that has increased to 158 at the present time. Huxley became its first director-general.

The aims of UNESCO are eloquently stated in Huxley's *UNESCO: Its Purpose and Its Philosophy*.[12] After adopting Prime Minister Clement Attlee's noble aphorism, "Since wars begin in the minds of men, it is in the minds of men that the defenses of peace must be constructed," Huxley listed three guiding aims, still embodied in UNESCO's constitution: (1) "advancing the mutual knowledge and understanding of peoples, through all means of mass communication," (2) "giving fresh impulse to popular education and to the spread of...culture," and (3) "to maintain, increase and diffuse knowledge."

No one could deny the relevance of these objectives to the troubled times in which we still live. The difficulty has been to discover effective means for accomplishing such nebulous ends. Throughout its history, UNESCO has been torn by conflicts as to how its goals may be achieved. Huxley presented the problems of advancing knowledge, making education a universal right, and diffusing information with eloquence and vigor. He also stressed the importance of *"coming to grips"* with the means to achieve these objectives. "Coming to grips" proved far more difficult than the composition of a statement of UNESCO's mission. Neither he nor any of his successors has managed to create a program on which all members of UNESCO could agree. As in every other United Nations forum, unanimity has rarely been possible in its governing bodies, the General Conference and the Executive Board.

The General Conference comprises delegates from all the member states. It meets every two years to consider the organization's achievements and problems and to determine future policies and programs. The conference elects the 50-nation membership of the Executive Board, which meets at least three times a year to supervise the execution of the program.

The actual administration of UNESCO is in the hands of a secretariat whose chief officer is the director-general, a position now occupied by Amadou-Mahtar M'Bow, of Senegal, now in his second six-year term.

In spite of the disagreements that surfaced in the governing bodies of UNESCO, in which delegates too often yielded to the temptation to allow rhetoric to dominate substance, UNESCO succeeded in mounting an active program. Its elements are discernible in its budgets for 1984–1985 and 1986–1987.[13]

Item	1986–87	1984–85
Major Programs		
I. Reflection on world problems and future-oriented studies	—	—
II. Education for all	21,746,000	23,983,000
III. Communication in the service of man	18,560,000	16,600,000
IV. The formulation and application of education policies	52,617,000	51,805,000
V. Education, training, and society	13,528,000	15,363,000
VI. The sciences and their application to development	36,325,000	36,203,000
VII. Information systems	8,357,000	6,900,000
VIII. Strategies for development	10,371,800	7,997,800
IX. Science, technology, and society	1,858,000	3,330,000
X. The human environment	26,810,000	26,461,000
XI. Culture and the future	25,455,000	30,550,000
XII. The elimination of prejudice, intolerance, racism, and apartheid	300,000	—
XIII. Peace, international understanding, human rights	250,000	260,000
SUBTOTAL	216,167,800	219,453,300
General Program Activities		
Statistics	820,000	817,000
TOTAL	$216,987,800	$220,260,300

The terminology used for most of the items on this budget of expenditures will be rather opaque to the uninstructed reader. To be as specific as I can about a program that ranges far and wide—both geographically and intellectually—UNESCO has been conducting four different kinds of activity. First, and generally con-

ceded to be important, valuable, and well executed, even by UN-
ESCO's detractors, is the campaign to eradicate illiteracy. This
takes two forms: the training of teachers and their support in countries where local resources are insufficient to recruit and pay
them.

Second, UNESCO has done much to preserve architectural and
artistic remains from ancient times, as, for example, the Abu Simbel
temples built by Ramses II in Egypt during the thirteenth century before Christ. These famous structures were about to be sub-
merged by the construction of the Aswan Dam. A campaign by
UNESCO to raise funds for their removal to high ground succeeded in preserving them for posterity.

Third, the work of UNESCO in encouraging and to some
extent supporting such coordinated scientific efforts as the International Geological Correlation Program, the International Hydro-
logical Program, and Man and the Biosphere is intended to
complete worldwide knowledge of the resources of the planet. The
necessarily international effort required to complete programs
such as these calls for scientific guidelines and the deployment of
field research personnel on a systematic basis so that findings from
different countries will be presented in a standard format, readily
accessible to scientists anywhere.

Fourth, UNESCO has been concerned increasingly with the
means to achieve its constitutional goals and with the identification
of the obstacles to its progress toward them. Hence, the emphasis
on studies of racism, apartheid, and the denial of human rights.

The goals of UNESCO have been consistent throughout its
history. Not many detractors have challenged their relevance to
the troubles and conflicts that have plagued mankind since World
War II. The means chosen to achieve them have been openly
derogated, and the quality of discourse in the General Conference
and the Executive Board has been a source of a great deal of criticism, especially from the Western industrialized nations.

That criticism led to notice by the United States, on December
28, 1983, of its intent to withdraw from UNESCO effective December 31, 1984. The reasons given for this action were set forth
as follows:

Politicization of UNESCO's traditional subjects in the introduction of programs, resolutions and debate on disarmament, "collective rights," and other extraneous themes;

An endemic hostility toward the basic institutions of a free society, especially a free market and a free press;

The most unrestrained budgetary expansion in the United Nations system; and

Poor management throughout the organization, prime reasons for which were a top-heavy, over-centralized bureaucracy and a structure wherein excessive authority had flowed to the Secretariat and away from the governing bodies and member states.[14]

In spite of numerous representations to the administration and to Congress by educational and scientific bodies protesting the withdrawal, the United States proceeded as planned, withdrew on the effective date, and terminated its 25% contribution to the UNESCO budget.

Almost as momentous was the notice on April 2, 1984, by the United Kingdom that it intended to take the same step. The special significance of this action was the original role played by the British government in creating UNESCO. Unlike the United States action, the British notice was accompanied by proposals for reform that, if put into effect, might lead to a change of heart. These proposals were as follows:

1. Implementation of the current programme should take account of continuing Western concerns about the programmes on communication and media questions and on human rights, peace, and disarmament. Lower priority should be given to the programmes of future studies.... The programme on human rights should accord with the Universal Declaration [of Human Rights] and the two covenants.... [T]here should also be a review of the operations of the Office of Public Information.
2. The workings of the Executive Board and the General Conference should be improved.
3. There should be economies, particularly at Headquarters.
4. There should be more concentration of programmes in the field and fewer studies.
5. There should be more decentralization. Personnel should be discussed in terms wider than geographical distribution.[15]

As this chapter is written, British withdrawal has now become final. It was a topic of intense debate in scientific and cultural organizations as well as in the press, and there are many cultural and scientific groups that are trying to reverse the government's decision.

No other activity of the United Nations has been so vehemently denounced by some partisans and so staunchly defended by others. I leave to later sections of this debate the discourse on the merits of the issues that UNESCO presents to the world it was created to serve.

The United Nations High Commissioner for Refugees (UNHCR). Ideology, fanatical religious differences, civil warfare, and wars between states large and small have created a new class of misery in the world. Millions of families have been displaced from their homelands to be thrust into alien and not always welcoming environments for periods of time that are almost always indefinite.

It is not a new problem. Refugees from European countries migrated to the New World from the seventeenth century onward, there to build new cultures and new nations. The world is more crowded now; there are no new continents to claim, and the numbers of displaced people are vastly greater than ever before.

To meet a need that grows constantly the UNHCR was established in December 1949 by the General Assembly.[16] There was a generally acclaimed predecessor. After World War I, the League of Nations created the office of a high commissioner to deal first with assistance to refugees from the Russian Revolution, and as misery went on to become more widespread, to cope with the problems of Armenian refugees from Turkey, Turkish refugees from the newly independent Balkan states and later to German refugees from the Nazi regime.[17]

Experience during the post-World War II years made it clear that refugees would continue to need help for a long time to come and that the United Nations had a responsibility to see to it that they got what they needed to survive. Drawing on the record of the League's high commissioner, a permanent agency was organized within the United Nations.

The office of the high commissioner is responsible to the General Assembly through the Economic and Social Council (ECOSOC) and is organized under a statute that provides him with considerable latitude. The statute begins with as specific a definition as possible of the refugee status, obviously a condition that can be and often is a matter of dispute. It is made clear that UNHCR's activities are to be nonpolitical and limited to humanitarian services. For eligibility for these services, a refugee must be a person "who is outside his own country owing to well-founded fear of being persecuted for reasons of race, religion, nationality or political opinion and is unable or...unwilling to avail himself of the protection of that country."[18]

The responsibility of the high commissioner is to provide for the protection of refugees by promoting the conclusion and ratification of international conventions and supervising their application. He is also expected to search for solutions to refugee problems by facilitating wherever possible the voluntary repatriation of those who have fled or been driven from their countries.

The budget of the United Nations provides for the direct administrative costs of the UNHCR. Voluntary contributions from governments and nongovernmental organizations provide for the assistance actually rendered to refugees. The funds allocated by the United Nations in 1985 were $14,117,800; voluntary contributions totaled about $445,303,400.[19] This sum is a reduction from a peak budget of about $500,000,000 in 1980; the high commissioner reports that there has been a "relative stabilization" of the major refugee situations. However, along with the stabilization has come the new necessity of providing massive relief and care for millions of recently uprooted refugees in "temporary asylums," i.e., situations where the host country does not propose to accept refugees as permanent residents. The formidable problems that have been generated in the large refugee camps created during the last two decades have required the UNHCR to call on many of the United Nations' affiliated agencies and services for cooperation. Thus, the World Food Program has provided emergency food assistance; the United Nations Children's Fund (UNICEF) has furnished support for education, health care, and sanitation; the United Nations Development Program has contributed funds and personnel for the establishment of programs leading to self-support by refugees. Other agencies working closely with UNHCR include the World Bank, the World Health Organization, the International Labor Organization, UNESCO, and the United Nations Center for Human Settlements. Probably in no other field of international activity are so many United Nations agencies collaborating with funds, personnel, and expertise.

It is estimated that since its activation in 1951, UNHCR has extended humanitarian relief in 90 countries to about 25 million people. Necessarily, the structure of an agency with responsibilities for millions of people in such widely dispersed situations requires considerable decentralization. The agency is, of course, under the administrative direction of the high commissioner, who is nominated for a term of five years by the secretary-general of the United Nations and elected by the General Assembly. As needed, the high commissioner appoints field representatives in those countries where refugee situations and programs are under way. His headquarters are in Geneva.

The importance and effectiveness of the UNHCR has been widely recognized. The organization and maintenance of enormous refugee camps for Afghans, Ugandans, Cambodians, and Vietnamese are spectacular containments of thousands of individual tragedies. Less known are the repatriation programs that UNHCR has arranged throughout Europe and Africa, and, to some extent, in Southeast Asia. Like most problems confronting international organizations, the desperate situations of modern refugees have no quick solutions in sight. For many, survival is all that can be expected in the short or middle terms. Repatriation or even resettlement is a distant goal. That UNHCR and the hundreds of governmental and voluntary agencies associated with it can keep the hope of these goals alive is in itself a gain for civilization in the face of twentieth-century barbarism. It is an achievement that has been properly recognized by the award of the Nobel Peace Prize in 1954 and 1981.

The United Nations Relief and Works Agency for Palestine Refugees in the Near East (UNRWA).[20] Surely no international organization faces so difficult a task as UNRWA. Founded in 1949 by the General Assembly to deal with condition of displaced Palestinians, UNRWA has become a permanent charge on the conscience and the patience of the international community. What began as temporary emergency services for 700,000 Arabs displaced from Palestine by the Israeli–Arab conflict has become, four decades later, a system for the temporary support of more than 2,000,000 people (half of whom are under the age of 21) for whom no permanent solution has ever been in sight. This total now stretches over three generations.

Because of the nature of its charge, UNRWA is an operational agency—unlike most United Nations organizations. Under a commissioner-general appointed by the secretary-general, UNRWA performs for refugees many services that are normally provided by governments, particularly welfare support, medical care, and educational systems. All this is done without territorial authority, legislative powers, or legal jurisdiction over the refugees in its care. The alarming growth of UNRWA's operations can be seen from a few statistics. In 1950 the agency operated 61 schools with an enrollment of 34,000 children. In June 1982 there were 645 primary and secondary schools with 338,000 pupils and 8 vocational and teacher-training centers with 5,200 trainees.[21] There are 120 health centers with 4,500,000 outpatient calls. The agency now has 17,200 employees, almost all of them Palestinian, and 120 internationally recruited staff.[22] The current budget for the support of UNRWA's activity is about $200,000,000, almost all of it coming from voluntary contributions by member states of the United Nations.

The history of UNRWA is the history of the Mideast troubles, too complex, too long to encapsulate here. At its inception, it was expected that the agency would not be needed for long. A vigorous program of repatriation for some and resettlement for others would end the need for its intervention. That expectation evaporated when it became clear that not many Palestinians would be able to return to their homes in Israel, none of the host nations had the resources to support so large a refugee population, and the Palestinians themselves did not wish to jeopardize whatever rights they might have to return to Palestine by accepting the nationality of the state in which they were "temporarily" residing.

UNRWA is an agency that has had to accommodate to conditions of warfare and turbulence. Near insolvency has been normal—indeed, it can be said that there never have been "normal" times for which administrators could plan with confidence. Until peace comes to the Middle East—and in the light of history, peace itself would be abnormal—UNRWA will continue to be needed. The plans of civilized nations should be made accordingly.

The United Nations Industrial Development Organization (UNIDO). Modern agricultural methods have greatly increased productivity, but at the cost of disrupting traditional cultivation and harvesting. Agricultural labor has been rendered surplus, and even in the developed countries of Europe and North America response to the movement from fields to city slums has been difficult and inadequate. For the developing countries the problems have been similar but especially intractable. The solution is obvious and extraordinarily difficult to carry out. Industrialization, if only it could be achieved in the twinkling of an eye, would transform developing nations into prosperous economies with entirely different sets of social problems than unemployment, maldistribution of goods and services, and the discontents that come with chronic poverty and hopelessness.

The desire of the leaders of the developing countries to move as rapidly as possible toward industrial economies led to the formation of the Center for Industrial Development (CID) in 1961 at the behest of the General Assembly. In January 1967 the CID was elevated to the status of an autonomous agency.[23] In 1985 it became a specialized agency within the Charter's definition of the term.

As defined by the General Assembly, the purpose of UNIDO is "to promote and accelerate the industrialization of the developing countries of the world, with particular emphasis on the manufacturing sector." This is a large order. Nations wishing assistance will need services ranging from choosing and setting up appropriate manufacturing facilities, through the development of technical and managerial expertise, to arrangements for transportation and marketing products. UNIDO's part is to recruit proficient and sympathetic consultants and to find sources of loans on terms that the developing borrower can afford. Neither the expertise nor the funds come easily. Through the World Bank and the United Nations Development Program both personnel and funds are made available, with UNIDO acting as planner and coordinator.

The target is ambitious. It is UNIDO's goal to increase the share of the developing countries in industrial production to 25% of the world's capacity by the year 2000. When UNIDO began operations in 1963, that share was 8.1%; by 1982 its share had increased to 11%.[24] Whether UNIDO can achieve its goal depends on many factors and future developments beyond its control. Its contribution of planning, training, technology transfer, and the arrangements for funding make the desirable possible. The world economy itself can make what is possible the reality needed by countries that are now too close to absolute and stagnating poverty.

The World Bank and the International Monetary Fund. Throughout World War II economists corresponded and conferred about the structure of the world economy after the peace. John Maynard Keynes, the English theorist whose analysis, *The Economic Consequences of the Peace,* all too accurately foretold the fearful consequences of Versailles, was the natural leader of an international group that was determined to assure that there would be no repetition of that calamitous settlement. With Harry Dexter White, an economist for the United States Treasury, Keynes proposed two institutional prophylactics against the economic debacles that followed World War I: the World Bank and the International Monetary Fund. Both of them have worked effectively, and both are essential elements of the intergovernmental arrangements essential for worldwide fiscal stability. They are related to the United Nations as specialized agencies and present annual reports through the Economic and Social Council.

The World Bank, more accurately known as the International Bank for Reconstruction and Development, was originally designed to channel capital flow from the United States, Canada, and the few other countries with relatively intact economies to the devastated nations of Europe.[25] Organized at Bretton Woods, New Hampshire, in 1944, it gave evidence not long after the peace that its resources could not possibly accomplish the tasks that Keynes and White had set for it. In 1947 the United States extended billions of dollars in credits through the Marshall Plan to hasten the reconstruction and to prevent the anarchy that threatened the nearly prostrate European nations.

The Marshall Plan relieved the World Bank of its role in the salvation of the ruined European economies. The second responsibility that had been assigned to it was the development of African and Asian economies that had been more or less protected by the colonial powers. Since its role was that of a very large financial cooperative to which all the non-Communist nations of the West subscribed, its business was with the developing countries to which the bank makes loans on terms that private banks cannot allow. Even at that, the World Bank found it to be unrealistic to lend on any commercial terms to the least developed countries, i.e., those nations whose per capita income was less than $375.

To solve this problem and to make possible World Bank assistance to these countries, the International Development Association (IDA) was formed, to be administered by the bank under an "elaborate fiction that it is a separate international organization."[26] With funds subscribed by the developed nations, zero-interest loans for 50-year terms are extended to the poor nations that qualify. Periodically the IDA funds are "replenished" so that the loans can continue.

For all its clients the World Bank and the IDA provide extensive consultative services, closely supervising the expenditure of funds for the projects for which the loans were made. In many cases, UNCTAD, UNIDO, IFAD, and the UNDP will have assisted borrowing nations in planning projects and recruiting technical personnel to carry them out, with major World Bank funds invested when the plans are complete.

A second offshoot of the World Bank is the International Finance Corporation (IFC), founded in 1956. Unlike the IDA, IFC is a separate legal entity with its own officers and staff. Its charge is to promote private investment in the developing world. Beginning with a membership of 38 countries and a capital of $78,000,000, it now has 119 members and a capital fund of $650,000,000.

IFC is a source for risk capital for private enterprise in the developing nations. It encourages the development of local capital markets and stimulates the flow of private capital from the developed nations to the developing. Its strategy now calls for the support of energy resource development and increased agricultural productivity.

The programs of FAO, IFAD, UNCTAD, UNDP, UNIDO, and the World Bank are of critical importance in making possible self-sufficiency in the Third World. Citizens in the affluent First World often fail to appreciate the significance of the United Nations effort to hasten development. For the United States, the Third World even now represents a major market for its exports. In 1981 "about 2 million U.S. jobs, or 6 per cent of all U.S. manufacturing jobs and one out of every four U.S. acres under cultivation [depended] on developing-country consumption, investment and import demand."[27] Economic growth in the Third World will expand markets sorely needed by most of the manufacturing nations.

In the First World we are accustomed to speedy change, sometimes so speedy that it disorients whole generations. In contrast, change in the Third World, especially economic change, is painfully slow. Impatient taxpayers and the politicians representing them sometimes argue that the developing countries become dependent and unwilling to bestir themselves in their own behalf as a result of First World bounty. This opinion is surely based on a misconception of the problem. In his Nobel Prize lecture, the Harvard economist Simon Kuznets puts the situation in a perspective that accounts for the difficulties of modernization:

.... [The] growth position of the less developed countries today is significantly different, in many respects, from that of the presently developed countries on the eve of their entry into modern economic growth (with the possible exception of Japan, and one cannot be sure even of that). The less developed areas that account for the largest part of the world population today are at much lower levels than were the developed countries just before their industrialization; and the latter at that time were economically in advance of the rest of the world, not at the low end of the per capita product range. The very magnitudes, as well as some of the basic conditions, are quite different: no country that entered modern economic growth (except Russia) approached the size of India or China...; and no currently developed country had to adjust to the very high rates of natural increase of population that have characterized many less developed countries over the last two or three decades.[28]

No one can predict how far the development of Bangladesh or Western Samoa or the Central African Republic can or will go. But such nations certainly cannot go it alone now. It is well that the United Nations system is there to help them along for as long as they need help.

The International Monetary Fund (IMF). At a time when the foreign debt of almost all Third World nations is out of hand and a cause of anxiety to central banks and lenders all over the First World, the IMF is famous as a lender of last resort, usually imposing on recipient governments conditions of austerity in return for its assistance.

Like the World Bank, the IMF was formed at the Bretton Woods conference of 1944 and formally began operations on December 27, 1945. Its articles of agreement specify that its aims are the promotion of international monetary cooperation and the expansion of trade. To accomplish these ends, IMF makes loans to member nations with balance-of-payments difficulties on conditions intended to resolve whatever economic crises caused the difficulties. The loans come from a revolving fund to which the borrowing nation is expected to repay its debt.

Unlike most United Nations agencies—including the General Assembly itself—the IMF's highest authority is a board of governors comprising representatives from each member nation, whose votes are weighted proportionately to a quota of contributions to the fund established for each country.

The success of the IMF in achieving its aims is generally conceded. In the words of Donald Regan, then the United States secretary of the treasury and *ex officio* a governor of the IMF:

> Many centuries [ago], a Greek mathematician discerned the vast power of the fulcrum. That man, Archimedes, said, "Give me a standing place and I will move the world." In a sense these two great institutions [the World Bank and the IMF] are here to provide nations a "standing place" and a fulcrum to be used to strengthen their own economies. But like the "standing place" and the fulcrum of Archimedes, they are only tools. In the long run, the true power will come from our own efforts and the dynamism of the market place.[29]

Like all international agencies, the IMF is a tool. It is a better used tool than most, perhaps because the world has learned that it cannot do without it.

The World Health Organization (WHO). In an address at Nairobi in 1973, Robert McNamara, then the president of the World Bank, distinguished between the relative poverty of the poor in rich countries and the absolute poverty of the poor in poor countries:

> Relative poverty means simply that some countries are less affluent than other countries, or that some citizens...have less personal abundance than their neighbors. That has always been the case, and granted the realities of differences between regions and between individuals, will continue to be the case....
>
> But absolute poverty is a condition of life so degraded by disease, illiteracy, malnutrition, and squalor as to deny its victims basic human necessities.
>
> It is a condition of life suffered...by hundreds of millions of the citizens of the developing countries....
>
> —One-third to one-half of the two billion human beings in those countries suffer from hunger or malnutrition.

—20% to 25% of their children die before their fifth birthdays. And millions of those who do not die lead impeded lives because their brains have been damaged, their bodies stunted, and their vitality sapped by nutritional deficiencies. . . .

This is absolute poverty: a condition of life so limited as to prevent realization of the potential of the genes with which one is born; a condition of life so common as to be the lot of some 40% of the peoples of developing countries. And are we who tolerate such poverty, when it is in our power to reduce the number afflicted by failing to fulfill the fundamental obligations accepted by civilized men since the beginning of time?[30]

The extent to which absolute poverty has been reduced is a matter for speculation. Statistics in such matters must be no more than roughly approximate. But McNamara's concern was the limited usefulness of economic development projects in countries where the population's ability to benefit was impaired by widespread disease and disabilities.

The literature of past centuries does not contain many references to absolute poverty and its consequences in the colonial world. Indeed, the relative poverty in the industrialized countries was often as debilitating and degrading as the absolute poverty now encountered so widely in the Third World. A smaller world with accelerating population increases has changed all that. No informed person needs to be reminded of the facts laid before the World Bank governors by McNamara. The media see to that.

It is clear that the ambitious plans for economic development depend for their fruition on improvements in the health of the peoples who are to be led into prosperity by comfortable altruists from the First World. This is the task of the World Health Organization. The need for a permanent international mobilization of medical resources was recognized at the United Nations conference at San Francisco in 1945. In the following year, representatives of 64 countries adopted a constitution for the WHO, which was ratified by 26 member states on April 7, 1948. The constitution calls for a typical United Nations governance. There is a World Health Assembly, comprising representatives of each of the

150 member states, which meets annually. An executive board, elected by the assembly, has 31 members and meets at least twice a year. The headquarters is in Geneva, but operations are decentralized to six regional organizations.

WHO's general strategy calls for eight basic aims: health education; proper food supply and nutrition; safe water supplies; maternal and child health, including family planning; immunization against major infectious diseases; prevention and control of local diseases; appropriate treatment of common diseases and injuries; provision of essential drugs. To accomplish these ends, the WHO campaign provides for the collection of data on health and morbidity, the dissemination of information on disease and the technology for its prevention and treatment, education of health personnel, and the standardization of drugs. Stress is laid on immunization programs. WHO is credited with a major success in the eradication of smallpox; cholera, diphtheria, whooping cough, poliomyelitis, measles, and tuberculosis are next on the list for extinction.

Whether WHO will achieve its goals of "health for all by the year 2000" remains to be seen. This is a campaign that requires a concerted effort by all nations. Fortunately, it is a campaign whose goals are accepted by all nations, regardless of ideology, religion, or economic condition.

In this chapter I have tried to present the programs of the United Nations that exist independently of the debates in the Security Council and the General Assembly. Their importance to the peace of the world and the conscience of mankind should be obvious. Each of the successes of these agencies is a step toward the peace that all nations profess to desire. Even the failures, of which there have been many, are occasions from which both politicians and professionals have learned.

This is the international system built around the central idea of the United Nations. Whether it is a system that could survive the dismantling of the United Nations itself is a question that my opponent and I will argue in the ensuing chapters.

Notes

1. Quoted in *Everyone's United Nations* (New York: United Nations, 1979), p. 352, from the IAEA statute.

2. For a brief account, see Louise Holborn, *Refugees: A Problem of Our Time* (Metuchen, New Jersey: Scarecrow Press, 1975), pp. 3–13.

3. For a full account of the ILO constitutional objectives, see Walter Galenson, *The International Labor Organization: An American View* (Madison: University of Wisconsin Press, 1981), p. 9. Galenson's history of the ILO is admirably comprehensive and probably the most easily accessible source of information about the organization and the United States' relations to it.

4. Ibid., p. 84, quoting a letter from Henry A. Kissinger, then secretary of state, to the director-general of the ILO.

5. Ibid., pp. 265–266, quoting White House press release, February 13, 1980.

6. Much of the material presented here concerning UNCTAD has been drawn from Eric Sottas, *The Least Developed Countries* (New York: United Nations, 1985).

7. For an account of the obstacles to commodity agreements among the developing nations, see Carlos Fortin, "UNCTAD and Commodities: Towards a new agenda for research and action," in *UNCTAD: The First Twenty Years,* ed. Carlos Fortin, Susan Joekes, and Leelananda de Silva (Brighton, England: University of Sussex, Institute for Development Studies, July 1984), pp. 33–37.

8. UNCTAD Bulletin No. 214 (August–September 1985), p. 2.

9. One United Nations official whom I interviewed, himself a national of a developing country with extraordinarily difficult economic problems, gave it as his opinion that such countries do not and need not expect an advanced economy to satisfy their populations. There are other values, he thought, and steel mills and freeways are not necessary to their enjoyment.

10. Alfred Maizels, "A Clash of Ideologies," in Fortin, Joekes, and de Silva, note 7, pp. 18–23.

11. Statement of Richard Kauzarlich, deputy assistant secretary of state for international and social affairs, UNCTAD *Bulletin* No. 206 (October 1984), pp. 7–12.

12. Julian Huxley, *UNESCO: Its Purpose and Its Philosophy* (Washington, D.C.: Public Affairs Press, 1948).

13. Estimated expenditures for 1984–1985 and 1986–1987 projections supplied by United Nations Secretariat. For further discussion of the UNESCO budget, see Amadou-Mahtar M'Bow, *UNESCO 1984–85: Introduction to the Draft Programme and Budget* (Paris: UNESCO, 1983).

14. Statement of Edward J. Derwinski, counselor, Department of State, to the

Subcommittees on Human Rights and International Organizations and on International Operations of the Committee on Foreign Affairs, House of Representatives, May 2, 1984, "U.S. Withdrawal From UNESCO," pp. 261–264.

15. United Nations Association of Great Britain and Northern Ireland, *U.N.A. Briefing No. 26, "The Case for UNESCO"* (London, March 1985).

16. General Assembly Resolution 319 (IV) A, December 3, 1949.

17. For a brief account of the high commissioner's work under the auspices of the League of Nations, see Holborn, note 2, pp. 13–20.

18. *Statute of the Office of the High Commissioner for Refugees,* Chapter II, Section A (ii).

19. *Report on UNHCR assistance activities in 1983–84 and proposed voluntary funds programmes and budget for 1985* (Geneva: Office of the United Nations High Commissioner for Refugees, August 1, 1984).

20. For this section, I have drawn from *UNRWA—A Brief History, 1950–1982* (Vienna: UNRWA Headquarters, no date).

21. All of UNRWA's educational programs have relied heavily on the collaboration of UNESCO for personnel and some financial support. See Edward H. Buehrig, *The UN and the Palestinian Refugees. A Study in Nonterritorial Administration* (Bloomington: Indiana University Press, 1971), pp. 147–166. See also *UNRWA—A Brief History,* note 20, pp. 113–155.

22. *UNRWA,* note 20, p. 289.

23. For this section I have drawn from UNIDO Monograph No. 21., *Technical Co-operation in Industry* (New York: United Nations, 1969).

24. *The United Nations at Forty: A Foundation to Build On* (New York: United Nations, 1985), pp. 176–179.

25. For an exhaustive account of the early years of the World Bank, see Robert W. Oliver, *International Economic Co-operation and the World Bank* (London: Macmillan, 1975).

26. Ibid., pp. 263–267. The officers of the IDA are the same as those of the World Bank.

27. Economic Policy Council of UNA-USA, *U.S. Policies Toward the World Bank and the International Monetary Fund; A Report of the International Financial Institutions Panel* (New York: United Nations Association, 1982), p. 6.

28. Simon Kuznets, "Modern Economic Growth," *American Economic Review* LXIII (3) (June 1973), p. 255.

29. Donald T. Regan, *Statement by the Governor of the Fund and the Bank for the United States, Summary Proceedings, Annual Meeting, 1983* (Washington, D.C.: International Monetary Fund, 1983), p. 114.

30. Robert S. McNamara, *Address to the Board of Governors, World Bank Group, Nairobi, Kenya, 24 September 1973* (Washington, D.C.: Interna-

tional Bank for Reconstruction and Development), quoted by Oliver, note 24, pp. 268–269.

ERNEST VAN DEN HAAG

John Conrad has described many U.N. agencies and bathed them in a rosy haze. Some deserve additional scrutiny.

Consider the famine in much of Africa fought by diverse U.N. agencies. Many factors contributed to it, but John Conrad does not mention the major contribution of destructive local government policies financed with development aid, multilaterally given through the U.N. (and all too often also unilaterally by the U.S.). The policies that contributed mightily to the African famine can be detailed as follows:

1. Centralized planning deprived farmers of initiative and supported a huge parasitic bureaucracy to waste and misallocate resources. Ghana and Nigeria, not to speak of Ethiopia, are instances, but there are many more. The U.N. bureaucracy itself, sympathetic to "socialism," encouraged "planning."

2. Price controls were used to reduce the price of agricultural products. This finally made food production unprofitable—wherefore famine. Price controls favored urban populations, which are politically important to African rulers, although most of the population is rural. People were attracted to urban centers, where they were unemployed and totally unproductive. Everyone starved.

The government policy so reduced incentives for agriculture that production was minimized. Relatively rich countries that were previously food exporters became poor. (The Nigerian oil bonanza was wasted.) The U.N. agencies aided the governments that had helped bringing the starvation about. This is still happening in Ethiopia.

3. Much development aid was used for showy projects, such as steel mills that did not produce anything at feasible prices.

Agriculture was neglected—as though the government did not know where the food came from.

It is true that the "Green Revolution" Conrad mentions did help India and other Asian nations to feed themselves. This invention of American scientists, which enabled Asian farmers to cultivate more productive kinds of rice and other grains, is credited by John Conrad to the U.N. The U.N. had nothing to do with it.

No doubt the Food and Agricultural Organization (FAO) has occasionally done something useful with the money Western nations contributed to it. But the major advances in agriculture had nothing to do with FAO, and the major disasters it tries to remedy had much to do with the governments in whose countries they happened. The Soviets introduced famine to Russia and made what had been the breadbasket of Europe into a country that imports wheat from the United States, Canada, and Argentina. The Soviets have been widely imitated in the Third World with the help of the U.N.

John Conrad is optimistic about the International Atomic Energy Agency (IAEA). I'm not. The proliferation of nuclear weapons probably cannot be stopped, and certainly multilateral treaties won't do anything to stop it. Possibly, the fact that small nations armed with nuclear weapons cannot prevail against better armed superpowers, and that these superpowers may retaliate against use of nuclear weapons, may deter actual use by small nations, though not the proliferation. IAEA can be of no help, except in hiding actualities to credulous naives. I wish Conrad's optimism were justified. It isn't. He seems to have read the treaties and neglected the actualities. Currently it seems likely that Israel, Pakistan, and India already have nuclear weapons, and that Egypt, other Arab states, Argentina, and other South American states will have them in the 1990s. There is no point in taking the IAEA seriously.

The International Fund for Agricultural Development (IFAD) committed the U.N. "to the protection of the right of all persons everywhere to be free from hunger and malnutrition." No one would disagree with the goal. But the commitment is hogwash.

(1) Wherein is protection from hunger a "right"? (2) How can the U.N.—for that matter, anybody—protect this "right"? How is the goal to be achieved? How can the U.N. determine domestic policies such as would make sure (a) that enough food is produced and (b) that it is distributed to the hungry? (3) Why, anyway, is the U.N. in charge of this matter?

The U.N. has never been authorized to create any rights and cannot do so. The "right" in question has no existence, unfortunately, except in U.N. declarations. At best it is an ideal.

A right such as the right of Americans to "life, liberty, and the pursuit of happiness" is protected by a government that will punish unauthorized interference (e.g., someone taking your life without "due process of law"). How can a "right" to be well nourished ("free from hunger and malnutrition") be enforced? Suppose Tanzania misregulates its agriculture, or Uganda is engaged in civil war, or China in the "great leap forward," and people starve. Just what is IFAD to do? Oust the Tanzanian government? Or the Chinese government? End the civil war in Uganda? The FAO has been smoking grass. And John Conrad shares its hallucinations.

Apart from silly declarations, IFAD may do useful things. I am not opposed to helping people to help themselves where that can be done effectively. I doubt that the U.N. bureaucracy is the best means of accomplishing this.

The International Labor Organization (ILO), about which John Conrad waxes enthusiastic, did help refugees after the First World War by issuing documents to persons left stateless after the Russian Revolution. It was useful in other ways long before the U.N.

But its "promotion of labor standards and social legislation" never amounted to anything. Where these things were accomplished they were the result of union activity, of domestic prosperity, and of domestic politics. ILO was, and remains, useless as far as labor is concerned. It has not even influenced the freedom of unions to organize and be independent of government. That freedom exists in democratic countries and doesn't exist in nondemocratic ones—the Soviet Union, its satellites, and assorted right- and left-wing dictatorships. The ILO has no ability to do anything about it. The main enemies of free labor are members of ILO and often muster a majority.

Nor can ILO do anything about "full employment" except wishing. We wisely withdrew from ILO when the Soviets used it too openly as a propaganda vehicle, but we unwisely rejoined when the ILO majority, afraid of losing our money, agreed to a less biased course. There is no reason at all for staying. The organization doesn't help anyone except its employees.

The United Nations Conference on Trade and Development (UNCTAD) is another useless agency. It has been trying to cartelize raw material producers on the model of OPEC. John Conrad thinks this restraint of trade (illegal within the United States) is a good thing. No economist does. Cartels are seldom successful, but when they are, they increase the price of the cartelized product by reducing production. This costs consumers money and makes what producers could produce artificially scarce. It transfers income from consumers to producers, as any monopoly does. Why John Conrad thinks this is a good idea is not clear to me. UNCTAD does, because it gives jobs to bureaucrats who would administer the cartel and increases the government income of the producing countries. (It does not in the end, but let that go; governments think it does.) Conrad prefers, in this instance, government-fixed prices, production, and market shares to free markets. Why? Cartels always have hindered progress, in favor of entrenched producers, and they are meant to do just that.

On the whole, UNCTAD (as usual we pay a disproportionate amount of the bills) simply has noted that some nations are poor and others prosperous. The UNCTAD voting majority consists of poor nations. So they try to redistribute the wealth and are displeased when the prosperous nations don't fall for it. Why John Conrad falls for this three-card-monte trick is up to him to explain.

The U.N. Development Program, Conrad tells us, is useful inasmuch as it made "arrangements for training" food inspectors for Kuwait, where there had been "concern about the quality of food inspection services." I am in favor of food inspection. Is John Conrad serious when he implies that Kuwait (a very wealthy country) could not have arranged to have inspectors trained without the U.N.? I think it could do as well, perhaps better, by direct action. Any English, German, French, or American university could have provided the training.

Certainly this U.N. agency must occasionally have been helpful. Conrad notes that it provided facilities to build fishing boats in Tonga where they were needed. Fine. But if they were needed they would pay for themselves in time, and, if so, a banker could earn money by lending the money. How does Conrad imagine the developed countries developed? Private initiative usually takes care of economically sound projects. And wasteful ones are not needed. Assuming that the Tonga project was useful, how economically was the U.N. service provided? Why did private industry not provide it?

Conrad's high regard reminds me of the uncritical admiration, prevalent at one time, of Mussolini's road-building activities. His admirers acted as though only Mussolini could build roads, or as though he did so more economically and better than others. None of this was true. Nor is it true that only the U.N. can provide fishing boats for Tonga, and that it does so better and more economically than alternative providers.

The United Nations High Commissioner for Refugees (UNHCR) has a mixed record. This agency helped many refugees from political violence and turmoil. But it also has kept some refugees on the dole indefinitely for political reasons. This has become a specialty of the United Nations Relief and Works Agency for Palestine Refugees in the Near East (UNRWA), which for many years has kept Arab refugees in camps (we, as usual, contribute disproportionately to finance them). These Arabs "did not wish to accept the nationality of the state in which they were 'temporarily' residing." They preferred to stay in the camps. They did not want to integrate into fellow Arab nations. The camps have become recruiting grounds and strategic positions for the P.L.O. and assorted terrorist organizations. Had it not been for the U.N., the Arabs in question would much more easily have reconciled themselves to becoming citizens of other Arab nations. The refugee problem in the Near East created by war is perpetuated by the U.N.

I do not see why the World Bank and the IMF could not function as well without the U.N. as they do with it. Therefore, I refrain from critical examination of their record, which is checkered. Some activities were helpful. Much money was and is being wasted in loans that will not be paid back. I do not share Conrad's enthusiasm for lending. When these agencies make loans "on terms that private banks cannot allow," one wonders why. Could it be that these loans are disguised gifts? If so, why are they disguised? Why, if they are American gifts, are they not given directly? Do those loans not encourage wasteful government activities by anti-American dictators?

JOHN P. CONRAD

So far as I can make out through all the sound, fury, and ponderous irony, Dr. van den Haag's case against the specialized agencies consists of the following not very clearly related elements:

1. The governments of the decolonized nations have made a lot of mistakes, and the United Nations must be held responsible.
2. Whatever good the United Nations may have done could have been done better by somebody else—a private bank, a university like Harvard or Cambridge, maybe a rich foundation, maybe a sound, conservative think-tank—somebody, *somebody else!*
3. Planning is an evil process insidiously foisted on unsuspecting Third World governments by wicked socialist bureaucrats whose aim is to remake the developing countries in the image of the Soviet Union.

Before amplifying the positive case for the U.N. specialized agencies, I had better deal with these strange notions cooked up from the thin book of neoconservative recipes. All my opponent's ripe wisdom flows from a fundamental principle of this sect's collection of not very carefully examined beliefs which runs like this: If the Third World will be patient, the free market will solve all problems. The free market made the United States the most prosperous economy the world has ever known. If Tanzania, Tonga, and Bangladesh will observe its simple principles, they will prosper too.

It follows that nobody needs the United Nations or any of its specialized agencies. There is an Invisible Hand that will take care of all the woes of people who inhabit deserts and swamps, and live at the mercy of typhoons and droughts. Good conservative Americans know that this is so because they have heard that this is how Adam Smith accounted for the wealth of nations. In the long run, Tanzanians can expect that their capital city will rival Washington, London, or Paris if they work very hard, pursue only their own individual economic interests, and abjure planning. In the long run, as John Maynard Keynes once reminded his fellow economists, all of us, including all contemporary Tanzanians, will be dead.

The doctrines of the free market were never applied to the European colonies, which were kept firmly closed by the imperial governments in London, Paris, Amsterdam, Brussels, and Lisbon. The transformation of a closed economy into the free enterprise system that we claim to have in the United States and Western Europe is not an easy trick to turn. It calls for the almost impossible in a country with meager natural resources, a largely illiterate population, and few, if any, technical personnel qualified to deliver government services. All these handicaps are compounded by the hostilities that seethe among tribes packed into arbitrary colonial boundaries drawn by nineteenth-century geographers who had never seen the territories whose fates they were settling for the ages. Even by hindsight it is hard to see how Uganda or Nigeria could have been decolonized into stable, prosperous, and tranquil nations—to say nothing of new nations born to destitution such as

Chad or Guinea-Bissau. That a few countries such as Zambia, Senegal, Cameroon, and the Ivory Coast have escaped the worst rites of the passage to independence is mostly due to their natural resources, not to the benign Invisible Hand that worked so well in Adam Smith's eighteenth-century Glasgow, and now, we insist, in the United States.

I shall proceed to the three charges that can be inferred from my opponent's case against the specialized agencies. They are a little difficult to deal with, since he provides us with very few details in their support. Sweeping generalizations can only be swept away by more generalizations. But here are my refutations, pending further particulars from my friend, who, so far, prefers not to be bothered with facts.

First, it is quite true that most, if not all, of the new governments of South Asia and Africa have made mistakes, some of them very serious. It is absurd, inhumane, and a grievous error for Colonel Mengistu to relocate a starving population of Ethiopians from a drought-stricken area as a means of dispersing resistance to his regime. The horrifying butcheries of Idi Amin and Milton Obote in Uganda do not even have that flimsy and unacceptable excuse. The Nigerian resistance to the secession of Biafra seems to have been a grave error that wasted people and resources with lasting effects on the economy. And so on—but on what continent have similar and even worse errors of judgment and crimes against humanity not been committed—and in countries far more advanced?

The United Nations cannot be held accountable for these dreadful mistakes. All that its agencies could do was to provide assistance in building sound economies and relieving distress brought on by drought, famine, and foolish warfare. These have been the services performed by WHO, IFAD, FAO, UNICEF, UNDP, and UNHCR, sometimes well and sometimes not so well. Professor van den Haag asserts that these functions could be better carried out by agencies not associated with the United Nations. He loftily refrains from saying why or how independent agencies would do better than those now on the job, and I will not try to set up arguments that he should make but doesn't.

Still there is one great advantage to assistance coming from a multilateral base. Last year I visited the director of the UNDP regional office in Fiji—one of the success stories of decolonization. After he had told me about some of the projects that had been carried out in his region, I asked why the United Nations should be responsible for such a program—would it not have been more efficient to make a bilateral arrangement with one of the developed nations? Not at all, he replied. What a former colony like Fiji or the Cook Islands or Western Samoa wanted was the sense of not being tied to any single benefactor, however kindly and enlightened. With UNDP assistance, the irksome colonial presence of alien masters was ruled out—a Swedish expert this year might be replaced by a Canadian next year and a Yugoslav in the year after that. All of the experts were hired for their skills, and none stayed with the UNDP program beyond the time for which they were needed.

I doubt that this diffusion of aid will impress a neoconservative as a sufficient reason for multilateralism—especially a pundit who sees nothing wrong with colonialism anyway. I like the idea of diffusion of support; I like the sense that the whole world is working on helping Africa or Asia—or North America and Europe, too—to be more peaceful and prosperous. We can be sure that a foundation in New York or Washington could do a great job in any country where they accepted a call, and so could our Agency for International Development. But from the standpoint of the recipient, it's one thing to be obligated to a rich nation like the United States or the Soviet Union. It's quite another to draw on the whole world, as represented by a U.N. agency.

If there's one governmental function that the typical right wing patriot detests more than any other, it's *planning*. He and his fellow guardians of the true ideology have all heard tragicomic tales of the Soviet five-year plans, and that's enough for them. I do not accuse Dr. van den Haag of such simplistic knee-jerking, but I note with concern his skepticism about the usefulness of planning, even for a country that has to start its course toward economic self-sufficiency from well behind square one. An example to shake his complacency about the *laissez-faire* whirlpool into which he wants the Third World to plunge—and sink or swim—is the Republic of Singapore. That nation has become one of the great successes of decolonization. Before World War II it was a British naval base, part of the Malay States, a British "protectorate." Because its population was predominantly Chinese, who don't get along with Malayans, in 1965 it was decided that it would be best for all concerned if it became a nation separate from Malaysia. That left Singapore to its own devices. It is an island of about 210 square miles, into which a population of about 2,000,000 is crammed. The ethnic mixture is mostly Chinese, with large Indian and Malay minorities, and no natural resources other than a well-developed harbor. The prospect of the withdrawal of the Royal Navy in the imminent future would remove the nation's principal employer.

In these discouraging circumstances the new Republic of Singapore embarked on independence. Its chief executive, Lee Kuan Yew, decided that there was no time for trial and error. Plans had to be made if Singapore was to survive and prosper. He called on the United Nations. A team of Scandinavian experts was sent to Singapore by the United Nations Development Fund. A long-range plan was drafted, some early financial assistance was received, and this southeast Asian city-state has become one of the world's more prosperous and stable economies. It is still a planned economy in which statism is accepted as a necessary requirement for survival. No UNDP funds have been spent in Singapore since 1983, the last year of a project jointly sponsored by UNDP and FAO to make Singapore self-sufficient in poultry and pork production.[1]

I interviewed Ambassador Mahubani, Singapore's permanent representative to the United Nations. He was emphatic that UNDP and the specialized agencies that worked with it had made the critical difference in Singapore's success. The stress throughout had been to make the country completely independent of outside aid. Mistakes had been made in other countries that had allowed themselves to become dependent on the United Nations and other sources of ecnomic support. Singapore had taken what it needed

from the United Nations, but the goal was always complete independence. This plan had defined success, aimed accurately, and
got it.

Contrary to the mythology of the New Right, planning is not
an invention of Josef Stalin. Individuals, sound business men running corporations, and large nations such as the United States do it
all the time, sometimes well, sometimes sloppily. Where resources
are abundant and capital no problem, as has been the case throughout most of American history, plans are loose and usually succeed
in spite of their obvious deficiencies. But in a country where
everything is short of what is needed, many decisions must be
made as to how what is available is to be used. I am puzzled that
such an elementary point has to be made, but the anti-United Nations literature is full of declamations about the waste of time that
UNDP and associated agencies spend on plans, when all that is
needed is to turn entrepreneurial talent and desire loose. It is never
that simple in sub-Saharan Africa, Bangladesh, or the South Pacific islands. I am sure that Professor van den Haag knows this;
his scorn for planners must be a polemic exaggeration for effect.

I want to conclude this response with a few words about the
idea of rights. In his discussion of the International Fund for
Agricultural Development (IFAD), he waives any substantive discussion and concentrates his fire on IFAD's commitment to ''protect the right of all persons everywhere to be free from hunger and
malnutrition.'' He protests: What a silly idea! How can there be a
right to be free from hunger? Hogwash!

Spoken like a learned legal positivist, a professor of jurisprudence who *knows* that the only rights anyone can have are those
that can be enforced by a court. What lawyers don't know isn't
knowledge.

What most jurists refuse to know is that moral philosophers
from Roman times on, including such eminent Romans as Cicero
and Ulpian, have been concerned with the problem of rights apart
from those that are proclaimed in the laws. There continues to be
a running argument, far too complex to recapitulate here, about
whether a natural right is absolute or qualified: Do all persons

have an absolute right to life? If so, how can capital punishment be justified? One famous legal philosopher, H. L. A. Hart, holds that all men have a right to be free, from which various subsidiary rights can be deduced.[2] Other writers argue that many other rights are implied in the social contract. Only the lawyers, and not all of them—as, for examples of exceptions, Cicero and Hart—deny the existence of natural rights.

The observance of natural rights is the very foundation of constitutional government in Western nations. Our Declaration of Independence, drafted by that superlative lawyer, Thomas Jefferson, asserts without qualification:

> We hold these truths to be self-evident, that all men are created equal, that they are endowed by their Creator with certain unalienable Rights, that among these are Life, Liberty, and the pursuit of Happiness. That to secure these rights, Governments are instituted among Men, deriving their just powers from the consent of the governed. . . .

It follows from this principle, generally accepted in civilized Western nations, that legal rights are limited and draw their authority not merely from a legislature but from a legislature that acknowledges natural rights. The Charter of the United Nations is generally conceded to be an American document, both implicitly and explicitly grounded in the idea of rights. The right to life is as self-evident to those who observe the Charter as it was to those eighteenth-century Americans who justified their revolution by appealing to the right to life, liberty, and the pursuit of happiness. Now, in the late twentieth century, we do well to keep in mind that the right to life is not to be restricted to those fortunate enough to be born in countries flowing with milk and honey.

With the IFAD covenanters, I claim that it is essential to recognize that there is a right to be free from hunger. It is a right that the comfortable and well-fed must honor in this shrinking world. The Communist party's indifference to starvation and famine instigated the worldwide contempt for Soviet governance back in the early 1920s, and the further iniquities of the regime came as unsurprising tragedies. A world that is indifferent to famine in a drought-ridden country has denied morality by denying the right to life itself. If Professor van den Haag prefers the systems-analysis jargon of "goals" and "targets" to moral discourse about rights and duties, he certainly has company. As for me, I prefer a higher ground and a concern about the condition of the human race. Considerations of expediency seem to limit my opponent's horizon. For him hunger is to be relieved not because we have a duty to the starving but rather because it is a goal to be chosen for some reason other than a sense of obligation.

But perhaps I infer more than Dr.van den Haag means.

Notes

1. A remarkable achievement, considering the area of the republic. The project created the capability of raising 200,000 pigs, converting the wastes into energy, water, and animal feed, with no environmental pollution. For details, see UNDP document SIN-74-006-Env-FAO-Aul-Can-E.
2. H. L. A. Hart, "Are There Any Natural Rights?" in *Theories of Rights*, Jeremy Waldron (Oxford: Oxford University Press, 1984), pp. 77–90.

ERNEST VAN DEN HAAG

Mr. Conrad correctly quotes J. M. Keynes, who once discounted long-run effects by saying that "in the long run we are all dead." Lord Keynes was a homosexual without children. Those who care for their children are interested in the long as well as in the short run.

As for the free market, it is no panacea and was not so described by me. It will not solve all problems. But it usually has proved better than government planning, which has led to disaster not only in socialist countries such as the Soviet Union, Poland, or Cuba (not to speak of China) but also in the Marxist African countries. Even the socialist countries that do relatively well, such as East Germany, do badly when compared with nonsocialist ones such as West Germany.

About planning Professor Conrad is confused. I am all in favor of individual planning and planning by firms. Therefore, I am opposed to central planning by the government: It supersedes individual plans and replaces market demand—basically consumer demand—with the preferences of government planners and, not infrequently, with their silly schemes. The effects of government planning even in nonsocialist countries should be available to Mr. Conrad if he will look at the history of public housing or government farm policies in the United States.

The U.N., contrary to the impression Conrad gives, played but a minor role in Singapore, which became prosperous under a government that fostered the free market. It made the country independent of outside aid. Same in Hong Kong and South Korea (which, as a result, does much better than North Korea). (On such matters I would not regard the American ambassador to the U.N. as an expert, nor the ambassador from Singapore.)

On natural rights Conrad is confused as well. Many lawyers, since before Cicero, believed in them. Others don't. I share Jeremy Bentham's view that natural rights are "simple nonsense." Not that it matters, but Conrad misunderstands H. L. A. Hart, whom he paraphrases. Hart has tried to explain the notion of natural rights, not to justify or support it.

There are few people left who believe in a social contract doctrine. Conrad does. I don't. It is true however that Jefferson believed in natural rights, as most eighteenth-century philosophers did. But nature never confided in me—as it did in Conrad—to tell me what rights it had bestowed on me: to hold slaves, as Aristotle thought, and as Jefferson did? It is society that determines the laws we live under, regardless of whether or not it justifies them by an appeal to nature (as though nature were a lawgiver and authoritatively tells us what to do). Society—but not the U.N., which has no authority to legislate—may grant everyone a right to be well nourished. I do not object. But how is society going to make it possible for people to exercise this right? It seems to me to have as much chance to be implemented as the rights granted by the Soviet

Constitution. I do wish Professor Conrad would once in a while descend from the clouds and at least look at what can be done to improve man's fate on earth. Certainly passing resolutions and granting rights that have little to do with what is possible won't help. Why not grant a right to be free from the weaknesses of the flesh and to live each for 200 years in peace?

JOHN CONRAD

Professor van den Haag's querulous negativism leads him into misunderstandings and errors that I have to correct—even though our readers will no doubt recognize them easily enough. Here goes:

On Planning

Neither I nor any United Nations agency favors centralized planning for any nation. The benefits of a command economy, if any, are reserved to the Soviet bloc. Specialized agencies will not interfere with a government's choice of this model, but not many countries have adopted this unpromising route to economic stagnation.

The position of the specialized agencies has been well stated by UNCTAD:

> ...most of the internal development planning, priorities and policies, even if they entail some external aspects, are essentially matters for decision at the national level, and do not fall into the category of problems calling for international negotiation. Questions arise such as: should there be any planning of development or should the economy be left entirely free to private enterprise? In planning, what rates of growth; what ratios of capital formation to gross domestic product; ...what priorities over time to heavy versus light industry, agriculture versus industry, *ad nauseam*? It is for the country concerned to take these decisions in the light of its political and socio-economic circumstances and available resources; and not

for any international agency in a multilateral framework to seek to
determine, particularly when such issues lend themselves to ideological and political disputations among the big powers.[1]

The unidentified author of this statement adds that "the primary responsibility for the economic development of developing
countries is their own."

It is one thing to create a planning bureaucracy like the one
with which the Politburo burdens the Soviet economy. It is quite
another to assist a brand-new nation, starting from scratch and
without a cadre of technical personnel, to make decisions about investments and capital formation. The question is not how to organize for central planning but rather: What plan should we make
to get the country off square one?

My polymathic opponent loftily denies the effectiveness of
United Nations Development Program services to the fledgling
Republic of Singapore. He does not tell us how it happens that he
is better informed on this matter than Ambassador Mahubani, a
citizen of Singapore whose business it is to be informed about its
political and economic situation. Perhaps Dr. van den Haag is
simply applying his distrust of diplomats to Mr. Mahubani—not a
creditable way of arguing his point.

van den Haag on Natural Rights

As an unreconstructable Benthamite (if I read him right), Dr.
van den Haag comes naturally to his resolute skepticism about natural rights. Jeremy Bentham was explicit: "natural rights is simple
nonsense: natural and imprescriptible rights, rhetorical nonsense,
nonsense on stilts."[2] Although Benthamite utilitarianism is no
longer a popular position in moral philosophy, Dr. van den Haag's
adherence to it is perfectly respectable. What is odd is his casual
misreading of H. L. A. Hart. I quote directly from the article that
my opponent thought I paraphrased: "I shall advance the thesis
that if there are any moral rights at all, it follows that there is at
least one natural right, the equal right of men to be free . . . ."[3] Hart
not only explains the notion but also supports it. His theory of nat-

ural rights is much more parsimonious than many other contemporary writers have advanced, but that is attributable to the scrupulous elegance of his thought. His essay ends with the following conclusion:

> ...[The] claim to interfere with another's freedom is justified because it is fair; and it is fair because only so will there be an equal distribution of restrictions and so of freedom among this group of men. So in the case of special rights as well as of general rights recognition of them implies the recognition of the equal right all men to be free.[4]

This position is not mine. I begin with the right to survival, or the right to life (a phrase I use cautiously and without reference to the current debate on fetal rights). If we all have a right to live, then we have a right to be free from hunger and malnutrition. But whatever the position from which we derive the idea of natural rights, both the renowned Professor Hart and my own modest self are in this camp—along with a great many famous philosophers, many of them long since the eighteenth century. That my opponent cannot hear some supernatural presence proclaiming the existence of rights is his problem. I can readily infer the idea of natural rights from the human condition.

The Social Contract Doctrine

Dr. van den Haag correctly supposes that I rely on the social contract doctrine, scoffing as he goes on at my adherence to an outmoded style of moral thought. I am not embarrassed. At a time when one can hardly pick up a philosophical journal without encountering references to the thought of John Rawls, I have no reason to suppose that social contract theory is in the decline that van den Haag assumes.

Descent from What Clouds?

Finally my earthbound opponent wishes I would descend from the clouds "and at least look at what can be done to improve man's fate on earth." I thought I'd been doing exactly that throughout this discourse. Even our discussion of natural rights is relevant to man's fate. If there were agreement on the right to life—or, following Professor Hart, the right to be free—man's fate would be substantially improved over the dreadful condition that prevails in the USSR, in Iran, or in Soweto.

But my opponent is bashful about what *he* proposes for the improvement of man's fate. Has he no positive ideas beyond the dissolution of the United Nations and, perhaps, the recreation of a truly *laissez-faire* free market in which the Invisible Hand would lavish benefits on everyone from Wall Street to Timbuctoo?

Notes

1. United Nations Conference on Trade and Development, *The History of UNC-TAD 1964–1984* (New York: United Nations, 1985), p. 29.
2. Jeremy Bentham, *Anarchical Fallacies* (Original published in 1843), quoted in Ross Harrison, *Bentham* (London: Routledge and Kegan Paul, 1983), p. 78.
3. H. L. A. Hart, "Are There Any Natural Rights?" in *Theories of Rights*, Jeremy Waldron (Oxford: Oxford University Press, 1984), p. 77.
4. Ibid., p. 90.

ERNEST VAN DEN HAAG

I'm not an "unreconstructed Benthamite." I do agree with Jeremy Bentham on some things, as I do with John Conrad. But I'm certainly not a "Conradian."

Contrary to Conrad, I don't believe that there are such things as "moral rights." I have not "misread" H. L. A. Hart, for, as quoted by Conrad, he says, "if there are any moral rights at all, it follows...." I do not believe there are "moral rights"; I believe there are moral *claims* that become rights when they are recognized by law. The notion of "moral rights" (a.k.a. "natural rights") capable of overruling law is absurd. Where did nature get the authority to decide what rights I have? How do we find out about its decision in any particular case?

I don't care whether "social contract doctrine" is in decline, or whether Mr. Conrad is not embarrassed about it. He should be. I think it's a misleading notion.

Mr. Conrad is quite right about my unwillingness to propose grandiose Utopian ideas about "the improvement of men's fate." Usually such ideas have led to disaster, as illustrated by the Soviet Union and China (not to speak of Eastern Europe), or to foolishness, as illustrated by the U.N. Yes, the "dissolution of the U.N." would help, though it would be a minor factor in improving man's fate. It would save wasting money and effort. Yes, *laissez-faire,* i.e., the free market, would help greatly, as shown by the United States. Sure, I have some other ideas. But, unlike the U.N., they are realistic and do not belong in this discussion.

JOHN P. CONRAD

The Importance of Natural Rights

Never in my most surrealistic flights of fancy have I pictured my dour opponent as a convert to Conradism. I inferred from his hasty discussion of moral rights that he is a close follower of Jeremy Bentham and the long and unproductive tradition of legal positivism. His contempt for the idea of natural rights would get a nod of approval from that benevolent old gentleman.

What is a right but a claim that someone has a duty to observe? All human beings have a right to life that others must observe. That right may be suspended as in the case of enemy soldiers in battle, or, as Dr. van den Haag never tires of urging, for a criminal sentenced to death. But the laws that protect that claim to life are enacted because of the common recognition of that right. When a government such as Stalin's Russia, Hitler's Germany, or Idi Amin's Uganda violates the citizen's natural right to life, its legitimacy and its laws are invalid.[1] Professor van den Haag may prefer to think of a natural right as a "moral claim," but not many moral philosophers will accept his quibble.

Anyone who has lived through most of the twentieth century, as both of us have done, should think hard before dismissing the idea of natural rights. The right to life and the other rights that flow from that right were denied by the Nazis and by the doctrines of Marxism–Leninism. Nazi law and Soviet law both proceed from the doctrine that the right of the state supersedes all individual rights, including the right to life itself. I reject this doctrine on the ground that it is in conflict with natural law. Professor Hart would find it in conflict with the natural right to be free; I prefer to invoke the elemental right to life. I have sufficiently exposed myself to my colleague's thought to be quite sure that he is as firmly opposed to the totalitarian principles of National Socialism and Marxism-Leninism as any other citizen of the West. On what basis?

The Social Contract Doctrine Again

In the company of the leading American moral philosophers of this century, John Rawls and Robert Nozick, I have no difficulty in using the social contract theory. Professor van den Haag loftily dismisses it as "misleading" but does not tell us why. I mention this matter again; I don't know whether his peremptory rejection of an old and respected philosophical paradigm represents a new and startling approach to the study of morals and justice or the inchoate intuitions of a neoconservative. I am curious and I am sure that our readers will share my curiosity.

The Realism of Professor van den Haag

"Sure, I have some other ideas," says my coy opponent. He isn't going to tell us his prescription for a better world because his ideas are *realistic*. I am disappointed. I hope that in the interest of international amity and tranquillity he will relent—if not in these pages then in some other medium. This is an age in which truly realistic ideas about international politics are sorely needed.

Note

1. For Jean Bodin, the legitimacy of Stalin, Hitler, or Idi Amin would not be open to question by their unfortunate subjects. "I conclude then that the subject is never justified in any circumstances in attempting anything against his sovereign prince, however evil and tyrannical he may be." *Six Books of the Commonwealth,* abr. and trans. M. J. Tooley (Oxford: Blackwell, no date), p. 68. Concerning this passage, Hinsley remarks that "because he feared anarchy more than he disliked tyranny,... Bodin insisted that misrule could constitute no right to restrain, depose, or assassinate the sovereign." (F. H. Hinsley, *Sovereignty* (London: Watts, 1966), p. 122. For better or worse, events since the eighteenth century indicate a consensus that natural rights must be observed by the sovereign.

PART III

USEFULNESS OR USELESSNESS?

CHAPTER 4

The Storm over UNESCO

ERNEST VAN DEN HAAG

I have just discussed the many U.N. agencies, and the reader may wonder why I return to UNESCO. The answer is simple. Although Professor Conrad thinks it is a great agency, I believe that even among U.N. agencies UNESCO is conspicuous for its sheer bureaucratic wastefulness and, on the other hand, for its politicalization, or, to put it bluntly, for its tendency to confuse Communist propaganda, to which it lends itself as an instrument, with culture, enlightenment, and intellectual progress. We have finally decided to stop paying for the anti-American and antidemocratic propaganda spread by UNESCO. In a fit of absent-mindedness our diplomats finally did what they rarely have the courage to do. We left and we stopped paying. This is further reason to devote extra space to UNESCO.

Those who wish to maintain, as does my friend John Conrad, that, despite everything, the U.N. is somehow useful and important find it hard to argue that the U.N. can do anything about world peace: Reality keeps breaking through. Often they fall back on second line of defense. What about the many useful things U.N. agencies do? they ask.

There are indeed a host of agencies associated with the U.N. Some are useful. Many are not. The useful agencies could and would exist even without the U.N. connection. Because they are useful they need no endorsement by, or affiliation with, the U.N. Thus, the Postal Union long preceded the U.N. Even the International Court of Justice—a much more doubtful institution—had predecessors before the U.N. So did the International Labor Organization. And, surely international health, demographic, agricultural, or scientific bodies can be organized easily and more cheaply and less politically without U.N. auspices. Some organizations, on the other hand, are intimately connected with the U.N. and derive their legitimacy from that organization. This certainly is the case of UNESCO.

UNESCO was founded in the belief that war arises in the minds of men, that it is in some way connected with cross-cultural misunderstandings. It was believed that better understanding among nations might help bring about peace. Other vague beliefs—that war is somehow rooted in culture or in psychology, that literacy and education in all its forms would help bring about peace—also played a role in forming UNESCO. Some more reasonable concerns were added. International cooperation in preserving archaeological or artistic treasures can be useful. The undeveloped countries in which many such treasures are located may need international help in preserving them. International relief organizations—such as the Red Cross—have proven their usefulness long before the U.N. Such additional organizations as were associated with the U.N. (the Red Cross preserves its independence*) could be useful on the face of it, although it is arguable that relief may be given on a bilateral basis as well as on an international one.

As I mentioned earlier, the notion that war arises from cultural or psychological hostilities and misunderstandings, and that, therefore, cultural understanding may help keep the peace, is contrary to the evidence. The Soviet Union did not invade Afghanistan or Hungary, nor did North Korea invade South Korea, or the Germans France, or the Japanese China, because of any

---

*It has not, however, escaped politicalization by the Third World countries, the majority of which have succeeded in expelling South Africa.

misunderstanding. The developing hostility between the United
States and the Soviet Union is not based on misunderstanding, although the previous amiability was. A cultural understanding, say,
of Russian literature and dance, or of American jazz, is not likely
to make any difference whatever in the hostility of the two governments to one another, nor can it contribute to the prevention of
war. Of course, speaking Russian, knowing Russian literature,
and appreciating Zen Buddhism are in themselves worthwhile
things. But they have nothing to do with war and peace.

There are always busybodies who believe that international
exchanges, personal acquaintance, the realization that Russians are
no more intrinsically evil than Americans will make a difference
to international relations. It won't, though it may get travel grants
for the busybodies. The belief that it will rests on a misleading
analogy between hostility among persons and hostility among nations. Hostility among persons occasionally rests on misperceptions. Often it does not. When two men want the same woman
there is no misunderstanding. Or when they are rivals for a promotion. Or when they criticize each other's literary output, or run
for the same office. Hostility among persons may rest on correct
perceptions, and often misperceptions are the effect of a hostility
that precedes them, not the cause. Still, it is possible that two persons are in conflict with one another—which but for the restraints
of the law might lead to violence—because of dislike or misconcep-
tions, or misunderstanding. Contacts can be useful in removing
interpersonal enmities—although, as often, they constitute the soil
from which mutual dislike grows.

Conflicts among nations have little to do with knowledge of
one another. The American Civil War and the War of Independence demonstrate as much. Conflicts are about power and expansion thereof and sometimes about ideologies or different ways of
organizing the world. There is no reason to believe that Stalin and
Hitler liked one another or cared for Russian or German culture.
Still, they were happy to promise peace to one another and invade
Poland together. In turn, Churchill cannot be accused of liking
Stalin. But after the invasion of Russia by Hitler he allied himself

with Stalin, as did President Roosevelt. Whereupon Americans were led to discover that they liked the Soviet Union. Misperceptions of one another's intentions may play a role—but correct perceptions will more frequently lead to war. Neither the correct nor the incorrect perceptions have much to do with culture, amiability, or the liking or knowledge of literature, music, dance, and science.

It follows that, to begin with, UNESCO grew from claptrap. Given these roots, it is not surprising that it spent its resources producing more of the same. It financed innumerable conferences where busybodies of all nations and sexes spouted claptrap at one another. We paid 25% of the expenses, including the salaries of numerous overpaid bureaucrats. However, except for the waste of money, UNESCO used to be as harmless as it was useless.

Nobody paid much attention to UNESCO, a minor waste of money as these things go, until U.S. patience was strained by persistent attempts to use UNESCO as an anti-U.S., antifreedom, and antidemocracy propaganda tool, and a manufacturer of apologies for the Soviet Union and assorted pro-Soviet Third World dictatorships. As time went on, these attempts succeeded and U.S. opposition became futile.

By this time Amadou-Mahtar M'Bow had become secretary-general of UNESCO, his decisive qualifications being (1) that he was black, (2) that he came from the Third World, and (3) that he spoke fluent French.

He had no other qualifications, unless one regards as qualifications his love of luxury and his determination to use Western money for Eastern purposes, chiefly Marxist pro-Soviet and anti-Israel propaganda.

Mr. M'Bow, living in truly grand style in Paris, where 70% of the UNESCO budget is spent on its headquarters staff, began to suffer from megalomania. He felt that no one should interfere with his expensive way of running things. He could rely on a majority of nations to support him. The Soviet bloc nations were in his corner since in effect he acted in their interest. So, for the same reason, were most of the Third World governments. UNESCO decisions are made by a majority, each nation, be it ever so small or big, having one vote. Thus, Mr. M'Bow could count on winning every vote just as the East and Third World blocs can and do win every vote in the U.N. assembly. UNESCO consisted mainly of myriad Third World nations, gladly acting as his myrmidons since he could provide them with some patronage. The patronage, immaterial to Western nations (except for diplomats), is important to undeveloped countries. How many people in Mali get the pay they get at UNESCO? Further, most Third World governments shared the secretary-general's ideological preferences. In addition, there was the Soviet bloc, delighted to spread Marxist notions at the expense of the West through an international organization. The Western countries—the United States and Western Europe—plus a few democracies elsewhere paid the bills. But they were a minority. Although they grumbled, seeing their money used for anti-Western propaganda, they did stick around. Who wants to leave a high-minded organization dedicated to culture, education, international understanding, and peace?

But M'Bow miscalculated. Realizing that UNESCO was not changing its ways, the United States threatened to leave. Here M'Bow miscalculated once more. He refused to budge, thinking the United States would be satisfied with minor cosmetic changes and would not dare to leave. But we did.

The U.S. move was opposed by a motley crowd. The usual timid souls in the state department were shocked. They think it is always better to be there—we might be able to influence things even if the evidence shows we are not. Besides, leaving any international organization seems so undiplomatic! They were supported by a crowd of diplomats and hangers-on who like to participate in useless conferences (at taxpayers' expense). To be able to say, "I was a delegate to an international meeting on..." gives some persons a sense of importance. But M'Bow had overplayed his hand. UNESCO was so obviously used for anti-Western propaganda that it had become almost indefensible in the United States.

Further, M'Bow made two tactical mistakes: He helped push proposals for government licensing of reporters and for UNESCO financing of Third World information services. Both proposals were transparently intended to hinder and restrict the freedom of the press, to facilitate the spread of government disinformation, and, not least, to help governments hide whatever they wanted to hide. This rubbed the U.S. media the wrong way and lost him the support he might otherwise have got from them. Secondly—and M'Bow could do little about this in view of the Arab and Soviet voting bloc—UNESCO took to passing wild anti-Israel resolutions of various kinds, often containing silly, outrageous, and untrue allegations. This did not help UNESCO with American public opinion, which tends to be solidly pro-Israel.

The United States left UNESCO and has been followed by Great Britain. There is a good chance that other democratic nations will also leave in due time. UNESCO will continue to grind out the usual anti-U.S. and anti-Western propaganda. However, the Soviet bloc and the Third World will have to finance these activities themselves instead of getting the Western world to pay for them. More important, UNESCO is in the process of losing its legitimacy as a neutral international organization, as it loses Western backing. It will become an organization flagrantly dominated by the Soviet Union and the Third World, with a few die-hard Western governments hanging on. UNESCO's antidemocratic propaganda will thus have less impact in the future, partly because it has less money, partly because it has less legitimacy. It will be clearly Soviet propaganda, no longer cloaked by an international disguise.

JOHN P. CONRAD

Professor van den Haag is not alone in his impatience with UNESCO. For the last four or five years there has been a drumroll of denunciation of UNESCO emanating from American conservative observers, who seem to infuriate each other the more they listen to each other on this subject. Indeed, my learned friend is so irritated at the thought of UNESCO's supposed iniquities that he cannot spare attention to the deeds and possible misdeeds of the other specialized agencies. He does not seriously consider the work of any other agency, except to comment that he thinks they would do just as well without the United Nations, an opinion that the agency personnel I have interviewed do not share.

In this response I shall confine myself to UNESCO, beginning with the farrago of assertions that Dr. van den Haag has offered in his contribution. I shall deal with those that seem most significant to me more or less in the order that they erupt in his essay:

1. *War does not arise from misunderstanding but rather from understanding a potential enemy all too well.* If we limit the idea of understanding to the immediate tactical situation, it is obvious that a strong Japanese military establishment was justified in the conclusion that an invasion of China could succeed for a while. Similarly, Mussolini correctly made the same estimate when he ordered the invasion of Ethiopia. Brezhnev's advisors underestimated the difficulties, but if the Soviet Union were willing to pour more resources into Afghanistan the Red Army could probably achieve a peace of the graveyard in that unhappy land. Apparently Brezhnev's successors know that there is a limit to the brutality for which the USSR can allow itself to be responsible.

In the long range, each of these examples demonstrates a misunderstanding of the strategic situation. Japan's generals dragged that nation into a foolish disaster from which she emerged better off than ever before because she was fortunate enough to surrender to a generous victor. As for the wretched Duce, the Ethiopian adventure strained the fragile Italian economy without realizing any benefits. The Russian adventure in Afghanistan has discredited the Kremlin not only with the non-Communist nations of Europe but also with European Communists, Chinese Communists, Muslims, and most of the nations of the Third World. For all of Mr. Gorbachev's winsomeness, he will be hard pressed to find any friends for Russia anywhere in an anxious world.

Can anyone seriously contend that General Tojo and his staff, the Duce and his bootlickers, or the senile old dodderers in Brezhnev's Politburo understood what they were doing to their nations and to themselves? What leader of what aggressive nation has ever understood the ultimate consequences of his actions? Ask the ghosts of Kaiser Wilhelm, who lived out his old age in contumely, of the Duce, strung up by the heels in Milan, or of those 22 Nuremberg defendants transformed from bemedaled heroes of the Reich to cowering common criminals in the dock.

What does all this have to do with UNESCO, and how could UNESCO make a difference? Since my impatient opponent has implied the question, I will explain. It used to be easy to induce the peasant youth of a country to leave the drudgery of the fields for the life of adventure that a foreign war seemed to promise. Illiterate, impoverished, and without hopes of bettering their lot at home, such young men could be inspired to flock to the colors by the prospect of the spoils of war and the image of a contemptible or hateful or inferior race to be conquered. Napoleon knew how to conjure up this grand illusion, and so did many less celebrated and less successful military men. It can still be done, as Hitler and Mussolini and Stalin have shown, if communications can be strictly controlled, if education can be tightly trammeled, and if the culture of the nation can be kept subservient to the leader's aims.

That is where UNESCO comes in as a substantial wager for peace. To further education, to spread science, to foster knowledge and respect for the cultural variety of the world will not alone preserve the peace. But a world in which all these values are raised and prized will be a world in which mountebanks, ideologues, and villains will have a harder time deluding the people.

Let Dr. van den Haag be careful in his reply. I have *not* claimed that all the world needs for perpetual peace is a college education and a seat at the opera for every man, woman, and child on the planet. But the idea of UNESCO is a good contribution toward the peace the world must have if the world is not to disintegrate before the next generation's eyes. To put that idea into practice, to ''construct the defenses of peace in the minds of men'' is a daunting assignment. There have been some very mundane obstacles to its achievement, none of which seem to have attracted Dr. van den Haag's attention. They can be surmounted. That they have not all been removed attests to their durability, and—alas—to the fallibility of the mortals who try.

2. *UNESCO and the straining of American patience.* My impatient adversary has noticed that in the conferences and assemblies sponsored by UNESCO a good deal of anti-American sentiment has come to the surface. If all these foreigners insist on biting the hand that pays for the microphone, he argues, then let some one else pay for the auditorium.

I have listened to a lot of rubbish in United Nations conferences. It is not uplifting to listen to the simultaneous translation from the Spanish and learn that my country is the "monster of the North." The boring clichés of the self-styled socialist delegates are even less appealing because they go on for so long. I haven't noticed, though, that these propaganda efforts win converts from the unconverted.

It is a problem that won't go away, even if the United Nations and all its works vanish into thin air. The United States is not a popular nation, for all our generosity and our good intentions. The reasons are well known—our affluence in a world of relative and sometimes desperately real deprivation, our support of "authoritarian" and oppressive regimes, and our occasionally bullying tactics in the Third World. One British diplomat reminded me, "That used to be our problem when we ruled the world—now it's yours."

It is a problem that we could handle a lot better than we have done in UNESCO. According to a review by the United States National Commission for UNESCO,

> ...there has been a decline in the quality of U.S. participation in UNESCO over the past decade or more. Unlike the delegations sent to represent the U.S. at earlier General Conferences, in recent years more than one delegation has included *no* recognizable representative of U.S. scientific, cultural and educational communities. It is not surprising that U.S. delegations which excluded the best American expertise were bewildered by the UNESCO program.
>
> In general, U.S. delegations have included too many persons being rewarded for domestic political purposes and not enough delegates or alternates with any understanding of, or interest in, the

UNESCO program. Moreover, they lacked experience in international conference procedures and in that sense, they were no match for the professional conference experts fielded by many other delegations, such as the Soviet Union.[1]

In the present divided world, any international organization under any auspices and serving any purpose—even so apparently nonpolitical an organization as the International Postal Union—will have to stage a conference from time to time and inevitably some of the agenda will be "politicized." So what? In our domestic politics, Americans have become crafty and innovative experts in partisan polemics, perhaps the most expert partisan politicians in recorded history. We have only ourselves to blame if we insist on sending fat-cat campaign contributors and party drudges to UNESCO to mobilize friendly delegates and stare down the seasoned conference-goers from the Soviet bloc and the Arab League.

The outstanding example of our ineptitude in the withdrawal is our sanctimonious distaste for UNESCO as a platform for anti-Israel propaganda. There is no question that UNESCO delegates have heard many denunciations of Israel, and it is not to be expected that the clamor will soon come to an end. However, Israel is the primary aggrieved party, and Israel intends to stick it out. Indeed, the Israeli government is said to have vehemently protested the American decision to withdraw on the ground that it will make its continued participation in UNESCO conferences more rather than less difficult. Israeli withdrawal from UNESCO might lead to withdrawals from other United Nations assemblies and to the "delegitimization" of the State of Israel.[2]

For the United States to decamp from UNESCO is to profess that we are a nation of political tyros, unsuited for the rough-and-tumble of international politics. We have senators, congressmen, and governors who could show the world how the UNESCO conference game should be played. We also have scientists and educators whose authority no competitors from Moscow or anywhere else could challenge. Instead of allowing the Russians and the Arabs the exclusive use of the UNESCO platforms for their tedious messages, we should be availing ourselves of every opportunity to tell our story to scientific and cultural leaders of other nations. I could choose a team to capture the attention of the UNESCO community, and so could any American president. Instead, we have withdrawn to our tents, depriving our best friends of our support.

3. *Mr. M'Bow and the management of UNESCO.* We come now to the stewardship of Amadou-Mahtar M'Bow, the director-general of UNESCO since 1974. Professor van den Haag correctly reports that Mr. M'Bow is black, African, and able to speak French fluently. He flatly says that Mr. M'Bow has no other qualifications, other than "his love of luxury and his determination to use Western money for Eastern purposes."

Not being acquainted with Mr. M'Bow myself, I sent for his *curriculum vitae.* It turns out that his qualifications, at least on paper, are considerable. He was educated at the Sorbonne, has been a professor of education in his native Senegal, was minister of education and deputy to the Senegalese National Assembly, and, before taking on his present position, was for four years under-director-general of UNESCO, charged with direction of the education program. He has published seven books and numerous articles, none of which have come into my hands.

Dr. van den Haag is particularly upset about the grand style in which Mr. M'Bow is said to be living in Paris. I do not have the advantage of having inspected Mr. M'Bow's quarters, situated directly above his own office on the fifth floor of the UNESCO building. It is further reported that this arrangement was authorized by the UNESCO executive board on account of security problems. This concern is not uncommon in European capitals, and the UNESCO solution of situating personal housing in an office building is often adopted. My informants have not told me how "grand" Mr. M'Bow's style is, but I assume that real austerity would be inappropriate for an official who must often entertain visiting congressmen and foundation fellows.

But the serious questions about Mr. M'Bow do not arise from his qualifications—as to which Dr. van den Haag may have more to tell us from his personal knowledge—but rather as to his stewardship of UNESCO. Here there are reservations in which UNESCO partisans reluctantly join with its critics.

The American criticism of UNESCO management begins with its "unrestrained" budgetary expansion and includes references to excessive salaries (more, my parsimonious opponent points out, than a Mali national can earn in his own country—as though that were an extraordinarily serious objection), nepotism, the employment of personnel with marginal qualifications, and too much work done in Paris, not enough done in the field.

Without firsthand knowledge of daily life at UNESCO, I have to rely on observers with opportunities for direct contact. Brigid FitzGerald of the United Nations Association of the United Kingdom has reported to the members of that organization as follows:

> The charges of budgetary excess, mismanagement, favoritism and nepotism seem partially justified, though it was largely pressure from the West which secured a reduction in the budgetary increase requested. . . in 1983—another example of "working from within." M'Bow himself has come in for particular criticism as far as mismanagement is concerned. UNESCO has always been difficult to manage. With over 160 member states, a heavy Executive Board and the permanent delegations all exercising pressure on the Director-General, it is very difficult to fulfill all the demands of the member states. The problem becomes worse in the Director-General's second term of office. Promises made in the run up to the second term have to be kept and the confidence of confirmed power in a post where it is difficult to challenge the authority of the Director-General tends to encourage a degree of megalomania. This seems to have happened not only with M'Bow but also with his predecessor. On the other hand, M'Bow's virtues are seldom cited in the Western press—he is hardworking, abstemious and strict with himself as well as with others. . . .
>
> "Criticisms of UNESCO for its bureaucracy, its autocratic style of government, its over-spending at Headquarters and other aspects of management appear to be justified. . . . However, Western governments must bear part of the responsibility for UNESCO's faults. Their level of representation at UNESCO has been low and, as M'Bow has pointed out, some responsibility must lie with the Executive Board, made up of government representatives, which has not, until recently, made any complaints. . . .[3]

It is a familiar story, one that can be duplicated in many large organizations, public and private. I have known much worse situations in American state governments. Readers of any business magazine are treated to frequent accounts of at least comparable problems in large corporations that don't have to compete to survive. The corrective is loud whistle-blowing, and a determined campaign to change the guard and issue new orders for its chief officer. According to all reports I have seen, we almost accomplished what was needed in 1983, but the White House was not to be persuaded to reverse its decision to get out.

Whatever Mr. M'Bow's failings may be, the actions of the United States do not reflect credit on the judgment of the officials who made the decision to withdraw. I cannot suppress the opinion that what bothered our decision-makers in the White House was not Mr. M'Bow's administrative errors but rather the petty bravado of some of the Third World delegates, and the stridency of the Soviet bloc. I am reminded of the children's jingle "Sticks and stones may break my bones, But words will never hurt me." Unfortunately, our neoconservative thinkers have much thinner skins than our kids in the playground.

Notes

1. "What Are the Issues Concerning the Decision of the United States to Withdraw from UNESCO?" An Advisory from the United States National Commission for UNESCO (New York: UNESCO, 1984), p.22. The commission consists of representatives of 60 scientific and cultural organizations, all of which have opposed the decision to withdraw. It is a quasi-official organization, established by Congress under Public Law 565, 1946, to provide "liaison between UNESCO and its programs with the major U.S. organizations interested in educational, scientific, and cultural matters." Two-thirds of the membership are designated by nongovernmental organizations, the rest are nominated by the White House.
2. Ibid., p. 9.
3. Brigid FitzGerald, "The Case for UNESCO," U.N.A. Briefing No. 26 (United Nations Associations, 3 Whitehall Court, London SW1A 2EL), pp. 6–7.

ERNEST VAN DEN HAAG

I do not share Mr. Conrad's nostalgia for UNESCO. The good things it did—helping to preserve Egyptian monuments or to spread literacy—are minor incidents in an unblemished record of waste and political propaganda. Mr. Conrad likes us to be members of, and pay for, useless organizations. I don't. Let me answer some of his points.

In response to my assertion that wars seldom arise from misunderstandings, cultural or otherwise, Conrad tries to prove that war in the long run does not pay. Perhaps. But this does not answer my point. Conrad's point is irrelevant, then. It is wrong too. Sometimes wars pay for the winner and sometimes they don't. Our wars against the Indians and against Mexico were profitable. Prussia's war against Napoleon III was also. (Not that I am in favor of war; I merely think that UNESCO has not contributed and cannot contribute to avoiding it.) Conrad shows that war does not pay by referring to the unhappy fate of losers such as Hitler or Mussolini. But victors can do quite well. Stalin got all of Eastern Europe. This doesn't justify war in Conrad's eyes or in mine. But it is inconsistent with his views that wars never pay, or that they are due to misunderstandings that UNESCO can help avoid.

Conrad does not mention that, if an aggressive mentality contributes to war, as he hints, UNESCO has no chance to do much about it. It would not have been allowed to "educate" in Hitler's Germany and it is not allowed to do anything to further pacifism (or freedom or democracy) in the Soviet Union. So UNESCO can only "construct the defenses of peace in the minds of men" where they are not needed—in the democratic nations. There, indeed, pacifists foster unilateral disarmament and thereby invite strongly armed totalitarian nations to risk war.

It is a little silly of Conrad to quote the U.S. National Commission for UNESCO, which complains that our representatives to UNESCO under President Reagan have not been as qualified or representative as before. They mean that our representatives were not chosen from their ranks. As a result we scrutinized what happened and realized (a) that the organization was costly and useless and (b) that the cards were stacked against us and against freedom.

According to Mr. Conrad, the secretary-general of UNESCO has considerable qualifications, having been a Senegalese politician and a professor of education. I regard the latter position as disqualification for nearly anything. M'Bow has shown his (dis)qualifications by the way he administered UNESCO—there is little point in arguing that his background was fitting. He has been a resounding failure.

UNESCO is now about to officially celebrate Lenin's birthday. Good luck. But why should we pay for this celebration? (Washington's birthday has not been celebrated by the organization.)

I agree with Mr. Conrad—a rare event—that the nonsense emanating from UNESCO about us, the Israelis, and others won't really harm us. I never said it did. But why should we pay for it? And stay in the organization that produces it, as though it can be taken seriously?

JOHN P. CONRAD

Even our most casual readers will have noted that in my response to Dr. van den Haag's case against UNESCO, I did not say that war did not pay. What I wanted to demolish was his notion that wars arise from understanding, not from misunderstanding. He has misunderstood me, and thereby has avoided the necessity of further defense of this untenable position.

Whether wars pay or not is quite another matter, but the United Nations and its entourage of agencies can do little about a country that sees a potential profit from conquest of its neighbor. It can do a lot to promote the practice of international cooperation, and that is the criterion by which the effectiveness of any specialized agency should be judged.

That UNESCO's programs in the last decade have been largely directed at the problems of the developing nations may or

may not have been a mistake. So far as I can see, it is in the Third
World that UNESCO can hope to have the most effective impact.
With my staunchly anti-Communist friend, I do not see how the
minds of men in the Soviet bloc are going to be changed by any
conceivable UNESCO program. Nor do I see how democracy
needs promotion in the Western nations, where education, science,
and culture are officially uninhibited.

In the Third World, schools are needed where none have existed. Illiterate men and women need to learn the three Rs that are
taken for granted in North America and Europe. Higher education
must produce scientists and technologists in abundance if the
developing nations are to advance beyond a state of arrested development. The cultural mission of UNESCO's triad should be addressed to helping people learn to think creatively about their
situations rather than to act senselessly. Men like the Ayatollah
Khomeini and Idi Amin would have more difficulty in attaining
and abusing power if they had to persuade an educated populace.[1]

There is much work for UNESCO to do. If it is not being
done as well as it should be (and surely, like any other human institution, its performance can be improved), the sulks of the
United States and the United Kingdom are not going to contribute
to its improvement. Vigorous response to the stuff and nonsense
that goes on in some UNESCO forums will be a lot more useful
than our petulant absence. What will be even more useful, if and
when we return, will be the presentation and aggressive promotion
of programs that we think will further the UNESCO objectives.
Nothing of the sort can be expected from the hacks and drudges
whom we have been sending as delegates to UNESCO. What is
needed are experts in the fields in which UNESCO is concerned,
experts who really believe that schools, science, and culture
should and can flourish everywhere. When this objective is
reached, the abuses of which Dr. van den Haag rightly complains
will be a lot less evident in the nations of the Third World.

One more note on Amadou-Mahtar M'Bow: I don't know Mr.
M'Bow, and Dr. van den Haag has not so far claimed an acquaintance with him. His paper qualifications are adequate. In scientific

renown he is no match for Julian Huxley, his famous predecessor, but to say that he lacks any qualifications for the job was unfair, and I am glad to see that in his own way, Dr. van den Haag has backed off from his scornful dismissal of Mr. M'Bow's eligibility for the job. Now he says that Mr. M'Bow has been a "resounding failure," but his bill of particulars is sketchy indeed. The director-general has not succeeded in attracting the admiration of the American right wing, but what United Nations official has managed to escape neoconservative denunciation?

To sum up, UNESCO has an important job to do, and it will not get done without strong and accepted leadership. It may well be that Mr. M'Bow has become an irretrievable liability, in which case the absence of the United States from the UNESCO councils makes the selection of an acceptable successor much more difficult. What is certain is that the apoplectic fury of the American right at the very mention of UNESCO does not enhance our reputation for concern about the welfare of the rest of the world.

Note

1. To forestall my opponent's natural question: What about Hitler and Mussolini? They took power over two of the best-educated nations in the world. The answer is obvious. Education is no panacea for all the ills of the world. A poor but educated people may be as desperate as, but more dangerous than, an illiterate mob. Education is only one of the necessary preventatives of conflict.

ERNEST VAN DEN HAAG

As Professor Conrad admits, education did not prevent a Hitler or a Mussolini. His idea that it could have prevented the Ayatollah Khomeini thus must be ascribed to faith. Underlying it is, perhaps, a common equivocation: "Education," the process, is thought always to lead to "education," the result, identified with rationality. This is not the case, as the views issuing from highly educated men, such as Professor Conrad, clearly indicate.

JOHN P. CONRAD

Without protest, I will leave it to the reader to assess Dr. van den Haag's claims to rationality as compared to mine. Whatever the verdict, the reader will surely notice that my opponent is not a close reader of simple prose. I am not so ingenuous as to suppose that the Imam Khomeini's rise could have been prevented by education alone, and I made that clear.

Throughout this phase of our debate I sense in my learned opponent's reasoning an implicit notion that education is a benefit to be reserved to Platonic guardians, not to be wasted on ordinary people, especially in the Third World. Indeed, I wonder if he doesn't consider education to have been a corrupting influence on those who haven't adopted positions close to his own.

Long before the world drifted into its present shambles, the English novelist and seer H. G. Wells remarked that the future of the world was a "race between education and catastrophe." I am optimist enough to believe that it's a long race and that catastrophe is not necessarily winning. However that may be, I want to allow education all the possible advantages. That is why the nonsense must be drained out of UNESCO so that it can get on with the work that has to be done. Fewer conferences, fewer studies, more teaching, and more learning should be the prescription. Vigorous participation by the United States and the United Kingdom can revive UNESCO and return it to its intended role. An illiterate world is the natural support of men like Khomeini, Qaddafi, and Idi Amin. It is a sign of American right-wing myopia that my opponent ardently pursues the goal of dismantling the first, and still the only, international agency committed to the increase of education.

ERNEST VAN DEN HAAG

Mr. Conrad endorses H. G. Wells, who believed that the future of the world is a "race between education and catastrophe."

This is a foolishly circular statement. If "education" is defined as that which will avoid "catastrophe," Wells's statement is true by definition and therefore trivial. If "education" is defined, more realistically, as the increase and spread of knowledge, there is no evidence that education will avoid catastrophe. If, most realistically, "education" is defined as a the spread of a mixture of information, belief, and ideology, it may well help "catastrophe" rather than avoid it. German education did not prevent Nazism; Nazi education did not prevent "catastrophe." Education among the Allied Nations, by fostering disarmament, invited it. So will the illusions Mr. Conrad somehow got through his education about the U.N. Certainly education in the Soviet Union is not going to help. Yes, I would like Mr. Conrad to descend from the clouds that he finds so comfortable, to at least look at the realities he has been hiding from.

About UNESCO, let me insert here a little piece that appeared in the April 14, 1986, issue of *Fortune* magazine. Perhaps it will help Mr. Conrad understand my lack of enthusiasm for UNESCO.

> Amadou-Mahtar M'Bow may well go around saying that *Mass Communications and the Advertising Industry* did not get a fair shake. It is a publication of the United Nations Educational, Scientific, and Cultural Organization and not only denies that more ad pages translate into an upwardly spiraling universe but affirms that advertising agencies are a major menace ideology-wise.
>
> Okay, okay, it does not hold advertising to be an unqualified evil. To be utterly fair, there are passages in the UNESCO publication depicting admen in a remarkably good light. In the Soviet Union, for example, they promote ads whose main function is "to form rational needs." Also "to form higher standards of taste."
>
> And yet M'Bow might even wonder whether we are biased against agencies favoring a New World Information Order, which would evidently require government licensing of journalists, this being one of the numerous last straws that led the U.S. and Britain to finally wave bye-bye to UNESCO in recent years, thereby forcing the agency to cut its staff, precipitating an all too brief hunger strike among certain employees accustomed to living high on the hog after being assigned to work at the Paris headquarters.
>
> But about the threat of advertising in Western countries. *Mass Communications* says, for openers, that agencies have a near mo-

nopoly on all human skills there. ("The advertising agency is the key assembly point of the society's most versatile talent in . . . writing, film, television, and drama.") Next the Unescoites postulate that Madison Avenue commits "systematic ideological reinforcement" of capitalist doctrine. Then they aver that ad agencies are dedicated to promoting the "consumer mentality that advanced capitalism requires." Why should we finance this nonsense?

JOHN P. CONRAD

In this last contribution we hear once more from my well-educated opponent that German education was not enough to forestall the National Socialists, whereas education in the allied nations led to the catastrophe of disarmament. Are we to understand that the advancement of education and the elimination of illiteracy are not goods to be sought? Is universal ignorance the true bulwark of lasting peace?

With all the faults that a multinational agency such as UNESCO may be heir to, its basic objectives are worthy of attainment. It is difficult to see how else they will be promoted. Before the creation of the agency, there was no worldwide effort to spread literacy and encourage the development of scientific communities in the less affluent countries. While pursuing these objectives, UNESCO did some foolish but harmless things, mostly because of the inexperience and poor judgment of some of its Third World delegates and staff. I repeat: if the United States and other Western nations that find these foibles objectionable could bring themselves to take a vigorous and responsible part in the development of the UNESCO program, the foolishness of which Dr. van den Haag complains would become less glaring.

I am surprised to find Daniel Seligman quoted as an authority on the UNESCO program, and quoted without attribution, too.[1] As for the significance of his persiflage, I must note that all large organizations will perpetrate foolishness and worse from time to time. As an American taxpayer, I do not relish paying for the nonsense purveyed by Edwin Meese and Patrick Buchanan—for two egregious examples—but on the whole I prefer to remain in our imperfect nation and do what little I can to improve it. That is the way things are in a pluralist system—the United States or the United Nations. Folly will always find a way into noble enterprises.

Note

1. Daniel Seligman, "Keeping Up," *Fortune*, 14 April 1986, p. 113.

ERNEST VAN DEN HAAG

The admirable novelist Shirley Hazzard worked for the U.N. Secretariat for several years. No one has described the deadening bureaucratic organization and its personnel of petty careerists à la Waldheim better than she has. I highly recommend her book *Defeat of an Ideal: A Study of the Self Destruction of the United Nations,* and her short stories (many originally published in *The New Yorker*, scarcely a conservative stronghold) to anyone who might want to learn about the actual working of the U.N. and its agencies.

CHAPTER 5

The Dream and the Reality

ERNEST VAN DEN HAAG

When Woodrow Wilson created the League of Nations after the First World War and pressed the victorious allies to join, the U.S. Congress, to his chagrin, had the wisdom to stay out. President Wilson was unable to muster the required two-thirds majority in the Senate. He had persuaded Americans that the (first) World War was "the war to end all wars" and "to make the world safe for democracy." After victory, he felt he had to offer something that at least might look as though these promises could and would be kept, something new that went beyond the traditional processes of diplomacy and international relations. Perhaps President Wilson actually believed that the League of Nations would be an instrument for peace. Perhaps he shared the hopes he stimulated. Whether one believes that he did depends on whether one rates higher his intelligence (which would lead him not to take the League, or his own slogans, seriously) or his honesty (which would lead him not to allege that he did when he did not). At any rate, wiser heads prevailed and we did not join.

Contrary to many myths, America's failure to join made no difference. These myths are still being fostered. Thus, the bizarre statement of Senator Daniel Patrick Moynihan at the 1984 annual meeting of the "Coalition for a Democratic Majority": "Had the Democratic Party not failed [to support the League] the world

173

would likely have escaped the Nazis.'' Yet, had the United States joined, the League of Nations would have been just as impotent as it turned out to be without the United States. It was unable to resist the Japanese invasion of Manchuria, Mussolini's conquest of Abyssinia, or Hitler's invasion of Czechoslovakia and Austria. Except for providing jobs to diplomats, America's membership would not have made a difference. After all, when Hitler's intentions were quite clear, Franklin Delano Roosevelt won reelection by promising not to enter the looming war, not to resist Hitler's conquests *manu militari*. Surely, even if the United States had been a member of the League of Nations, Roosevelt would not have favored sending American troops to Manchuria or Abyssinia or Czechoslovakia. Nor would any American president. The League could have resisted only by means of troops sent by its members. Its proclamations merely made it ridiculous. Declarations of disapproval do not prevent an aggressor from attacking if the declarations are not bolstered by military force. Between the two world wars the world was less safe for democracy than before, and many small wars occurred. Of course, the League did not prevent the Second World War and could not have done so had the United States been a member, Senator Moynihan's absurdity notwithstanding.

Nonetheless, during and after the Second World War, FDR insisted on reproducing Woodrow Wilson's fantasy. The U.N. was founded. This time Congress did not have the wisdom to stay out. As a result, American taxpayers now pay *de jure* 25%, *de facto* much more, of the expenses of a fundamentally anti-American organization, which, for the foreseeable future, is useless in preserving peace and unlikely to be helpful in fostering any other goal of American foreign policy, such as making the world ''safe for democracy,'' protecting human freedom or human rights, or indeed doing anything that, if it can and should be done, could not be done better (and more cheaply) by other means.

The founding of the U.N. expressed and fostered unrealistic hopes in the United States. Many Americans thought that, somehow, the U.N. would make it possible for the United States to dispense with any foreign policies of its own. All problems would be settled by the U.N. "Support the U.N." was the slogan used widely—as though it meant supporting any particular policy. Support the U.N. meant to support dreams and ignore realities. Somehow Americans got the impression that the U.N. could settle international conflicts on a consensual, semilegal basis, so that we could avoid "power politics," which always had seemed morally doubtful to us. Nobody worried much about how consensus would be produced, or how legal decisions would be taken and enforced. Wherever a problem did arise, there was an outcry: Let the U.N. deal with it. Conversely, wherever an administration was suspected of having failed to consult with the U.N., it was regarded as derelict and could count on editorials recalling it to its moral duty.

The delusional hopes attached to the U.N. seem to have been shared by much of the American foreign policy establishment. Nothing was done to bring Americans down to earth. To be skeptical of the U.N. was to be labeled a cynic. The phrase "the last best hope of mankind" was on everyone's lips. Among liberals the phrase amounted to a dogma. Who wants to disappoint or downgrade the last best hope of mankind? Yet it should have been obvious that the U.N. could not possibly make a difference, affect the factors that shape the foreign policy of nations, or help secure peace.

The ineradicable uselessness of the U.N. is rooted in four factors that should be clear to anyone not preferring to dream. These factors are as follows: First, the structure of the U.N. prevents it from making decisions on any conflict among major powers. Second, if it did, decisions opposed by a major power could only be imposed on it by the war they were to avoid. Third, the nature of international relations makes violence (war) *ultimately* unavoidable. Fourth, the Soviet Union's expansionary aims require the rest of the world either to surrender and accept Soviet domination or to prepare for armed resistance.

Consider first the structure of the U.N. It is an international organization. The powers retained their powers, including their war-making powers. They promised one another to act in accordance with certain principles, to meet regularly, to discuss problems peacefully; they set up a Secretariat and bureaucracies to execute decisions and deal with ancillary matters, and a General Assembly to debate things and pass resolutions. Every member was given an equal vote, and decisions were to be taken by majority. Further, a Security Council was created in which the major powers would have permanent seats. Smaller powers would be elected to fill a seat for a term. Each permanent member could veto any decision of the Security Council. The Security Council would make all decisions involving war and peace, but a veto would cancel any majority decision.

This elaborate structure keeps people busy but is of no other use. Whether they are vetoed or not, there is no way of enforcing U.N. decisions short of going to war. One, or several, of the powers favoring a U.N. decision would have to send military forces to impose it on the powers that do not consent to the decision. This is what we call war. The U.N. does not have any power of its own. No power will send military forces to carry out U.N. decisions it does not like. These forces are sent, at best, by supporters of a decision. This happened in the Korean War. The U.N. made the decision to resist the attack by North Korea. But the U.N. banner was but a decoration. The war was fought by one group of allies—the West in this case—against another—in this case North Korea, China, and the Soviet Union. Except for the emblem, the war was not different from what wars have been for the last 2000 years, an attempt of one power or group of powers to conquer another, resisted by the latter. And certainly the war was not less bloody. The truce (no peace has ever been concluded) was agreed to by the attacker when he did not feel he could overcome the defense, which is usual.

Since the U.N. is an international organization in which each country preserves its power and sovereignty, it really is no more than all the nations meeting together. Each made some promises. But there is no way of policing, let alone enforcing, such promises—e.g., of peaceful behavior—and the "United" in U.N.

expressed hope, nothing more. The nations are not united. There is nothing in the U.N. organization or procedures to unite them. At best the U.N. offered a convenient meeting place and debating rules. Even these are but kept in the breach, as Israel and South Africa can testify. Anyway, as I've noted, the idea that conflicts necessarily rest on misunderstandings, removed by clarification, is untrue. Often conflicts are caused by understanding, and misunderstanding is caused by conflict. But if it is communication that is needed, we have telephones, embassies, and meetings, all of which can be used without the U.N. At worst, the U.N. exacerbates existing conflicts and creates new ones.

An international must be distinguished from a supernational organization, an organization superior to the powers, which can resolve conflicts among them and enforce its decisions. A supernational organization, though possible, is not probable in any foreseeable time. (It has never existed.) The U.N. as an international, not a supernational, organization is no more than all the nations together, associated in a club, and, at times, pretending that they are governed by club rules. But the club rules, at most, determine the schedule of meetings.

There is nothing above, or independent of, the member nations. The members may try to agree. The club (i.e., the members under a different name) cannot make them. They seldom do agree on important matters. The club may admit new members and, possibly, expel rambunctious ones. This last has not been tried, but it would hardly make a difference. Some diplomats would lose employment. Thus, on the whole, the power of the U.N. consists in offering a forum for national delegates to make speeches to one another and, occasionally, to pass resolutions that have no more effect than the speeches. And no less. For both, although unlikely to affect the foreign policy of any power, can have propaganda effects, of which more below.

The citizens of every country are subject to its laws. Conflicts among them are decided by courts according to the laws made in the country. The courts are independent of the parties before them and impartial as between them, and, above all, their jurisdiction is compulsory. No person can effectively refuse to submit. The decisions of courts are enforced by the government through its police force, which has power superior to that of any citizen or group of citizens. No citizen is allowed to impose his will on others by violence, and if any citizen tries, the courts can restrain him. Thus, peace is kept among the citizens. This permits them to go about their business unarmed, and to be able to pursue it without engaging in, or being subject to, violence.

Unlike citizens, nations are sovereign. Sovereignty, to reiterate, was defined in the sixteenth century by Jean Bodin as *potestas legibus absoluta*, power independent of law. A sovereign nation does not need to obey laws other than those it legislates or approves itself. And it can change its laws at will. It cannot be restrained by laws other than those it wishes to be restrained by. Bodin's definition did then, and still does now, fit the facts. The U.N. has not altered them; it has not affected the sovereignty of nations. To be sure, there is now, and there existed in Bodin's time, a body of international law (*jus gentium*). But it has only the form of law, not the function. International law, unlike municipal law, is followed by the consent of those who want to follow it, or not at all. Even submission to an international judicial authority and recognition of its decision is by consent in each case or not at all. Each nation is its own supreme lawgiver and law enforcer. No sovereign nation is subject to law from any other source, national or international. None recognizes any law superior to it. Hence, if there is a conflict among nations, they decide how to resolve it—by negotiation, if possible; by voluntarily submitting to arbitration, occasionally; or finally, by organized violence against one another—war.

Each nation in effect reserves the authority to determine how to resolve conflicts. Nations may decide on negotiations, or arbitration, when the potential gain is not worth the cost of an armed conflict, when no vital interests are involved, or when they feel unsure of winning such a conflict. In negotiation or arbitration, international law can be of help in formulating the arguments brought to bear and the principles appealed to. The international law that may be involved consists of traditional principles and procedures, of precedents and customs that have been established—as are treaties—because they are mutually convenient. However, any nation can violate such principles without being held to account if it is powerful enough, or if nobody wants to go to the trouble of correcting its behavior. As I am writing, the Soviet Union is too powerful to be corrected (without world war), and, rightly or wrongly, nobody seems to wish to take the risk of correcting Libya or Iran.

Even such well-established principles, useful to all concerned, as the inviolability and extraterritoriality of ambassadors and embassies are readily violated if any power finds it convenient, perhaps for domestic reasons, to violate them. Thus, Iran stormed the American embassy and held American diplomats hostage for a lengthy period. The U.S. government, though not sponsoring it, currently tolerates a relatively minor violation by, in effect, allowing demonstrators to hinder access to the South African embassy. Americans could do little about the situation in Iran other than go to war. We didn't. (We seized Iranian assets though, and after a long while our diplomats were released.) South Africa could interrupt diplomatic relations with the United States, but it would not gain thereby. Generally speaking, nothing can be done about enforcing the rules of international law against a recalcitrant power—whether the rules are interpreted unilaterally by one party, or time-honored and generally accepted, or, finally, proclaimed by some international body such as the International Court of Justice or the U.N.—unless the enforcers use their own military force and go to war. Perhaps this could be done with minor powers such as Albania. But it is done rarely. Great Britain obtained a verdict against Albania from the International Court of Justice for blowing up British shipping in peacetime. But nobody enforced the verdict. It was not enforced because Great Britain did not think it worthwhile to send an army to Albania. If the Soviet Union violates international law, little can be done unless one wishes to start the war that international law, or the U.N., is meant to prevent. This goes as well for any of the Soviet dependencies or allies or, analogously, for the United States or any of its allies.

There is a difference though: On the whole the United States is willing to follow international law. When it does, one party, the United States, regards itself as bound to international law and the other does not, with consequent harm to the United States. The party that follows the rules when the opponent does not and cannot be made to will normally suffer.

Basically, the U.N. is a charade. So is the International Court of Justice and similar bodies. But rather than entertain, as some charades do, the U.N. misleads, and the less one understands that it is a charade, the more it misleads.

As long as the nations are sovereign, this situation cannot be changed. And nations show no inclination to give up their independence, and the ability to go to war, should they decide it to be necessary. The U.N. could not even prevent Argentina from trying to conquer the Falklands by military force any more than it could prevent England from defending them. That is why both countries, indeed all countries, keep armed forces ready for defense or attack.

As I am writing, a rather bloody war has been going on between Iran and Iraq. It is continuing with no end in sight. All the U.N. could do was to pass resolutions. The same has been true for wars between Israel and Egypt (and assorted allies at the time). The same has been true for the invasion by the Soviet Union of Czechoslovakia, Hungary, or Afghanistan, or the invasion of Cambodia and Laos by Vietnam (a Soviet ally), and such little wars as between India and Pakistan (over Kashmir). The small wars that have occurred since World War II are simply too many to list, even if one does not count minor local events such as the invasion of Cyprus by Turkey. In all these events the U.N. has been unable to do anything but pass resolutions. Occasionally, the U.N. will hire troops from neutral nations, with the consent of the *quondam* belligerents, to keep them apart and help them, if not to make peace, at least to keep a truce. However, when the parties (or one of them) decide to go to war once more, the U.N. obligingly withdraws these troops (which anyway could not much more than observe). U Thant did so in Egypt on May 18, 1967. This facilitated the attack of Egypt against Israel. There is not much else the U.N. could have done. Yet the U.N. bureaucracy has done nothing to discourage its followers from believing that it can keep the peace, or contribute to keeping it, or be useful in this respect.

The alternative to the international anarchy the U.N. cannot disguise would be some form of world government, to which conflict resolution would be delegated and which, having a monopoly of armed force, could impose its decisions on all parties. Of course, all nations would have to give up their military forces and allow the world government to enforce its decisions. It does not seem likely that the United States, the Soviet Union, China, South Africa, Albania, or Nicaragua are likely to get together, give up their independence and their armies, and submit to such a body. It is hard to figure who would do the governing. Would the world government be elected? By whom? By what means? Most of the world does not now have free elections. Would they be introduced in China and the Soviet Union, Chile, Vietnam, South Africa, Syria?

Even if such problems could be solved—and I don't believe they can be—it is doubtful that a world government could really govern peacefully. Surely sooner or later there will be national rebellions. After all, there are rebellions all the time in multitribal Uganda; the Irish do not get along with the English or with Irish Protestants, the Greeks in Cyprus with the Turks. India barely manages to keep its states together. The United States, despite a central government, went through a wrenching civil war. Could a central world government do better? Wouldn't its various constituents declare their independence almost immediately so that they could have a go at others—leaving the central government to go to war against them? We would have the same international conflicts in different form; wars would become civil wars without reduction in ferocity, as the American Civil War or, more recently, the Spanish Civil War has shown.

It may as well be said that wars are as unavoidable in the life of nations as death is in the life of individuals. As long as there are independent entities, not subjected to effective superior power, they will occasionally have conflicts; at times they will use violence to resolve them. This does not mean that specific wars cannot be avoided. They can be, just as specific illnesses can be. However, war cannot be avoided any more than death can be.

We are usually grateful to physicians who often succeed in prolonging our life. We seldom picket hospitals demanding that death be abolished. Yet we are resentful of diplomacy and of the military because, although they can prolong peace, they cannot ultimately avert war altogether.

It is as though death were attributed to doctors. Certainly they make mistakes. In some cases, had the treatment been correct, the illness could have been avoided or cured. Death could have been postponed. But not avoided in the end.

Diplomats do make mistakes. And so do the governments of nations. Some wars could have been avoided. Even the war against Hitler might have been avoided if Hitler had been confronted with well-armed and resolute Allies. But France only thought it was armed. England clearly was not. America said it would not enter the war. And the Soviets made a deal with Hitler, promising to let him take as much of the West as he wanted.

However, prolonging peace—nothing could be more important—has nothing to do with the U.N. It has to do with avoiding and settling conflicts and with discouraging attacks. Attacks are discouraged if the prospective attacker is convinced that he will be defeated, or that the attack is unlikely to be cost-effective, regardless of victory or defeat. Switzerland is not attacked for the second reason, the United States for the first. That conviction depends on the strength the prospective victim can muster through its own military preparation and that of its allies, and, not least, on the resolve to defend itself.

The U.N. is at best a distraction. If there are powers willing to go to war for some purpose—as Argentina was for the Falklands, or Egypt to conquer Israel—they can be discouraged only by the certainty, or high likelihood, of defeat. Wars happen either if the attacking nation underestimates the resolve and power of the victim and overestimates its own (this was the case of Egypt and Argentina) or if the prospective victims actually are sufficiently weak to make victory likely. This was Hitler's case, although it turned out that in the end he had miscalculated by attacking the Soviets and underestimating them, and by failing to take account of the likelihood of American intervention. He turned out to be wrong, but his initial calculations were by no means unreasonable.

To avoid similar miscalculations by any aggressor one must remember the Roman dictum *Si vis pacem para bellum*—If you desire peace be prepared for war. If the prospective victim is well enough prepared, attacks are likely to be discouraged. Unfortunately, the forces in the world often are so balanced that the aggressor feels he has a good chance. Diplomacy and agreements must strive to avoid this situation and remember that apparent weakness invites attack.

Given the situation, it is hard to see what role the U.N. can play in avoiding war, or even to imagine that it can play any. John Conrad appears to think it can. The reader will share my eagerness to find out what he thinks the U.N. can do that cannot be done as well, or better, without it.

JOHN P. CONRAD

Professor van den Haag has taken us on a circuitous ramble from the dream of perpetual peace to the specter of *unavoidable* war, which he insists is the reality we must all face. War must come to nations as death comes to us all. Along the way toward this depressing conclusion, he tells us that President Wilson was either a fool or a charlatan—we can take our pick—that Jean Bodin, back in the sixteenth century, pronounced not only the first but also the last word on the subject of sovereignty, that Senator Moynihan was guilty of a bizarre absurdity when he contended that if the United States had joined the League of Nations World War II might have been avoided. A good many other insights are to be seen on this tour of political philosophy, the history of ideas, the recent course of international relations, and what readers are to take for the stout common sense of a neoconservative. A blithe stoic is my fatalist friend; the end must be nigh and nothing can save us, especially the United Nations. We hear again that understanding leads to conflict. We learn from his doom-laden assertions that there are four reasons for expecting the United Nations to fail.

A liberal internationalist must be excused if he is a little breathless at this fast clip, but I will do what I can with the prophecies of this latter-day oracle of despair. I have not given up hope, and I want to restore the reader's faith that we may yet muddle through, perhaps by the skin of our teeth, as the human race always has.

Woodrow Wilson and the League of Nations

I will begin with President Wilson, one of our few truly great presidents, an intellectual who passionately believed that the League of Nations could become an effective instrument for maintaining the peace. The "wisdom" that Dr. van den Haag so readily attributes to the Senate "irreconcilables" was the party politician's foresight that a victory for Wilson on the issue of the League would jeopardize Republican chances to regain the White House in 1920. Anyone reading Senator Lodge's intemperate letters and speeches about Wilson will recognize a resentful Republican determined to end Democratic occupancy of the White House at the earliest possible opportunity and at any cost—not a wise and patriotic statesman eager to promote world peace.[1] As a matter of fact, the senator was a staunch advocate of a League to Enforce the Peace until President Wilson decided to include the formation of such a league as one of his Fourteen Points for the settlement of World War I and then engaged in an exhausting whistle-stop campaign across the nation to amass support for the Covenant. At that point, sinking the League became a matter of national urgency in the minds of the "irreconcilables." Dr. van den Haag's hindsight may find wisdom in the pettifoggery of the willful men who torpedoed the League, but not many of their contemporaries would have agreed with him.

The idea of a League to maintain the peace is old, going back at least to the early seventeenth century, with the publication of *Le Nouveau Cynée* by a French monk, Emeric Cruce, who was obsessed with the seemingly interminable Thirty Years' War and the violence of his times. Various thinkers of the first rank have tried their hands at elaboration of the idea, including Jean-Jacques Rousseau, Immanuel Kant, and Jeremy Bentham. What was an exercise for intellectuals preferring peace to armed anarchy became a popular movement in England and the United States during the nineteenth and early twentieth centuries.[2] Wilson was not an early convert, although at Versailles he became its most zealous exponent. There is no reason to suppose that he did not fully believe in the idea, nor is there any basis for Dr. van den Haag's argument that the idea of the League did not have unimpeachably auspicious credentials in political philosophy. On the contrary, there was a general revulsion at the record of conventional diplomacy that led to World War I. Secret treaties, the negotiation of ententes and alliances to balance each other, and an arms race of surreal and uncontrolled momentum brought about a condition of international anarchy that made that terrible war inevitable. What was so unwise about a strategy to create commitments to collective security? What was so statesmanlike about the pandering of Senator Lodge and the Republican "irreconcilables" to partisan hostilities, ethnic mistrust, and the deliberate misreading of American history that led to the rejection of the League?

Lost in the acrimony of this unedifying debate are the principles by which Wilson thought the League should be organized:

...Only free peoples can hold their purpose and their honor steady
to a common end and prefer the interests of mankind to any narrow
interest of their own.

A steadfast concert for peace can never be maintained except by
a partnership of democratic nations. No autocratic government
could be trusted to keep faith within it or observe its covenants. It
must be a league of honor.[3]

Opinions will differ as to the effectiveness of a League—or
the United Nations—from which totalitarian governments would
be excluded. Wilson seems to have expected that the League
would be a club of victors. That was not the prospect that the "irreconcilables" and Senator Lodge disliked. What was important to
them was the humiliation of President Wilson and the defeat of the
Democratic Party in 1920. American rejection of the League of
Nations was an example of American politics at its unedifying
worst—parochial, unreasoning, ill informed, and demagogic.

Senator Moynihan's Speculations

Is it really so bizarre to suppose that American membership in
the League would have forestalled World War II? It is idle to pretend to certainty one way or another. The notion that we Americans could have made a crucial difference because of our idealism
or our economic power assumes that statesmen of minimal vision
like Warren G. Harding or Calvin Coolidge could and would have
brought both these characteristics to bear on the exhausted and impoverished Europeans.

Nevertheless, had President Wilson's health been spared, had
he been able to lead the nation into the League, it is not beyond
the realm of possibility that economic sanctions could have been
applied to Japan and Italy that would have made their adventures
in China and Ethiopia impractical. American power might have
stiffened British and French backbones when Hitler began to rearm Germany.

We shall never know. History does not allow nations to replay
their hands. But those were years when economic sanctions might

have been enough to prevent the successive disasters that led, step by obvious step, to the catastrophe that was World War II. We could not have lost much by participation in the League, and we might have saved the world.

I doubt that Senator Moynihan, one of the most learned and thoughtful politicians of our time, meant that with American membership the League could have mobilized an armada to head off the Japanese in Manchuria and another expedition to block Mussolini from his assault on Ethiopia. Such measures would have been unnecessary, even if they had been practical, given the shaky condition of the Japanese and Italian economies in those days. All that would have been necessary was a firm set of embargoes.

A Note on Sovereignty

For me, as for most of our readers, I suppose, Jean Bodin (1529–1596) is a figure in the pantheon of jurisprudence, not a household name and not a writer whose *Les Six Livres de la Republique* are well thumbed or likely to become so. Probably I should be grateful to my opponent for bringing this character onto our platform, but I don't intend to devote much more time to his antiquated discourse. In Chapter 1 I have already given my views on Bodin's interpretation of the idea of sovereignty, and I stand by what I said.[4]

It is quite true that international law is different from municipal law, and Dr. van den Haag correctly notes that compliance cannot be coerced in the settlement of disputes between sovereign nations. It is also true that throughout history disputes have been settled with tragic frequency by military violence.

No news in all that but a long-standing state of affairs that must be changed. As political philosophers have told us for centuries (including the redoubtable Bodin), this condition amounts to anarchy. As the scale of violence rises from lances and pikestaffs to nerve gas and multitargetable nuclear warheads, the need to bring anarchy to an end becomes terribly urgent. Too slowly we are discovering that by common consent sovereignty can be limited, that machinery can be designed for the routine settlement of disputes that in earlier times might have become *casus belli*. The world is learning the processes of multilateral diplomacy by which cooperative endeavors in strengthening the international economy, preventing disease, and fostering the productivity of industry and agriculture can prevent the traditional causes of war from boiling to the surface.

The crude idea of sovereignty as the seventeenth century knew it is giving way to the necessity of international cooperation, a necessity that even the Soviet Union grudgingly acknowledges. Two examples: In the Cyprus situation, the USSR joined a unanimous Security Council in its resolution of the conflict between the Greek Cypriots and the Turkish minority.[5] That does not solve the Cyprus problem, but it keeps the peace. It may be argued that this is not an area in which crucial Russian interests are at stake, but it does not take much imagination to conceive of mischief that might be planned in the Kremlin to create new interests out of the Cypriot ferment. A second example is the willingness of the Russians to allow its Eastern European satellites to participate in the International Monetary Fund—an absolute necessity for Poland, and probably for Czechoslovakia and Romania as well. Internationalism in the Western sense of the term comes slowly to the self-styled socialist nations, but necessity is the mother of economic reform. The Soviet bloc will find that other necessities will change their repellent ways.

In a later chapter I intend to examine the meaning of sovereignty in the twentieth and twenty-first centuries in more depth. Meanwhile, let us allow Jean Bodin's shade to return to the comfortable obscurity from which Dr. van den Haag has summoned him.

The Roots of Uselessness

Professor van den Haag exposes his central argument by defining four factors that, he says, account for the "ineradicable uselessness" of the United Nations. I doubt that the disposal of these factors will shake his hostility to multilateralism, but it's worth a try; at any rate I cannot ignore them.

The Structure and the Enforcement of the Peace

So far as I can make out, these phases of the argument rest on the contention that the only way that United Nations decisions can be enforced is for troops to be sent to impose the collective will on the offending nation or nations. This is manifestly not true. The Charter is explicit. Article 41 provides for the Security Council to consider "measures not involving the use of armed force to give effect to its decisions" and goes on to specify "complete or partial interruption of economic relations and of rail, sea, air, postal, telegraphic, radio, and other means of communication...." Only in Articles 42–47 is provision made for deployment of military forces to bring about compliance with the directives of the Security Council, and then only if economic measures are considered inadequate for the purpose.

I will concede that economic sanctions should be more freely used. Argentina's use of force to invade the Falklands should have been met with an immediate embargo, supported if necessary by a naval blockade. In the present conflict between Iran and Iraq, the United Nations could do these persistent adversaries a great favor by isolating both countries from sources of military and civilian supplies. The means to end small wars between small nations exist, and it is not inconceivable that in some of these conflicts the concurrence of both superpowers might be obtained. What is lacking is a failure of nerve, an unwillingness to use the United Nations as it was meant to be used.

It has been done. Security Council mandates were honored by the Netherlands in 1949 when Indonesia was granted its independence. Similarly, actions by the Security Council served to pacify the Congo and Cyprus and to abort a conflict between Indonesia and Malaysia. The failure of the United Nations to bring order and stability to the Middle East merely demonstrates the impossibility of doing the impossible. Eventually the conflicting religious warriors will weary of the needless bloodshed, just as Catholics and Protestants wearied of the Thirty Years' War. At some point in a future that we hope will be sooner rather than later, the good offices of the United Nations will be welcome in bringing about a lasting settlement.

In passing, Dr. van den Haag offers the opinion that the United Nations "exacerbates existing conflicts and creates new ones." This comment requires two kinds of supporting examples, but my opponent offers none. The reverse is more likely the case. Conor Cruise O'Brien, an Irish veteran of the Congo imbroglio and now a sharp observer of events in the United Nations, remarks:

> The Security Council—following appeals to it by parties in regional disputes—brings together the superpowers and medium powers and others in relation to every crisis. What the public is then treated to, almost invariably, is yet another "failure of the United Nations"; another local scrap, followed by some rather forlorn patching up; a token force along a peace-line, later to be bundled out, perhaps, by one of the local parties which has decided that it no longer needs a peace-line. But there is a positive aspect even to the failures. The Security Council usually fails either to avert or to end local conflicts. But the contacts of the superpowers of the Security Council, in respect of each such crisis, have also certainly helped in limiting the tendency of local conflicts to spread, and in minimizing adversarial superpower involvement. Furthermore each exercise in regional "crisis management"—and especially each *failure* [O'Brien's emphasis] in "crisis management"—is a practical lesson for each superpower about how the other perceives its own vital interests; and each lesson reduces, just a little, the dangers of unintended confrontation. If the equivalent of a Security Council had existed from, say, 1875 on the Balkan wars would not have been avoided or abbreviated; but enough might have been learnt from them to make it possible to avoid the First World War.[6]

That argument is going to seem tenuous and easily dismissible by my rough-and-ready adversary. But the texture of diplomatic relations in the complex contemporary world has to allow for a fine weave. A perfect example of the superpowers feeling out each other's interests under the auspices of the United Nations is Resolution 242, unanimously passed by the Security Council in 1967 as the framework for peace between Israel and her Arab neighbors and adversaries. That that resolution has not been fully implemented as yet is not relevant to O'Brien's argument. His point is that the United States and the Soviet Union learned a great deal about each other's interests in the eastern Mediterranean and, as far as that area was concerned, have stayed out of each other's way ever since 1967.

To put the matter in different language, the United Nations Charter is a new and unfamiliar instrument in the hands of nations that have for centuries managed conflicts by negotiation and trickery and always with intimidation and coercion as potential alternatives so long as the means for resorting to them have been unavailable to the parties in confrontation. The instrument is used cautiously and often clumsily, but as experience is gained, as the various *casus belli* lose sway over ethnic, religious, and ideological partisans, the instrument will gain in effectiveness.

So much for the first two "roots of uselessness" discovered by Dr. van den Haag. Intertwined as they are in his presentation, I have not troubled to disentangle them. Arthur Goldberg, once our ambassador to the United Nations, remarked to me in an interview that the present condition of the General Assembly and the Security Council reflects the unruly world that is represented in those bodies. For the powers with worldwide interests, the structures in New York, Geneva, and Vienna are arenas where much may be learned about the anxieties of the lesser nations and the ways in which we can avoid making matters worse for them—or, possibly, sometimes improving conditions. The small powers come to listen as well as to give voice to their frustrations. We should have the modesty to do likewise.

The Inevitability of Doomsday

After a bewildering digression on the idea of world government, a prospect that neither entices me nor seems in the least relevant to our discourse, Dr. van den Haag assures us that war may be delayed, some specific wars can be prevented, but, in the long run, (I suppose it's a long run, but my gloomy friend is not reassuring), war cannot be avoided "any more than death can be."

The wisdom of Vegetius, whose maxim on the preparation for war my Latinist friend quotes so approvingly, but without crediting the source, was well suited to the fourth century, A.D., when that master of the military arts wrote his text on the organization of a Roman legion. Times have changed. Warfare was the natural state of affairs for the Romans, and anyone who hoped for a breath of peace had to hope that his side was better prepared for war than his enemies.

His maxim, all that commemorates his name in an age of missiles, tanks, and submarines, was certainly applicable up to the onset of World War II. It was only with World War I that it became apparent that wars were no longer to be won, that there was no longer glory and honor to be gained in the field of battle. *Dulce et decorum est pro patria mori*—"Sweet and honorable it is to die for one's country." Horace could compose the line, and many young men have believed him, but the misery of the Somme and the terror of aerial bombardment in World War II have drained the sweetness and honor out of warfare. Hitler and Mussolini clung to the notion that master races could win wars, and it is clear that the incentives of honor and glory could stir the hearts and minds of young Germans and, perhaps, some young Italians. The rest of us did our duty as best we could, but there was little zest and not many of us aspired to heroism, though heroes there were.

We know now that nuclear warheads will drain the human race from the planet. We cannot allow war to be inevitable, and if we give thought to the subject, we know that it need not be. Professor van den Haag's analogy between death and war is absurd. Death is a part of our biological condition, but there is no natural law that requires war.

But the habit of war will die hard. Both the United States and the USSR seem convinced—at least for the present—that they cannot allow themselves to be directly engaged in battle. The danger of a nuclear exchange is too real. Lesser powers that cannot manufacture a bomb are still free to fight, and a superpower can engage such a lesser power if it seems necessary. We are the beneficiaries of mutual assured destruction, and that doctrine will keep us safe for as long as rational men are in power in Washington and Moscow. I have no doubt that Vegetius would nod approvingly.

For my part, I hope that we can do better. If potentates in Washington and Moscow can summon up enough rationality to abstain from ultimate hostilities on account of the hydrogen warhead, their successors may eventually become rational enough to rely on the give and take of negotiation for the dispute of superpowers, and to join in whatever measures may be necessary to discipline the unruly lesser powers. The machinery of the United Nations was intended for this purpose, and I am not such a pessimist as to believe that it cannot be used with success.

If you want peace, prepare to negotiate.

Sweet and honorable it is to negotiate for one's country.

The Expansionary Aims of the Soviet Union

Professor van den Haag is certain that the Russians intend to require the rest of the world "either to surrender and accept Soviet domination or to prepare for armed resistance." Many Americans devoutly believe that this is the prospect ahead. It certainly is a plausible worst-case scenario, and well worth resisting. To my opponent the prospect is so self-evident that he does not discuss it further.

I think it deserves some further consideration. If world domination is the Russian objective, the strategy is not going well. Precarious control is maintained in Eastern Europe, where sullen nations are held in place by might and main, not by gratitude, respect, or even economic advantage. It is a serious question for Kremlin strategists as to whether they can count on the troops of the satellite nations to march under the Soviet banners. There is an expensive foothold in Cuba, a foot in an unpromising door in Nicaragua, an interminable war in Afghanistan, some unprofitable adventures in Africa, and few if any true friends anywhere. With a military establishment that the nation can ill afford, the expansionary aims that the Politburo has inherited from the tsars are destined to failure. It was one thing for the tsars to expand from the Urals to the Pacific; it seemed as manifest a destiny as it was for our forefathers to expand from the Appalachians to California. It is quite another to conquer and control a populous and organized modern state. It can be done at enormous expense, but why?

The answer lies in the dying faith in Marxism. The prophets of communism believed that history was on their side and that capitalism would eventually collapse. Their duty was to hasten the dawn of socialist justice. The Kremlin commitment to these dogmas has lasted too long and is too unreserved for easy reversal, even though not many Russians truly believe it. To turn loose the Eastern Europeans, to reject the pleas of Ethiopian and Cuban opportunists would be to jettison an important body of doctrines by which the Russian Communists have gained power and kept it. As for Afghanistan, I persist in my belief that this was a decision made by a collection of senile bumblers and abetted by the vain and overconfident marshals of the Red Army. It will take all of Gorbachev's wit and adroitness to extricate the Soviet Union from Afghanistan, but eventually he will.

So why not keep the United Nations on an alert for a helping role in the Afghan morass in which Soviet honor and credit have sunk? For the last couple of years, an under-secretary-general has been negotiating with the Russians, the Afghans, and the Afghan resistance. Some day all the parties to this process will find a formula for bringing an end to the misery. It will not be a triumph for which the United Nations could possibly claim sole credit. But because the machinery is there, it is being used, and an end can be expected. Would Professor van den Haag prefer that everyone should take the unlikely chance that the military outcome will be favorable to the unfortunate Afghans? Does he have a better suggestion?

History moves, and the Russians will have to move with it. That practical Communist, Deng Xiao-Ping, saw what had to be done and is doing it. Eventually someone in the Kremlin will attain power and see the value of Russians' minding their own business, just as the remarkable Mr. Deng has done. When that day comes the Russians will find the United Nations a splendid vehicle for coming to terms with the rest of the world as a friendly power rather than an instigator of nightmares, the world's bogeyman.

But the nightmare is still on. We are still dreaming, sometimes in a cold sweat. The reality is that the world can and should be a peaceful and harmonious planet if we transfer the effort we put into preparing for a war that everyone knows must never happen into preparations for an entirely possible peace.

Notes

1. The complex and tragic history of the Senate's rejection of the Versailles Treaty, and with it the League of Nations, has been often told. For a detailed account, outlining the obduracy of both sides in the conflict, see Thomas A. Bailey, *Woodrow Wilson and the Great Betrayal* (New York: Macmillan, 1945), especially pp. 38–52. The sympathetic narrative by Herbert Hoover, himself a president who also suffered a humiliating defeat, reviews these events with much admiration for Wilson and little for the "irreconcilables." See *The Ordeal of Woodrow Wilson* (New York: McGraw-Hill, 1958), pp. 265–303. Note that Hoover worked closely with Wilson during the war and had personal knowledge of Wilson's thinking about the League.
2. For a brief account of the history of the idea, see F. H. Hinsley, *Power and the Pursuit of Peace* (Cambridge University Press, 1963), pp. 13–149.
3. Quoted by Hoover, note 1, pp. 302–303.
4. See pp. 32–33, 147, above.
5. See Chapter 2, pp. 88–90.
6. Conor Cruise O'Brien, "The Very Model of a Secretary-General," *Times Literary Supplement*, No. 4,320, 17(January 1986), pp. 63–64.

ERNEST VAN DEN HAAG

John Conrad takes me to task for many things. Often his objection is that I don't agree with him—a capital crime no doubt, to which I simply will plead guilty. Yet some things do warrant a rejoinder.

Throughout, in many variations, John Conrad calls me an "oracle of despair." This seems silly. I know that I will die, that the human life-span, including mine, is unlikely to exceed, say, 100 years by much. This certainty does not lead me to despair. Nor does it, as far as I know, Professor Conrad, who will die, just as you and I will. I know, similarly, that war is unavoidable. It seems silly to deny either certainty. There has hardly ever been more than a century of peace for most nations. This does not drive me to despair either. Why should it? I am satisfied to enjoy life during peace despite death and war. So, apparently, is Professor Conrad. Why then does he represent me as gloomy and despairing because I acknowledge the certainty of death and war? Is it because I am realistic and John Conrad prefers to dream? Nothing wrong with dreaming, as long as one does not confuse dreams with reality, or call anyone who prefers it to dreams—or nightmares, such as the U.N.—"an oracle of despair," just because he has benefited from reading history or analyzing international relations, including the notion of sovereignty, which Mr. Conrad does not like. The main function of dreams is to keep the dreamer sleeping. Yet sometimes it is better to awaken and to face reality without being diverted by dreams. To be concrete: Some wars can be avoided—not by dreaming about an ideal world, or the U.N., but by working in the world we have—just as some illnesses can be avoided or cured, not by dreaming about panaceas, or life without death, but by taking care of one's health and exploring how to improve it. All this can be done fully knowing that neither death nor war can be avoided in the long run. Beware of dreaming physicians, and of professors who dream that the U.N. can secure peace.

President Wilson was a dreamer. He did nothing for the peace of the world besides dreaming of it. The Versailles treaty to which he contributed so much guaranteed the next war and would have done so if all his ideas had been implemented. John Conrad is impressed by Wilson's dreams. I am by his fatuity. The motives of his opponents may have been every bit as bad as John Conrad thinks. But the effect of their opposition and of our subsequent failure to join the League of Nations not only was harmless, it was fortunate and saved us money and illusions. The League was as useless as the U.N. is, even though Conrad refuses to learn from the experience. I wish someone had prevented our joining the U.N. just as Senator Lodge managed to prevent our joining the League. We would have saved ourselves billions and the presence of numerous Soviet spies with diplomatic immunity in New York. And we would not be compelled to finance anti-American and antidemocratic propaganda as we are now. John Conrad asks about the League: "What was so unwise about a strategy to create commitments to collective security?" The answer is simple. It is unwise to create such "commitments" if there is no way to enforce them. There can be no way as long as nations are sovereign. Hence, the "commitments" are deceptive, at best self-deceptions. It is better to face reality rather than to hide it dreamily beneath illusory "commitments."

Conrad goes on to quote Woodrow Wilson to the effect that only democratic nations care for peace, that "no autocratic government could be trusted...." Perhaps. But if either the League or the U.N. had excluded "autocratic governments" such as, at present, the Soviet Union, China, Vietnam, East Germany, and all of Eastern Europe, the U.N. would simply be an alliance of the Western nations. We already have that. It is called NATO. We might as well give up the U.N. then. (Perhaps I agree here with Conrad and Wilson, except, neither being consistent, I cannot be sure.) Conrad seems to want the U.N. even if, in lucid moments, he allows that it is useless.

As Mr. Conrad says, Senator Moynihan is a gentleman and a scholar. Still he can be wrong. Since becoming a senator he has made a habit of it. His idea, that World War II might have been avoided had we joined the League of Nations, is too absurd to warrant further discussion. I hope he was joking, although John Conrad, in endorsing him, appears to be serious.

Conrad believes that, somehow, sovereignty no longer is what Jean Bodin in the sixteenth century thought it was. I used Bodin's concept and his definition because it succinctly describes the present situation. John Conrad to the contrary notwithstanding, there is no legal power or authority, only brute force, that could compel any sovereign nation to do what it does not want to do, be it Albania, the Soviet Union, or the United States. If there were a supernational legal authority, with enforceable verdicts, there would be no national sovereignty. This is what Jean Bodin found 300 years ago. This is why sovereignty remains *potestas legibus absoluta*, power not limited by law. The facts have not changed; therefore, the definition is no less correct than it was. That much remains true, even if John Conrad prefers that it weren't and decides that what he prefers must be true *eo ipso*.

Sure, as Conrad says, Poland *et al.* try to profit from the International Monetary Fund (i.e., in effect, to borrow from it). If this has to do with the U.N., it constitutes another argument against it, not, as Conrad thinks, an argument in its favor. Why should we be induced to strengthen bankrupt Soviet allies with loans unlikely to be repaid, extended at below market rates of interest?

I cherish one passage in John Conrad. After paraphrasing me (correctly) to the effect that the only way U.N. decisions could be enforced on "the offending nation or nations" is "for troops to be sent," Conrad triumphantly rejoins, "This is manifestly not true. The Charter is explicit," and goes on to explain that all kinds of other sanctions (mainly economic) are listed in the Charter. They are. So? Have they ever worked? Could they work? Not even Albania has yielded, or will yield, on anything because of sanctions, other than invasion and defeat. Nor will Poland or South Africa, let alone the Soviet Union. The Charter does list these remedies. But they are ineffective, wherefore I did not bother to mention them. There are no effective remedies other than force, as, say, in Korea. And whether or not the U.N. banner is used, that force, or that war, does not differ from the force or the war which according to Conrad the U.N. is designed to avoid, and which according to me it cannot avoid. Conrad's argument about U.N. remedies is like saying, "It is not true that there is currently no cure for the common cold. Why, physicians can prescribe *x, y,* and *z.*" Sure.

But these medicines won't cure a cold, although they keep physicians busy; some patients believe in placebos till they die. Moreover, no U.N. remedy could ever be used against any major nation threatening the peace, for that nation and its allies are in the U.N. They would use their votes and vetoes to prevent the use of such a remedy. The U.N. is not an independent authority (let alone power) above the litigants. It *is* the litigants.

Conrad goes on to say that the response to Argentina's invasion of the Falklands should have been an "immediate embargo," perhaps "a naval blockade." A naval blockade can be enforced only by acts of war. Further, Argentina is largely self-sufficient and could survive a blockade—which would strengthen its resolution. Anyway, there is no way to enforce a blockade against Argentina with its enormous coastline. Finally, South American nations would have sabotaged the embargo. The U.N. certainly would not have supported any of John Conrad's odd dreams; the majority would not have voted against Argentina. The Soviet Union might well have vetoed a Security Council resolution in favor of sanctions and certainly it would not have observed it. Britain had only the choice of surrendering the Falklands or defending them. The U.N. was useless, of course, except as a transparent cover for surrender, which the British decided against.

It strikes me as absurd to contend, as John Conrad is foolhardy enough to do, that the Netherlands granted independence to Indonesia because of "Security Council mandates." (Nothing happens if these are ignored.) Independence was granted to Indonesia, as it had been granted to India before and to other former colonies, because it became too costly to keep the colonies, as nationalism of various sorts spread throughout the world. The U.N. had about as much to do with it as the weather. Of course, if the U.N. passes a resolution on the weather every day, once in a while the weather will be whatever the U.N. mandated. John Conrad then will explain that we owe the sunshine to the Security Council.

Far from pacifying the Congo, as John Conrad contends, the U.N. started a civil war there, while pretending to prevent it. There was only one armed faction; it takes at least two to have a

war. The U.N. provided the second. (I was there and took pictures
of the horrendous atrocities committed by the U.N. troops in
Katanga.) The U.N. made war to make sure that the Congo did
not, as it might well have, split into different independent units.
The result was to deliver the Congo to one of the most inept and
cruel dictatorships now existing, that of Mobutu Sese Seko. Incidentally, I shouldn't rely on Conor Cruise O'Brien as a witness,
as Mr. Conrad does, for that Irish politician admittedly has lied in
the past when it suited his purpose (see his *To Katanga and Back*).
Still, what he says may be true, though it does not help John Conrad. To wit, "The Security Council usually fails either to avert or
to end local conflicts. But the contacts of the superpowers at the
Security Council...have almost certainly helped...in minimiz-
ing...." The first point is correct. About the second the witness
(a) speculates and (b) fails to indicate why the U.N. is needed for
these "contacts." Don't we have embassies? Telephones? Airplanes? What makes meeting in the U.N. building different from
meeting anywhere else? Is the coffee better? To attribute everything helpful to the U.N. and everything harmful to there not being enough of it is not an argument, or even speculation. It is
sheer obfuscation—which is what the U.N. is all about.

Let me conclude with a few historical asides.

John Conrad seems to believe that at one time it was great to
die in war but that things have changed and it is no longer great.
Things have changed. But the suffering that war inflicts and the
sordidness of the circumstances have not, except, perhaps, that the
wounded are cared for to a greater extent and that prisoners are no
longer killed automatically or enslaved. The suffering of civilian
populations—and the proportion that suffers—probably has
declined too. War remains supremely undesirable and harmful.
But it always was.

There is no natural law that requires war, as it does death,
and, contrary to Conrad's implication, I don't think there is. Yet
war is as unavoidable as death because of the unavoidability of
conflicts among independent entities (states) and the impossibility

to compel nonviolent resolution. Natural laws are not, contrary to Conrad's implications, the only unavoidable things in life. Crime is just as unavoidable as death, as Conrad certainly knows, but it is not a natural law. So with war.

I am ambivalent about John Conrad's naiveté. On the one hand it is endearing. On the other it is dangerous. What can one say of someone who writes about "the expansionary aims that the Politburo has inherited from the tsars" being "destined to failure." I hope Conrad is right, but I wonder how he knows. Surely the U.N. will not help to cause these aims to be "destined to failure." Could it be our armament? I hope so, but I wish I could be as certain as Mr. Conrad. Is he right in stating that these "expansionary aims" of the Soviets are simply "inherited" from the tsars? About as right, I think, as it would be to say that Hitler's aims were "inherited" from Imperial Germany. It leaves out the whole unprecedented Messianic ideology and dynamics of nazism and communism.

What is one to say about Conrad's writing, "It will take all of Gorbachev's wit and adroitness to extricate the Soviet Union from Afghanistan, but eventually he will"?

How does Conrad know (a) that Gorbachev has "wit and adroitness" (Why is wit needed?); (b) that he has more than Stalin or any other of his predecessors; (c) that he wants to use whatever he has to get out of Afghanistan (or does Conrad mean to conquer it when he writes "extricate"?); (d) indeed, that Gorbachev thinks as John Conrad would if he were in Gorbachev's place?

Such assumptions are never more than half right, and they are founded on wishful thinking. Why assume that a Soviet dictator or oligarch has "wit and adroitness" when all we know is that he must have some cunning to become a dictator? Why assume that he would be as naive (and as reasonable) as John Conrad and interested more in peace than in domination?

Since John Conrad asks me: I have no suggestions about Afghanistan except that we should help those who fight for its independence. Unlike Conrad, I cannot predict the ultimate outcome of the fight but I would not rely on Gorbachev's goodwill or wit, or on the U.N. Both are images that do credit to Conrad's creativity but have no counterpart in the reality in which we live.

JOHN P. CONRAD

I have ruffled the sensitivities of my pessimistic friend by suggesting that he is an "oracle of despair." He protests that he enjoys life even though he must accept the inevitability of death, war, urban crime, and various other unpleasant prospects. I can contemplate the inevitability of my death with equanimity, I concede that there is no prospect of eliminating crime altogether, but I will not reconcile myself to the inevitability of war. At my age, I know that I will not be called to the colors, and neither will Dr. van den Haag. I have sons and grandchildren who might face that prospect should the United States become involved again in a non-nuclear war, the kind of interminable bloodletting that we found so intolerable in Korea and Vietnam and which, I suspect, ordinary Russians find no more appealing in their country's effort to confer the blessings of Soviet socialism on Afghanistan.

My unflinching colleague does not say whether he includes nuclear war under the rubric of inevitability. If so, neither of us can be sure of how long the two of us will continue to enjoy life in the gardens of the West. We have both had good and interesting lives, and if both of us are vaporized in a nuclear exchange, we will not have much to regret on our own accounts. What distresses me about the certainties that my prophetic friend proclaims is the implied termination of the lives of my children in the middle of their journey, and the lives of my grandchildren when they have scarcely set forth.

For these personal considerations, considerations that most parents and grandparents all over the civilized world must share, I will not resign myself to the dread certainty that Professor van de Haag accepts with such calm. Whatever can be done to assure peace—if not in our time (for we can see wars and omens of wars in every direction), at least in our children's time—should be done. For this reason, I want to strengthen the United Nations rather than hobble or dismantle it. I want to search for the means to forestall the disasters that will surely befall us unless the human race can change its ways.

A likely prospect? Dr. van den Haag notes that he has read history and analyzed international relations. Wherefore he is entitled to assert that war, bloody, stupid, and needless war, has always, is now, and always will be the ultimate resolution of conflict. Efforts to prevent war may succeed from time to time, but in the end young men and women will go to battle, some to die, some to be maimed, and some to march home in victory or defeat. In the shadow of the colors is the ultimate weapon that some national leader, not necessarily an American or a Russian, may fire off in desperation or mere impatience.

Is it not worth our while to take every possible step to assure that peace becomes more general? What have we to lose from bending every effort to reinforce the United Nations? Professor van den Haag is annoyed with the espionage that undoubtedly goes on, and he can't stand the puerile and ineffective propaganda churned out by the Arab League and representatives of the USSR. American talents at public relations have not begun to be used on the East River. For the most part our recent permanent representatives have specialized in surly derogations of nations that do not unquestioningly follow our lead. The General Assembly is an international forum. We should not be so maladroit in using it.

To sum up my rejoinder so far, we have a lot to gain from the strategic use of the United Nations. Dr. van den Haag has not as yet advanced any but trivial reasons for our departure. (It costs too much. There are spies all over. Some nations send delegates who say awful things about the United States, Israel, and South Africa.) It is really too bad for a student of history and an analyst of international relations to present such arguments to the uninstructed. As he well knows, there are a lot of Americans out there who are susceptible to xenophobia, who want to get those foreigners out of New York and get on with the business of bashing the Communists wherever we can and the consequences be damned. Such people will be grateful for the authoritative voice of a foreign affairs analyst to support their inclinations. They may fulfill his prophecy of inevitability sooner than he would like.

Senator Moynihan and the League

As I said in my earlier comment, neither Senator Moynihan nor I can prove that the League of Nations might have prevented World War II had the United States been a member. Let us reason this thing out with as much hindsight as history will allow us. There were three, and only three, possibilities: (1) the League without the United States as a member, (2) the League with the United States as a member, (3) no League. With (1) we got World War II. With (2) we might have still had World War II, but the chance of preventing it might have critically increased, assuming the influence of a strong secretary of state like Charles Evans Hughes or Frank Kellogg. But with no League at all, what earthly reason is there to suppose that World War II would not have come along, and probably sooner? I vote for (2), believing that we should at least have tried to join in keeping the peace. I don't know about Senator Moynihan, but I suspect that that was his reasoning, too. Professor van den Haag, clothed in his impenetrable pessimism, prefers to let human nature take its inevitable course. Who's bizarre?

Poland and the International Monetary Fund

It sounds very reasonable for my opponent to ask, "Why should we be induced to strengthen bankrupt Soviet allies with loans unlikely to be repaid, extended at below market rates of interest?" This is a question that we are likely to hear rather frequently in the immediate future. Not only Poland but the Soviet Union itself is short of hard currency and will have to start borrowing larger amounts on much longer terms. I suppose that Dr. van den Haag would let the whole lot go whistle.

Tempting though that option might be, it's likely that present militaristic and oppressive policies would continue, and at the expense of the quality of life for ordinary people in the Eastern bloc. If the IMF and the Western banks will refuse to lend unless agreements are reached on the limitation of arms and, perhaps some restraint in foreign adventurism, the West *may* be a gainer. The IMF has been a hard-nosed lender in the Third World, as most of the South American nations are painfully aware, demanding drastic budgetary austerity and other economic strong medicine as a condition for its loans. There is no reason to suppose that it would be more lenient with Poland, or with the USSR, if that nation should apply for a loan. Western nations cannot control their private lending institutions so rigorously in these matters, but the banks and other funds can be encouraged to adopt a conservative lending policy aimed at the kind of leverage the IMF has always used.

If we refuse to lend to an Eastern bloc nation we certainly have no chance at influence. Western lending policies by themselves will not topple the Communist regimes, but every small step in the right direction should be taken. In a general way, we understand the economic troubles of the USSR fairly well. There is no reason to believe that they are so serious that a new Russian revolution is in sight, but they may worsen so that domestic policies will be even more oppressive than they are now and foreign policy may become more adventurist. Lean and hungry, the Soviet Union is more of a danger than when it's fat and comfortable. Either way it's not an attractive place.

The Aims of General Secretary Gorbachev

I won't trust the General Secretary any farther than my suspicious friend. The world has been too often disappointed by the gulf between the words and deeds of the Soviet Union and its brutal and cynical leaders. Mikhail Sergeyevich Gorbachev could not have climbed to the top of the greasy pole with immaculate hands. Those "iron teeth," so much admired by Andrei Gromyko, were made for biting.

What leads me to suspect that the General Secretary may have other matters on his mind than the expansion of the USSR to all the continents is the probability that he has more good sense than his senile and poorly educated predecessors. He has been frank enough to say that

> ...the problems in the country's development grew more rapidly than they were being solved.... Signs of stagnation had begun to surface in the life of society. The situation called for change, but a peculiar psychology—how to improve things without changing anything—took the upper hand in the central bodies and, for that matter at local levels as well.... That sort of attitude is much too costly for the country, the state, and the Party. So let us say it loud and clear! The top-priority task is to overcome the negative factors in society's socio-economic development as rapidly as possible, to accelerate it and impart to it an essential dynamism, to learn from the lessons of the past to a maximum extent, so that the decisions we adopt for the future should be absolutely clear and responsible, and the concrete actions purposeful and effective.[1]

If Mikhail Sergeyevich does not mean what he said, he should. Except in armaments, the Soviet Union is falling farther and farther behind the West. To increase investment in domestic production, the Politburo must curb its foreign adventurism, even if some Red Army marshals will be embarrassed. Gorbachev's frantic efforts to stop President Reagan's Strategic Defense Initiative do not arise from his concern that nuclear war should not be conducted in outer space; he dreads spending the money to match this American initiative.

So I do not see the expansionary aims of the Soviet Union as an immediate threat to peace. The nineteenth-century tsars could keep the British and French Empires concerned about Russian expansion in Afghanistan, or a possible invasion of India and the Middle East—all at quite tolerable expense. For the Soviet Union the costs are vastly greater, as Gorbachev is finding out.

It is to the interest of the Politburo to contribute to world calm rather than turmoil. The General Secretary's wit[2] and adroitness will certainly be needed to get the Red Army out of the Afghan mess, but the interest of his country will be served if he extricates it, as soon as possible, from an expedition that costs money, lives, and the unyielding hostility of China and the Muslim world, as well as the contempt of the Western nations.

Can Sanctions Work?

The ever so conventional wisdom, so cheerfully adopted by my opponent, is that sanctions cannot possibly work. When President Reagan wants to impose sanctions on Libya, our allies reject the idea with a pragmatism born of concealed self-interest. Like our good professor, Prime Minister Thatcher patiently explains that they cannot work because they never have. She doesn't mention that the United Kingdom has a large investment in Libya, which would be jeopardized if it joined the United States in economic sanctions, and an even larger stake in South Africa, which might be wiped out in the successful application of embargoes.

I am not sure about Albania, cited by Professor van den Haag as an example of a country against which sanctions could not succeed. The late Hoxha regime managed to do without the rest of the world for over 40 years, but not many countries are prepared to accept the sacrifices that such an austere polity imposes—only North Korea comes to mind. It is becoming clear that the sanctions now being imposed on South Africa—and very limited sanctions they are, too—are having their effect. As for Poland, the modest economic pressures brought to bear by the West have prevented General Jaruzelski allowing his hard-line Communist ministers to work their will on Solidarity and the Catholic Church. The general's complaints about American hostility toward Poland speak volumes.

The nasty problem with sanctions is that investors in foreign economies are reluctant to make economic sacrifices to bring pressure on rogue nations. They would rather see the banners flying, the troops marching, the bombers in formation, and the fleets at full steam ahead. As a result, sanctions have never been seriously tried. Instead, young men die in battle and whole economies are ruined in nations that have won empty victories at the end of a long run, but in the short run balance sheets are in balance.

The United Nations and Indonesia

In spite of its weakness after World War II, when it was a completely occupied nation, the Netherlands spent four years of diplomatic maneuvers and a dogged military effort to regain control of the Dutch East Indies.[3] Pressure from the United Nations, fueled by the Truman administration, forced the Dutch to relinquish their tenacious effort to resume their colonial control. The American position was forthright. Senator Brewster and Senator Vandenberg offered amendments to the Economic Cooperation Administration Bill (the Marshall Plan), which would cut off all funds from any government failing to comply with the Security Council's request until the ECA administrator was "advised in writing by the President of the Security Council that such compliance had been effected."[4] The Dutch government got the point.

Professor van den Haag has arrived at a contrary view of this generally forgotten episode, but I don't know of any historians who will agree with him. Once again, he is content to assert the validity of his interpretation of events by virtue of his own assumed infallibility.

Rescuing Conor Cruise O'Brien

Until Dr. van den Haag called attention to Dr. O'Brien's "admitted" lies, I had not been aware of the mendacity that so shocked my opponent. He has referred us to O'Brien's report on his experiences in Katanga in 1961, *To Katanga and Back.*[5] It is a harrowing account of the experiences of an Irish civil servant plunged into the chaotic decolonization of the Belgian Congo. The United Nations had taken the firm position that that unusually oppressed colony should not be dismembered. The Belgian interest was in preserving its Union Minière de Haut-Katanga, a lucrative copper-mining corporation situated in the province of Katanga, the mainstay of the Congolese economy. To do so, the Belgians had supported Moïse Tshombe, a son-in-law of the paramount chief of the dominant Lunda tribe, as provincial president with a view to claiming its complete independence from the rest of the Congo. In July 1960, the Congo army mutinied and Tshombe declared that Katanga was an independent state.[6] A Katangan army was put together, consisting of Belgian regular army officers, several hundred foreign mercenaries recruited by the Tshombe government, and Katangan foot-soldiers. The main support of the central Congolese government at Leopoldville (now Kinshasa) was the United Nations expeditionary force consisting of Swedish, Irish, Indian, and Sudanese troops rapidly assembled by the secretary-general.[7]

Regardless of the Katangan situation, the anarchic condition in this newly liberated colony required the introduction of foreign troops. In spite of the desperate effort of the Belgian government to detach Katanga from the rest of the new nation, it was seen by other African governments and by the Third World in general as an effort to maintain Belgian authority through a puppet government. The Soviet Union saw an opportunity to ingratiate itself with the decolonizing world and sanctimoniously supported the main Congolese government, then led by Patrice Lumumba, its prime minister.

O'Brien was seconded from the Irish foreign service in May 1961 at the request of Secretary-General Hammarskjöld and detailed to Elisabethville to perform a mission that he understood to be "to see to the implementation of the resolution of the Security Council, and specifically of the resolution of February 21st [1961], which called for the immediate withdrawal and evacuation of all foreign military and para-military personnel, including mercenaries and foreign political advisers."[8] His performance of this obviously difficult—if not impossible—mission was complicated by the implacable hostility of the Belgians, the British, and the French. Urquhart relates in his biography of Hammarskjöld that "whenever he seemed to be making progress, he had been frustrated by the intrigues of Tshombe, Munongo [Tshombe's "minister of the interior"], the European consuls, and the mercenaries, while the European population held him up to Western press correspondents as an object of execration and the author of all misfortune."[9]

By September O'Brien believed he had a plan with some chance of success to terminate the Katangan secession without bloodshed. He rounded up the principal members of the Tshombe government, with the exception of Tshombe himself, and informed Hammarskjöld and his staff that the operation had succeeded and the secession was at an end.

It wasn't. Fighting broke out between the Katangan and the United Nations troops. O'Brien had made two mistakes. He had wrongly said that the secession was at an end, and he had been imprudent in the use of the word *secession*. He was recalled to New York and arrangements were made for him to return to the Irish foreign service.

Dr. van den Haag seems to have made at least two misinterpretations of the extraordinarily confusing history of the United Nations intervention in the Congo. First, he implies that had the United Nations not intervened, there would have been only one armed faction in the Congo. In a sense that's true, but it was a faction that was devoted to preserving as far as possible the valuable section of the Congo economy for the benefit of Belgian, British, and French investors. It was not interested in the rest of the Congo, which, so far as Tshombe and his sponsors were concerned, was a foreign country. There was a Congolese army, of sorts, which was incapable of dealing with the Katangan forces led by professional officers.

ONUC[10] had been sent there under a unanimous resolution of the Security Council that the United Kingdom or France could have vetoed but did not. Its purpose was to maintain law and order until the fledgling government of the new nation could get on its feet.

The second misinterpretation is that Dr. O'Brien lied. In his book he expresses his embarrassment:

> ...at a Press conference...someone raised the question of what I had said on September 13th. I gave an answer based on what I had said, but with some fine-spun legalistic qualifications....
> ...Mr. Latz...kept a laundry in Elisabethville, and was a part-time correspondent for the Associated Press.... He was, of course, hostile to the UN.

> He had been at my earliest Press conferences during the fight-
> ing...and when I had finished this rather carefully worded exposi-
> tion, he shook his head. "That," said he, "is not what you said."
>   ...Mr. Latz had over me at that moment the immense moral
> authority of the man who is telling the truth over the man who is
> dodging it.

There is the lie and the admission. If Dr. van den Haag really believes that Dr. O'Brien can never again be trusted because of this incident, his standards for the probity of others are such that scarcely any man or woman in public life today could escape his denunciation. O'Brien's is the rare case of the public servant who has admitted his fault. I cannot bring myself to censure his conduct so severely on the facts that I have been able to ferret out. Dr. van den Haag seems to be made of sterner stuff.

As for the atrocities that Dr. van den Haag witnessed and photographed, I must respond that I was not there. However, when men take up arms against each other terrible things happen. My opponent does not tell us what he was doing in the Congo, under whose auspices, and where. His pictures, which I have not seen, seem to have been taken from one side of the lines. While the United Nations troops were certainly rough at times, the Katangan side was certainly not an immaculately scrupulous soldiery. Brian Urquhart, who succeeded O'Brien, was nearly beaten to death by Katangan commandos.[11]

The Congo imbroglio was a messy affair that did not end with the tragic death of Hammarskjöld. Mistakes were made by everyone involved and the country continued in a chaotic condition for nearly two years after that mysterious event. Dr. van den Haag complains that the outcome has been the inept and cruel dictatorship of Mobutu Sese Seko. That was about what had to be expected as the aftermath of the Belgian version of colonialism, one of the most cruel, greedy, and exploitative imperial governments ever to impose itself on an African people. The exposure of the conditions created by Léopold II shocked the world, requiring that control of the colony be transferred from his personal administration to the Belgian government in the early years of this century. Although that adjustment improved the situation and ended some of the abuses of the native population, the government itself was centralized in Brussels. There were no elections, no Congolese civil service, no Congolese with administrative experience. There was no chance for any Congolese to acquire any political experience. It is little wonder that the nation of Zaire got off to a rocky start. Would Professor van den Haag prefer that the Belgians continued their oppressive control?

Inevitable but Undesirable

Now and then my opponent and I find a point, or part of a point, on which we can agree. I think the course of history can be changed so that war will not be inevitable, and that the United Nations is one of the vehicles for that change. Professor van den Haag will not accept that position; let's arm to the teeth and keep those silos filled. Nevertheless, he concedes that war is "supremely undesirable and harmful," but perhaps less undesirable and harmful than in former years. I can at least agree that war is undesirable, "supremely" so, and whether it is more or less undesirable than in years past hardly seems to be a question worth exploring.

What gives me a little encouragement is the change in attitude toward military glory. One of our most popular presidents was Theodore Roosevelt, a fundamentally decent and intelligent man who did many good things for our country. Yet here was a great national leader who yearned for war and bitterly regretted that it fell to Woodrow Wilson to lead the United States into World War I. He could exult when American soldiers reached the trenches in the spring of 1918: "They are the men who have paid with their bodies for their soul's desire. Let no one pity them, whatever their fate, for they have seen the mighty days and risen level to the need of mighty days."[12]

He brooded over the absence of great events during his presidency which, he thought, kept him from attaining the heroic stature of Washington or Lincoln. Those were simpler days, and the unthinking naiveté of one of the more remarkable men of his times had not been affected by the succession of terrible wars that have bloodied the rest of this century. Not many contemporary Americans or Western Europeans yearn for heroism and glory in combat. The Japanese, once one of the most martial of peoples, have decided that they no longer want to die for their emperor or seek heroism in a "Co-Prosperity Sphere." Few men and women nowadays will accept the belief held by so many of our own forefathers that war was essential to the moral discipline of a nation. Theodore Roosevelt could say, "This country needs a war," a statement that no present-day politician would care to make, even if he thought it.[13]

The nightmare of war still goes on, but as never before in history there is a growing consensus among civilized nations that the nightmare must come to an end. We can rouse ourselves from the horrors that convince my friend that some conflicts can only be resolved in blood, or we can direct our policy toward the attainment of lasting peace. It will be a long time before the world can be sure that the scourge of war has been finally put aside. There will be brush-fire wars, border skirmishes, and atavistic predation for many years to come. But if the United Nations can prevent a few of these murderous occasions, as it can if it is put to the use for which it was intended, our investment of faith, goodwill, and a little money will have been well rewarded.

If we believe in war, we will certainly get it. If we believe in peace, we *may* begin a process that will get us there, perhaps in my grandchildren's time. It's worth the difficult effort.

Notes

1. Mikhail Sergeyevich Gorbachev, *Political Report of the CPSU Central Committee to the 27th Congress of the Communist Party of the Soviet Union*, February 25, 1986 (Moscow: Novosti Press Agency Publishing House, 1986), p. 4.
2. My use of this word seems to upset my opponent. For the benefit of his vocabulary: "*Wit* 1. The seat of consciousness or thought, the mind. 2. The faculty of thinking and reasoning in general; mental capacity, intellect, reason" (*Shorter Oxford English Dictionary*). I do not mean that Mr. Gorbachev is in any way an amusing man.

3. At the time of the transfer of power from the Dutch government to the new Indonesian Republic, the Netherlands was maintaining an army of 80,000 home troops and 65,000 indigenous troops, mostly Indonesian. Alistair M. Taylor, *Indonesian Independence and the United Nations* (London: Stevens, 1960), p. 413.
4. Ibid., pp. 211–212.
5. London: Hutchinson, 1962.
6. No nation, not even Belgium, recognized the independence of Katanga.
7. For a more detached and briefer account of the intricate situation in the Congo, see Andrew Boyd, *United Nations: Piety, Truth, and Myth* (London: Penguin Books, 1964), pp. 121–159. For all the details, see Brian Urquhart, *Hammarskjöld* (New York: Harper & Row, 1984), pp. 389–515, 545–597.
8. O'Brien, note 5, p. 347.
9. Urquhart, p. 567.
10. *Opération des Nations Unies au Congo.*
11. For an eye-witness account, see O'Brien, note 5, pp. 320–326.
12. Quoted in John Milton Cooper, *The Warrior and the Priest* (Cambridge: Harvard University Press, 1983), pp. 327–328.
13. Ibid., p. 36.

ERNEST VAN DEN HAAG

Professor Conrad will not "resign himself" to what I regard as inevitable. He may not resign himself to death either, and this is nice, if a little foolish and totally irrelevant to the issue I addressed of whether death and war are unavoidable. I don't think either will be postponed, let alone avoided, by Mr. Conrad's romantic defiance. Which brings us to the U.N. Mr. Conrad asseverates, over and over, that he thinks the U.N. is wonderful. I don't doubt that he thinks so. I don't doubt either that the U.N. is quite useless in international relations of any sort and that Conrad's illusions about it are quite dangerous.

About the International Monetary Fund and the help it extends to Eastern Europe, Conrad feels that somehow help will lead to a liberalization of these Communist dictatorships and to a weakening that will increase our influence. He presents no evidence. There isn't any. Nor is there any logic to the belief. Dictatorships do better in a prosperous country. Finally, Conrad believes that if we don't help the Soviet Union it will act worse domestically and internationally. There is no evidence for this either and Conrad does not attempt to present any. No need therefore to respond. But the whole thing strikes me as too absurd to let go. It is like saying that if we were to pay a subsidy to criminals they would stop committing crimes. No evidence for this, although we have tried it in some ways (unsuccessfully). No subsidy is known to be high enough to change the behavior of criminals or of the Soviet Union.

It's nice of Mr. Conrad to tell the Soviet Union what is in its own interest. For all I know he's right. But he's not in power, and what may be in the interest of the country may not be in the interest of the leaders.

Conrad doesn't see the expansionary aims of the Soviet Union as "an immediate threat to peace." Apparently he has not heard about Afghanistan, Nicaragua, Angola, etc. I guess he won't be satisfied until we are directly attacked. We will not be, because we are stronger than Afghanistan.

In a footnote Conrad explains why he attributes "wit" to Mr. Gorbachev. Using the *Oxford English Dictionary* he defines wit as intelligence. I think it's better to say intelligence when that's what you mean. Wit, in American usage, is not quite the same as intelligence. I would call Mr. Conrad intelligent. I'm not at all that sure about his wit. Moreover, we know that Gorbachev must have cunning, as Stalin did. We know nothing about his intelligence, let alone wit. (Conrad does not disclose his sources.)

About sanctions Mr. Conrad has his usual illusions, and I'm getting tired of trying to take them away from him. It is quite unsupportable to believe as he does that Western sanctions against Poland had anything to do with the course the Polish government adopted. It was determined on the one hand by the Soviet Union and on the other by Polish popular resistance, organized largely by the Catholic Church in that country. I wish sanctions could be effective instead of being empty gestures. Life would be easier.

On Conor Cruise O'Brien *res ipsa loquitur*. I don't think he makes a good witness for Mr. Conrad. If Conrad thinks otherwise, let it be.

I think I know a little bit more about the Congo,* having been there and studied the matter, than Mr. Conrad does, but the U.N. war in the Congo is so marginal to our debate that I will forego correcting Mr. Conrad's clichés on the matter.

JOHN P. CONRAD

In the eight paragraphs of his final reply, Professor van den Haag has set up some irresistible targets. I hope our readers will bear with me while I take careful aim and fire. There are too many sitting ducks out there, and I won't have the space to shoot them all down. I'll leave some for the reader's marksmanship.

1. *The Obsessive Analogy:* The professor is set in his ideas, firmly committed to the notion that death is the supreme example of inevitability. I don't suppose that anyone can convince him that the analogy between war and death is false. Death is our common destiny. No one can avoid it. Throughout history, many people in many countries have been fortunate enough to escape the curse of war. As I said in my earlier statement, I can contemplate the prospect of my own death with equanimity, knowing that I cannot escape it. History and reflection provide ample reason to believe that warfare can become more infrequent and eventually become entirely obsolete. Every possible effort should be made to achieve this state of affairs and hasten its arrival. The support of the United Nations is one such effort. To foster the recognition of the interdependence of all nations is another.

The incantation that death and war are somehow equivalent in their ineluctability is dangerously false. We all must resign ourselves to death and live as well as we can. No one should resign himself to the inevitability of war or any other evil that afflicts humanity. Resignation to the inevitability of violence is the self-fulfilling prophecy that has been too often fulfilled in the past. The

---

*See my article, "War in Katanga," in the March 27, 1962 issue of *National Review.*

analogy between death and war is false, but because superficial minds can swallow it whole, nations have reconciled themselves to the avoidable evil of war.

2. *Prosperous Dictators:* "Dictatorships do better in a prosperous country," pontificates my opponent. Perhaps they do, although I don't think of a really good example. Actually, as Professor van den Haag should know, dictatorships ordinarily depend on maintaining a command economy, never a likely avenue to prosperity.

What is depressingly repetitive in the history of autocracy is the inclination of the autocrat in economic trouble to find an external enemy to whom the attention of his people can be diverted. Mussolini found Ethiopia, Hitler demanded *Lebensraum* as the solution to the intractable problems of the Third Reich, and Tojo convinced the Japanese people that the prosperity that had eluded them would be theirs if the Chinese could be forced to turn over Manchuria and other useful territories. More recently, the Argentine generals hoped to distract their tormented people by mounting a glorious invasion of the Falkland Islands.

Given the commitment of the Communist party to an unworkable economic doctrine, it is unlikely that Russia can improve its economy in the near or middle range of the future. If it deteriorates further, the Politburo and the Red Army may not resist the temptation to resolve the nation's difficulties by a "patriotic war." After the Russian experience in Afghanistan, that decision may be harder to make, but desperation often clouds good judgment.

All that leads to my modest hypothesis that assistance by the International Monetary Fund, if firmly and properly administered, may impose some limits on the aggressive behavior of the Warsaw Pact countries. I can't prove that it will, but it's worth a trial.

After all, Western banks, including some American banks, lend to these nations without the stringent conditions that the IMF has characteristically imposed for many years. Perhaps it's *Schadenfreude* on my part, but I'd like to see how the ministries of finance in the Communist bloc would respond to the intrusiveness of the IMF approach to the resolution of their difficulties.

In this phase of our discussion, my incautious friend tries to set up another analogy—this time between common criminals and the Soviet Union. That won't work, either. Neither thugs nor the Politburo are in the least lovable, but that's as far as a similarity can be carried. Thugs can and should be restrained by the police. The Politburo is restrained by mutual assured destruction and, to some slight extent that any reasonable person would like to see increased, by the necessary interdependence of humanity. In avoiding untenable analogies, a fastidious thinker does not concern himself with the relative wickedness of a Communist leader and a street mugger. They are just different, and the difference is important.

3. *The Expansionary Aims of the Soviet Union:* Nobody, not even Professor van den Haag, and certainly not I, can say for sure what the aims of the Soviet foreign policy really are. I have read Gorbachev's address to the Central Committee of the Communist party. My inference is that Mikhail Sergeyevich is a worried man, and his worries are focused on the internal problems of the country. After the Chernobyl disaster, these anxieties have probably become even more acute—that event throws into stark relief the political, technological, and administrative malfunctions of an inherently defective system of government. I suspect that Gorbachev's reference to the Afghanistan adventure as a wound that must be healed indicates his perception that the Politburo has to cut its losses. A nation that is led by insecure men running a very shaky system cannot easily withdraw from its foreign adventures, especially when its military men have been allowed enormous power. As for Angola and Nicaragua, the Politburo has been very cautious. Its Cuban surrogate can be sent back to Havana without loss of Russian face. Ortega in Nicaragua has been allowed a very short leash. Gorbachev knows that he can annoy the United States by modest shipments to Nicaragua, but I doubt that in his fondest dreams he supposes that Nicaragua can become a Soviet satellite.

4. *The Professor and the Congo:* Let us agree: Dr. van den Haag has been to the Congo and I haven't. He says he knows more about what happened in the early 1960s that I do, but he

doesn't say what he knows that conflicts with the version of the events in Katanga that I extracted from my review of the literature. Having lived in foreign countries myself, I know how easy it is to conclude that one knows more than one really does about an unfamiliar environment, even when nothing special is happening. The complexities that confronted Dr. O'Brien, Mr. Urquhart, and Dr. van den Haag himself would be difficult indeed to sort out in the absence of channels of information that nobody seems to have had.

It's a more relevant matter than it seems to Dr. van den Haag. The United Nations intervened to bring about a regime that would be oriented to the West—to the vast irritation of Nikita Khrushchev—and to suppress the secession of Katanga for the benefit of some European corporate interests. It was a prolonged process. By hindsight we can see that many mistakes were made. From all I have heard, President Mobutu is no bargain, but neither was the Belgian suzerainty. At the present time, Mr. Mobutu's government has had to submit to the tutelage of the IMF. There is a reasonable prospect of responsible government. In Africa, as everywhere else, patience and intelligent consideration of future consequences are usually rewarded.

So much for the targets that Dr. van den Haag has set up for me. It may seem to the reader that we have strayed some distance from the essence of our debate. The abstraction to which I am committed is that in an interdependent world conflicts must be resolved by negotiation. As the human race has struggled up from savagery we have learned to negotiate differences that formerly led to war. We have a lot more to learn, and education of all kinds must be the foundation on which a reliable and lasting peace is built. The topics that Professor van den Haag and I have addressed in this section are germane to the development of a safer world. As nations and their citizens learn that interdependence is the prospect from which no nation can escape, it will be more difficult to delude them into the belief that war is inevitable or even possible. No one on the planet should have to wake up in a cold sweat in the morning, fearful of what terrors and miseries the day will bring.

The nightmare will be over, but the reality of interdependence does not imply an easy world. There is no Utopia ahead for this country or any other. There will be plenty of conflicts, but wise leaders will accustom their peoples to resolving them by negotiation. Pending that access of wisdom, the United Nations is needed so that nations can practice the art of multilateral negotiation and thereby to make possible conditions that remove some of the causes of bitterness and desperation.

ERNEST VAN DEN HAAG

Hitler, Conrad notwithstanding, first made Germany prosperous, then brought war and misery. It was the prosperity he produced (largely through rearmament) that got him the allegiance of the Germans. Conrad's idea that Hitler went to war because of "intractable" domestic problems is a fantasy (incidentally, of Marxist origin: Marxists always have economic explanations) unsupported by evidence—indeed, refuted by it. Nor does Conrad's mechanistic explanation of Japanese imperialism make much sense to non-Leninists. Conrad is probably right on Argentina, although here too I think that he oversimplifies. As for the Soviets, they were least aggressive when they were worst off economically, i.e., up to the Stalin–Hitler pact.

Conrad's method of trying to find out about the aims of Soviet foreign policy by reading Gorbachev's speeches strikes me as bizarre. Does he expect Mr. Gorbachev to announce the actual aims?

JOHN P. CONRAD

Professor van den Haag has a point, but not much of a point. Hitler knew, or should have known, or his banker, Hjalmar Schacht, should have told him, that some day the books would have to be balanced. An economy cannot prosper forever on the manufacture of munitions. The Third Reich was spending far beyond its means on Stukas, U-boats, and Panzer divisions. It was a distortion of Keynesian economics: Government spending stimulated the economy and a false prosperity resulted. I am sure that Hitler's reply to any worried economist brave enough to remonstrate would have been to the effect that spending on the Reichswehr was an investment in future *Lebensraum* for the *Herrenvolk*. (How those repellent words resound in the ears of persons of our age!)

Marxist fantasy, indeed! We are all Marxists if the indelible sign is an economic explanation of political and social events. Professor van den Haag should spend some time in a review of the essays of contemporary conservative economists. As for his inability to find an economic rationale for Japanese imperialism, I will invite him to provide us with an alternative explanation.

Along with better informed observers of the Soviet scene than either of us, I think there is plenty of evidence that General Secretary Gorbachev has a lot to worry about. His speech betrays a great deal of concern about a state of affairs that should cause any responsible Russian much anxiety. He is not informative about the foreign policy aims of the Politburo, but in his speech to the CPSU Central Committee he had a lot to say about the dismal condition of the Russian economy. As any practitioner of military intelligence could tell Dr. van den Haag, the first task in assessing an adversary is to determine his capabilities, which will certainly limit his aims. At this stage of the Russian adventure with Marxism, expansionism makes no sense. That doesn't mean that in changed circumstances the Politburo may move toward aggressive policies. Mrs. Thatcher to the contrary notwithstanding, I do not think we can "'do business,'" in any ordinary sense of the phrase, with the present Russian regime.

I had not intended to continue this exchange so far, but really, one has to bring the professor down from his high horse.

CHAPTER 6

The Veto

ERNEST VAN DEN HAAG

The uselessness of the U.N. having become fairly obvious, those who thought that it would free the world from war look for explanations. The explanation for the uselessness of the League of Nations—that the United States wasn't there—won't wash: This time we joined. The true explanation is not acceptable to U.N. supporters: In a world of sovereign nations, no international organization can prevent war, and in a world divided into two hostile camps led by the United States and the Soviet Union, no organization containing both camps can be united. The true explanation would suggest that the whole enterprise was flawed and condemned to futility *ab initio*. looking for a more inspirational if less realistic explanation, many U.N. supporters have decided that the veto is the fatal flaw. Without it the U.N. could have lived up to the expectations they placed on it.

This is about as far from the truth as one can go. The veto is actually what did and does keep the organization going. The U.N. has not accomplished much besides existing. But without the veto, even its existence could not continue.

The U.N. consists of a General Assembly comprising all member countries. The General Assembly permits members to make speeches at one another and to pass resolutions, to have lunch, and to organize parties for one another. Nothing the

General Assembly does, except the budget it passes, is binding on the members *de jure* or *de facto*. Its impact is purely propagandistic.

The U.N. also has a Security Council with five permanent members (China, Great Britain, France, the United States, and the Soviet Union) and a changing cast of temporary members elected by the General Assembly. The permanent members—and only the permanent members—can each veto any decision of the Security Council they don't like. A vetoed decision is invalidated by the veto.

The Security Council is charged with all matters of peace and war. Since the U.N. was founded by the victorious Allies after World War II, the previously important powers, which were defeated and have since become important once more, were allowed to join only later. They did not become members of the Security Council. Japan and West Germany (East Germany is a Soviet satellite and has no independent power) to this day are not members of the Security Council. Yet either is certainly as important and powerful as France or Great Britain. It makes no difference because, although the Security Council is charged with important matters, it is as impotent as the General Assembly, even if somewhat more representative of the power distribution in the world.

The veto was instituted at the behest of the Soviet Union. It upset American democratic sensibilities. (The Ukraine and Byelorussia were also accepted as independent members of the U.N. to please Stalin, although they are less independent of the Soviet central government than, say, Georgia and Alaska are of the U.S. federal government. Neither Soviet republic has ever been known not to vote with the Soviet Union.) Stalin feared that he would be outvoted in the U.N. Therefore, he wanted the veto to annul any displeasing majority vote. His fears were well founded at first and the Soviet Union used the veto frequently, nullifying decisions of the American-dominated majority. Given the veto, Stalin, in effect, dropped his emphasis on the General Assembly voting power (he had wanted at first all Soviet republics to have a vote) since he realized that General Assembly votes were irrelevant to foreign policy. But in a sense his original insistence underlines the lack of realism in the U.N. structure. How can questions be decided by a majority vote when the answers must depend either on power or on principle? Neither has anything to do with majority votes. And in the Assembly votes each country counts equally, regardless of population, strength, culture. Thus, Albania or the Seychelles have as much voting power as the United States or China.

Only in one case did the veto not prevent an important Security Council decision. It was a freak case worth recounting because it illustrates the futility of the U.N. with and without the veto. When Communist North Korea invaded pro-American South Korea and the United States decided to come to its aid, we decided to do so under the U.N. banner. We proposed resolutions in the Security Council branding North Korea as an aggressor and inviting members to help South Korea to resist. They were passed. The Soviet Union could have vetoed them, but was engaged in a six-month boycott of Security Council sessions because of the failure of the Council to allow the People's Republic of China to occupy the Chinese seat. In the absence of the Soviet Union, the Council, on June 27, 1950, declared North Korea to have invaded South Korea and authorized U.N. action. Hence, the U.S. effort in Korea was officially a U.N. effort. It was carried on in the main by U.S. and South Korean military forces aided by small Turkish, British, and other contingents. These U.S. allies might have helped with, or without, U.N. resolutions, and, although welcome, their aid was not essential. Despite the Security Council resolutions, the Soviet Union not only refused to help but supported the North Koreans. Essentially, the Korean War was fought by the same protagonists and antagonists in the same manner in which it would have been fought had the Soviet Union vetoed the Security Council decisions—indeed, in the same manner in which it would have been fought had the U.N. never existed.

After the Second World War decolonization proceeded at a rapid pace. India and Pakistan became independent nations. Many other nations in the Pacific, in Africa, in the Caribbean, in the

Near East, and all over the world became sovereign and were accepted as members of the U.N. Their independence was ideologically and financially supported by the United States. But most of the leaders of the new nations found democracy uncongenial and preferred to run their countries dictatorially, while engaging in semi-Marxist experiments, although still largely supported by the Western powers. These leaders had absorbed notions of nationalism, antiimperialism, and anticapitalism in the academic institutions of the West in which they had been educated.

Soon the U.N. had a fervent anti-American majority. Many undeveloped nations discovered that they could vote with the Soviet bloc and against the United States without jeopardizing the generous help they received from the United States.* They did so enthusiastically. It is always fun to bite the hand that feeds you (one resents being dependent on handouts). If one can do so without risking anything, why not? Fortunately, all the voting did not matter except for propaganda purposes.

Since the United States will now be in the minority, it may have to make use of the veto as the Soviet Union did before. Since our government is less realistic than the Soviet government, it is harder for us to do without concensus, but we may finally learn not to be afraid of going against the views and votes of the government of Uganda.

Does the veto make a difference? It is indispensable for the continued existence of the U.N. But since that organization makes no difference, except to diplomats, hotel owners, and newspaper reporters, one may conclude that there is no difference. If, however, one wishes the U.N. to continue—I guess it makes John Conrad sleep better at night—the veto is indispensable. Suppose the Security Council makes a decision that the Soviet Union considers contrary to its important interest. If it could not veto it, it could only leave the U.N. (or boycott it, as it has done several times). With the veto, the decision it opposes is invalidated. Even

---

*No reasonable description of the behavior of our policy makers would fit into a book that may fall into the hands of minors. Hence, none is attempted here.

when decisions were made that the Soviet Union did not like but could not prevent—e.g., to financially support "peacekeeping forces" hired by the U.N. in the Near East—the Soviet Union simply refused to pay its share. Who is going to force it? The same is true for the United States. It can veto instead of leaving. Thus, the veto assures the continuance of the U.N. organization by assuring its impotence. Without it, the U.N. might act contrary to the interests of either superpower, and would immediately fall apart. Thus, the veto is essential to the permanent bureaucracy of the U.N. It guarantees its livelihood. It is not important to anyone else, any more than the U.N. is.

JOHN P. CONRAD

In this trenchant analysis of the veto powers of the permanent members of the Security Council, Professor van den Haag has traveled straight to the heart of a fundamental issue. He follows a well-trodden path—he is far from the first to perceive that the survival of the United Nations depends on the veto. Indeed, I have yet to discover a supporter of the United Nations who fancies that the veto could be deleted from the Charter. Some day it may fall into disuse, but not soon.

Practical optimists can afford to entertain illusions even less than tough-minded pessimists. We build on small victories for international reasonableness, preferring the realization of some of our hopes to the helpless contemplation of the catastrophes that my stoical friend considers inevitable. We know that in a world in which power is distributed so unequally, hegemony will be claimed and maintained by the nations with the largest economies and the most nuclear warheads. With or without the United Nations, the rival hegemonies of the two superpowers would be the basic elements of international diplomacy.

That being the case, the hand raised in dissent from a proposed Security Council resolution must be explained and is open to challenge. The permanent representatives of the United States and the USSR know this and so do the governments that send them. Our government has apparently decided to refrain from exercising its veto with respect to resolutions having to do with apartheid in South Africa; nothing we can say in explanation will expunge the negative effect of a veto on the rest of that unhappy continent. The USSR, which in the past has vetoed resolutions on terrorism, has decided that it gains nothing in world opinion by its acceptance of terror as the right of lesser powers to impose their will on greater powers. In addition, of course, Soviet emissaries to the Middle East have recently been found to be fair game by Arab fanatics.[1]

We will continue to have the veto, and the veto will have the practical effect of assuring that the Security Council cannot impose its will on its permanent members. There is, however, an escape from the veto, the "Uniting for Peace Resolution," designed by that ingenious secretary of state, Dean Acheson.[2] Under the provisions of that procedural circumvention of the Charter, when the Security Council fails to act on a threat to the peace, the General Assembly may "unite" to consider collective measures—including armed force—to "restore international peace and security." This resolution was adopted at the time of the Korean "police action"[3] in 1950 and was used again during the Suez crisis when the United Kingdom and France jointly vetoed Security Council actions calling for withdrawal of their forces from Egypt. Where there's a will a way can be found. The world's misfortune in these uneasy years is that the will is lacking.

We can see how the lack of will protracts the Iran–Iraq war into a distant future when it may well be that the youth of both nations will have been entirely wasted. The secretary-general can and does negotiate with both sides, aiming toward the achievement of a peace that neither side can bring itself to accept. That is all the secretary-general, acting for the United Nations, can do. Resolutions calling for a cease-fire can be passed by the Security Council and the General Assembly and will be ignored as so much wind from a distant shore. The collective will of the international community represented in these bodies is neither firm enough nor close enough to a consensus to take the obvious actions prescribed in the Charter: economic and political sanctions and, if the sanctions are not enough, the dispatch of armed forces under the provisions of Articles 41 and 42.

Why? Not because the apparatus for ending the war is not on hand in the United Nations Charter and its organized political agencies. We have to account for the lack of will. For some nations, this war to mutual extermination may be politically convenient. For others, there's good business in the sale of arms to both sides. For still others, it's a matter of indifference—who really cares about these distant peoples and their bloody quarrels? For all these interests and noninterests, a spurious claim to tough-minded pragmatism justifies doing nothing, aside from drafting resounding statements for the Security Council to pass as resolutions. Pragmatism is invoked by cynics who insist that sanctions never work. If they are voted anyway, these cynics will be in the forefront of those who will see to it that they are violated.

It is not the United Nations that is useless and ineffective. It is the international family of quarreling nations, which will not use the principal tools available to assure peace and prevent war. Ours is an age in which international anarchy survives. The United Nations is an attempt to bring order into a world that has drifted too often into disaster. To dismantle it on account of its failures could not possibly lead to a more peaceable community of nations.

The apparatus of the Security Council is there to be used by nations that desire peace and prefer negotiation to threats and ultimatums. The veto has little or nothing to do with the futility of a Security Council resolution. Professor van den Haag should explain the failure of will and nerve by the nations represented there.

On Anti-Americanism in the Third World

In passing, Dr. van den Haag voices a peculiar explanation of the anti-Western behavior that he ascribes to the leaders of the new nations released from colonial status under the auspices of the United Nations. These leaders, he says, came to their misguided notions under the influence of "the academic institutions of the West in which they had been educated."

This is as good a place as any to dispose of this simplistic argument, so appealing to antiintellectual conservatives in the United States. I have never understood why Dr. van den Haag, an exemplary product of these same academic institutions, so firmly believes that they are the prime source of anticapitalist iniquity. They are not, and no serious observer of Third World politics can entertain so naive an explanation. Is it really to be supposed that an African or Asian politician can honestly accept American capitalism as a way of life for a nation that has practically no capital at all—simply because the United States furnishes his military with rifles, artillery, and a few fighter aircraft?

Why is the feeding hand so often bitten? There are three reasons that carry a lot more weight than the influence of radical professors at universities in London or New York. First, we have to recognize the painful and inevitable resentment of the poor for the rich, the small for the large, the powerless for the powerful. When the United States sets itself up or is thought to set itself up as the arbiter of political and economic wisdom, it is not surprising that smaller nations try to demonstrate their independence of this mighty arbiter. Sometimes these demonstrations will be obviously foolish and contrary to their own interests, especially when such nations are represented by diplomats with little or no experience of international give and take.

Second, and much more substantive, the Third World nations are economically disadvantaged and many do not see how free-market capitalism can be a realistic way out of their predicament. Throughout the 1970s, the consensus of Third World diplomacy was that the United Nations should commit itself to the creation of a New International Economic Order.[4] While this consensus has gradually disintegrated, partly because of the vigorous objections of the developed countries, there continues to be a general belief that the Third World countries should have a better share of the global economy than they now enjoy. For those countries that depend on the export of raw materials for survival, the fluctuations of earnings are a distressing affliction that must be remedied. That many of them are former colonies that have been exploited by their northern masters adds to a sense of grievance and alienation that no amount of foreign aid will assuage.

Third, the governing elites need scapegoats. Poverty, hardship, and sometimes starvation are the lot of the peoples they must govern. It is convenient for Third World politicians to fix blame on rich European and North American nations for conditions that they cannot possibly remedy. Legitimacy must be maintained by whatever means are at hand; an explanation that American interests or multinational firms are the cause of impoverishment of newly liberated peoples is mostly untrue, but all too understandable.[5]

I share Dr. van den Haag's distress about the anti-Americanism that is so often evident in the deliberations of the various bodies of the United Nations. I do not have the illusion that anti-Americanism is a phenomenon that would somehow vanish if the United Nations disappeared into the sunset, as one of our representatives so tactfully suggested. The reality of American unpopularity in the Third World may not be erased by any measures our government can take, but at least we could avoid making matters worse. For years our geopoliticians have taken the stand that at all costs the Republic of South Africa must have our undeviating support. We have adopted a policy of "constructive engagement," we have obstructed Security Council resolutions condemning apartheid and calling for sanctions, and we have affirmed an alliance with that otherwise isolated nation. Is it any wonder that the African nations are less than appreciative of what little we have managed to do for them?

In the Middle East our policy toward the contending interests has been less than even-handed in spite of claims to the contrary. No one knows a way out of the labyrinth of lethal hostilities that pushes young men into madness in that part of the world. But our government could be much more insistent on negotiations than it has been throughout all these terrible years. Arab hostility takes forms that are impossible to accept. Terrorism arising from a sense of impotence is still terrorism. If we persist in the search for a *modus vivendi* in the Middle East, we may some day achieve it and the Arab world will be less vociferous in its denunciations of our iniquities.

Not even its most zealous advocates claim that the United Nations can be the panacea for all the problems of a troubled world. Not all the diplomacy that this world needs can be carried out on the banks of the East River. There will always be a vital role for the quiet diplomats to play in bilateral negotiations. What our nostalgic conservatives fail to understand is that as the world shrinks into a global village there are some issues that are too large to handle in polite negotiations between a foreign minister and an ambassador. The United Nations exists to open discourse on the great issues of the times to all nations that are concerned with conflict and its resolution.

Notes

1. General Secretary Gorbachev made the Soviet policy on this issue quite explicit in his opening speech before the 27th Congress of the Communist Party, in which he denounced "the hideous face of terrorism which its instigators try to mask with all sorts of cynical inventions. The USSR rejects terrorism in principle and is prepared to cooperate actively with other states in order to uproot it." Mikhail Gorbachev, *Political Report of the CPSU Central Committee in the 27th Party Congress* (Moscow: Novosti Press Agency Publishing House, 1986), p. 87.
2. General Assembly Resolution, 377 A, 3 November 1950. See Chapter 2, p. 64 for further discussion.
3. As it was referred to at the time, at first hopefully, then sardonically.
4. In 1974–1975, the General Assembly passed "A Declaration and Program of Action on the Establishment of a New International Economic Order," and a "Charter of Economic Rights and Duties of States." The context of the times is often forgotten. In 1973 the Organization of Petroleum Exporting Countries (OPEC) was formed and almost immediately the price of petroleum rose vertiginously. What was a serious problem, now half forgotten, for the industrialized economies was and still is desperate for the developing countries.
5. For a more complete discussion of the sources of Third World political positions, see Edward Luck and Peter Fromuth, "Anti-Americanism at the United Nations: Perception or Reality?" in *Anti-Americanism in the Third World: Implications for U. S. Foreign Policy*, ed. Alvin Z. Rubinstein and Donald E. Smith (New York: Praeger, 1985), pp. 219–248.

ERNEST VAN DEN HAAG

John Conrad has granted my first point—that the U.N. would fall apart without the veto, which prevents it from taking action against any major power or its allies (all of whom are U.N. members). This implies my second principal point: The U.N. can do nothing about restraining any major power or its allies from war. It is useless in preserving peace (John Conrad does not grant this consequence).

Still, I think it interesting to take up some of Conrad's *obiter scripta*. Throughout, Conrad deals with "the rival hegemonies of the two superpowers" with "the largest economies and the most nuclear warheads." He means the United States and the Soviet Union, as though they are not only rival powers but also morally equivalent and equally likely to be actual peace breakers. This reminds me of Abraham Lincoln's tale of a woman who, seeing her husband struggle with a bear, shouted, "Go to it, husband. Go to it, bear!" Since I know Conrad not to be pro-Communist, I think he simply confused objectivity and neutrality. The former is, the latter is not required in any analysis of foreign policy affairs. Yes, we are both superpowers. But in every other respect the United States differs from the Soviet Union. We are for freedom at home and abroad. Our government depends on the consent of the governed. The Soviet Union has a despotic government that does not depend on the consent of the governed. It opposes freedom at home and everywhere. Where it has power, it imposes strict censorship on political expression. It sends dissenters to the Gulag, or to psychiatric hospitals, and does not permit its citizens to leave. Why does Mr. Conrad treat the two superpowers as morally equivalent?

And why does Conrad appear to give weight to dubious procedures to circumvent vetoes when he knows as well as I do that, veto or not, the U.N. can do nothing against the will of a major power without simply becoming an old-fashioned military alliance of one group of powers against another (as in the Korean War)—a way of fighting, but not of preventing war? Why does Conrad pretend to believe that France and Britain were stopped from retaking the Suez Canal from Egypt by U.N. resolutions, when they were stopped by Eisenhower's refusal to support them? Why does Conrad dish up the old cliché suggesting that there is "good business in the sale of arms," wherefore wars are stirred up? Might as well say that hamburgers are good business, wherefore eating them is stirred up. The appetite existed before the hamburgers. So does the appetite for arms exist before they are supplied—indeed, that is why they are produced and sold, and why it is profitable to do so.

The U.N. is not an independent organization possessed of authority or power over the member nations, but simply a silly name for all the nations together pretending to do things they have no intention or ability to do. Conrad writes, "It is not the U.N. that is useless and ineffective" but "the international family of quarreling nations," as though they were not the same. A moment's reflection shows that it is silly to pretend that the U.N. has an existence apart from the nations that constitute it. Hence, if the nations quarrel, the U.N. is riven by quarrels about which it can do nothing, for the U.N. *is* the nations.

Sure, Conrad is right that "to dismantle it [the U.N.] could not...lead to a more peaceable community of nations." Dismanteling would make no difference one way or another, with respect to anything except (a) the considerable waste of (mostly our) money, and (b) the illusions dear to Mr. Conrad, and finally (c) the amount of anti-American propaganda produced, which we continue to finance, and also perhaps (d) traffic and spying in New York.

Conrad also writes that "former colonies...have been exploited by their northern masters." This is a canard. Some were indeed oppressed culturally or politically (although most former colonial populations are more oppressed by their own governments now, after independence) but most benefited economically from being colonized. Certainly that was the case for India, Pakistan, Uganda, Ghana. Conrad is right, though, that these countries tend to resent their former masters. Most people cannot forgive help they received. Nor do I believe, as asserted by Conrad, that

"anti-Americanism...would somehow vanish if the U.N. disappeared." But we would stop paying for it—which is enough for
me. Incidentally, Ambassador Lichenstein did not suggest for the
U.N. to "disappear into the sunset" (though it sounds like a fine
idea) but merely for it to leave New York, if, as asserted, New
York was not hospitable enough. Too bad his offer has not been
accepted.

I do not believe that our "unpopularity in the Third World"
should cause our policy makers sleepless nights. Foreign policy is
not a popularity contest, and nations that are powerful and rich are
not likely to be popular.

Nor do I see why we should vote for "sanctions" against
South Africa, which has not invaded and occupied independent nations as the Soviet Union has. We may not like the domestic order. I don't like that of the Soviet Union either. I am not in favor
of "sanctions" against the Soviet Union or South Africa.

JOHN P. CONRAD

Of course I won't grant Professor van den Haag's conclusion
that the United Nations is useless for the preservation of the peace.
Neither the United States nor the USSR has been motivated to
make serious use of the United Nations machinery in recent years,
and the consequences have been awful. On the occasions when the
interests of the two superpowers have converged, the Security
Council has been a useful instrument for creating a world consensus and bringing it to bear on the conflicts that lead to war.
Unfortunately, superpower interests are usually opposed, and a
deadlock takes place in the Security Council.

At this point it will be useful to consider the reasons for superpower dissonance. I hope that my suspicious friend can restrain
his neoconservative intuitions: I do not regard the United States
and the USSR as "moral equivalents." Unlike him, I do believe
that it is a useful exercise to organize our limited knowledge of the
Soviet Union to arrive at a tentative understanding of how that na-

tion has become so obnoxious. The effort requires as much objectivity as one can bring to it. It will not do to throw up one's hands, as van den Haag is so prone to do, and proclaim that the USSR is run by a gang of villains and that is all one needs to know about the dynamics of Kremlin policies.

From the time of the 1917 Russian Revolution, the Soviet leadership has been committed to the threadbare Marxist ideology that holds that a Communist society is the inevitable outcome of history. For true believers certain policy implications inevitably follow. They *know* that the luck of the Russians is that they are the first builders of a socialist state, and hence the objects of the implacable, but logical, enmity of powerful capitalists who see that their interests are threatened by the success of the revolution. It therefore follows that the Soviet state must be strong enough to defend itself and to protect other socialist states from aggression by reactionary forces. The national interest of the Soviet Union is the defense of socialism—and as any military man knows, the best defense is a powerful offensive capability.

The Soviet leadership has been committed to this ideology for nearly 70 years, during which time the course of history has refuted most of the Marxist political dogma. The fidelity of the Communist party, though unrewarded by fulfillment, has ossified Marxist-Leninism. The party's immense power depends on continued and unquestioning acceptance of the pure ideology, whether one privately believes it or not. "Revisionism" is the ultimate heresy; resistance to change has become the test of loyalty. In such a climate, adjustment to events and examined experience is impossible, even within the leadership.

In the beginning, the perceived national interest of the USSR was the protection of socialism at home and its promotion abroad. That is still the perceived interest of this unfortunate but talented nation. The true national interest, of course, is the realization of the vast economic potential of the Russian land and its people. Until the ideology is replaced by liberal pragmatism, the USSR will be at odds not only with the United States but with the rest of the world. Once the ideology has withered away, there is no special reason for conflict between Russia and the United States. Working

together, both within the United Nations and without, the two superpowers could make the prevention of war a realistic goal. The
veto will become obsolete.

Let me anticipate my skeptical friend's derision. The nearly
Utopian state of affairs that I predict will be a long time in
coming—if ever. He may be right, but this is the goal we should
be working toward. In the dire present we live in incessant confrontation. Our best hope is a standoff; our lurking fear is anni-
hilation. The world needs leaders who can help the uneasy Mr.
Gorbachev and his entourage change their perception of the interest of their nation.[1]

On the Merchants of Death

Before World War II some simpleminded idealists supposed
that World War I might never have begun had it not been for the
economic interests of armaments manufacturers and their sinister
sales representatives, typified by the mysterious Sir Basil Za-
haroff. I suppose that my opponent refers to that childish reasoning when he asks about my "dish[ing] up the old cliché" about
good business in the sale of arms.

My hypothesis is intact. There *is* good business in the sale of
arms, and armaments manufacturers are going to resist the imposition of an embargo on such nations as Iraq and Iran and do their
damnedest to evade it if it is imposed. Governments whose trade
balance depends on the export of munitions will faithfully support
the freedom of commerce in Exocet missiles and Mach 2 bombers.
Since the Soviet Union is a major supplier to Iraq and possibly to
Iran, too, it is not likely that the United Nations can block supplies
to either nation. But if the half dozen nations that are significant
producers of munitions could be prevented from satisfying the
appetite of these cruel belligerents for airplanes, missiles, and
tanks that they could not manufacture themselves, that endless war
would have ended long ago.

There is no possible objection to selling hamburgers to people
who like fast foods. I assume that my libertarian opponent will
agree that there are serious objections to opening the free market

for the distribution of heroin to people who want that commodity. And there is at least as serious an objection to supplying offensive munitions to nations that can have no legitimate use for them.

A Moment's Reflection

Professor van den Haag should reflect longer than a dismissive moment; I hope that our readers can give more thought to definitions. The United Nations exists as an instrument, a machinery for the resolution of quarrels between nations. It is a name for that instrument, that machinery; it is not the nations, as Professor van den Haag brashly and carelessly asserts. As I have said before, building on Noel-Baker's metaphor about the spade that does not work,[2] when the United Nations doesn't work, it's because it hasn't been used.

The present drift back into the old way of conducting foreign affairs is alarming. We rattle bombs and missiles instead of sabers; we shout imprecations and denunciations at volumes amplified by media unknown in the nineteenth century. Even our diplomats learn to believe our simplicities. Mutual assured destruction has so far kept us out of a fatal conflict, but the road to reconciliation and assured peace is not in sight. I say that the first steps in that direction must be taken in the United Nations. Does Professor van den Haag have a better idea? Does he even care?

The White Man's Burden

Nothing exemplifies van den Haag's world outlook so starkly as his contention that colonialism was good for the colonies and better than independence can ever be. I might leave it at that; not many readers will agree that we should all resume the "civilizing mission" of the British, French, Dutch, Italian, Belgian, and Portuguese empires. At the risk of restating what should be obvious, I have three points to make.

First, the civilizing mission didn't civilize. Except in India and Pakistan, the imperial masters didn't bother to create administrative cadres capable of government. In every colony the behavior of the imperialists displayed the expectation that the colonial status should be permanent. The assumption on which this expectation was based was the innate inferiority of the "natives." The "civilizing mission" was to help them appreciate the benefits of subordination to their betters, and incidentally to make the most profit out of the mission for the home offices in Europe.

Second, the abuses, incompetence, corruption, and oppression of which some of the governments of liberated colonies were certainly guilty might have been expected. The world economy is still not organized to accommodate the urgent needs of the Third World for equity in trade. It must be added that there has been a lot of foot-dragging by the northern nations with respect to cooperation with such United Nations agencies as UNCTAD, IFAD, and UNIDO. As an American I am embarrassed by the leadership of the Reagan administration in begrudging support for these altruistic initiatives.

Predatory greed thrives in an environment where there is never enough to go around. Monsters like Idi Amin, clowns like the Emperor Bokassa, and compulsive embezzlers like Ferdinand and Imelda Marcos are made possible by the deprivation and misery of the populations they govern.

Third, after shaky starts, many of the new nations are doing rather well. In Africa, Cameroon, the Ivory Coast, and Kenya, for three examples, are paying their way and are competently governed. The growth rate of Botswana exceeds that of the United States and most of the other developed countries. India's economic condition continues to improve, and would improve even more were it not for the endemic religious hostilities—which the British Raj was unable to resolve during its two centuries of domination. Pakistan would be in comparable shape if the unspeakable General Zia could be persuaded to take early retirement.

The days of wine and roses have not yet arrived for the Third World, but enough promising experience has accumulated to reassure my atavistic friend that his disdainful pessimism is unwarranted. The white man's burden can be left to the historians. The rich northern nations now lavish military aid on countries in no need of it. If some of those funds could go for education and economic development, the postcolonial struggle would be an earlier success.

Notes

1. Those who doubt my assessment of the General Secretary's uneasiness should read his address to the CPSU Central Committee. In spite of his seemingly ebullient expectations of a millennium to come, if only some administrative reforms are put into effect, it is apparent that he knows that something is dreadfully wrong and that changes must be made.
2. See Chapter 1, p. 6.

ERNEST VAN DEN HAAG

As Conrad correctly says, knowing that "the USSR is run by a gang of villains" is not all one needs to know. But it is something one should not forget, as Mr. Conrad has a tendency to do.

On the arms business, it is perfectly true that arms merchants are in it for profit just as funeral directors are in their business for a profit. It does not follow that funeral directors cause or contribute to death, however profitable. It is no more true that arms merchants contribute to war, or cause it, as Mr. Conrad seems to suggest.

The war between Iran and Iraq will go on. It has very little to do with arms merchants. Financially solvent nations always can get arms just as financially solvent drinkers always could get liquor, and drinking is not caused by the liquor industry that profits from it. This war, like all wars, is regrettable but there is nothing we can do about it. Certainly there is nothing the U.N. can do about it since it can't do anything about anything. Why does the U.N. exist? To make Conrad sleep better. A sleeping pill may be cheaper and actually less addictive and dangerous.

Conrad says the U.N. is "an instrument, a machinery for the resolution of quarrels between [sic] nations." Sure, that was the purpose, but the instrument doesn't work, the machinery is useless and costly and counterproductive. The machinery does not produce anything. Nothing is remedied by saying that the intentions were good.

Unlike Conrad, I don't believe that "reconciliation" between the Soviet Union and us is any more possible than "reconciliation" between the Nazis and us. But war could have been prevented then, and can be prevented now, if the prospective aggressor learns, or understands, that he has nothing to gain from attack and will be defeated. That is why our armaments may keep the peace. As indicated, the U.N. merely fosters illusions among such people as Mr. Conrad and thereby endangers the peace.

I did not assert, as Conrad suggests, that "colonialism was good for the colonies and better than independence *can ever be*" (italics added). (How could anyone know what will "ever be"?) I did assert that independence has *so far* been worse for the ex-colonies, particularly for the average man in the ex-colonies (not for the leaders), than life under the rule of the colonial power was, at least in the last 25 years. Colonial expansion by European countries began with major atrocities in many cases. But by the time they became independent, the colonies, even the Congo (now Zaire) under Belgian domination, were better off than they have been since, and better off, I'm afraid, than they are likely to be in the near future. This is no justification for colonialism. It is simply a statement of fact, which Mr. Conrad could easily check if he weren't so busy defending the U.N.

I'm not in the least embarrassed, as Conrad is, by our diminishing support for the "altruistic" U.N. initiatives. These initiatives amount to waste and have not helped anyone but U.N. bureaucrats. Charitable activities in famine-stricken and undeveloped countries have preceded the U.N. and are more sensibly undertaken without it. The International Red Cross has a good record. The U.N. does not.

CHAPTER 7

Mischief on the High Seas

ERNEST VAN DEN HAAG

So far I have argued that the U.N., contrary to the views of John Conrad, is not and cannot be of any importance in international relations or in preserving peace. Yet, although unimportant materially, it can do some mischief in morally misleading people and in confusing issues. One clear instance is the scandalous resolution by which the Arab bloc succeeded in getting the U.N. to label Zionism a form of racism.

But the U.N. can do mischief in other less obvious ways. Consider the treaty of the sea elaborated under U.N. auspices in numerous international conferences. The U.S. and Great Britain finally refused to sign it when policy makers realized what the diplomats had wrought. The treaty is an interesting instance of what the U.N. can do to complicate and exacerbate international relations. The treaty consolidates, codifies, and modifies a number of useful customs relating to freedom of the seas, the sovereignty of nations over adjoining bodies of water, transit rights, and other customs.

It is reasonably suspected that the bottom of the sea contains metals that might at some future time be mined, just as oil is now, in areas under the sovereignty of adjoining nations. Some of the recoverable metals (or, for that matter, some oil) may be found in the middle of the Atlantic or Pacific Oceans; therefore, it does not belong to anyone. Many nations not adjoining the oceans decided they want part of the bonanza they envisioned. They suspected that for practical purposes the United States and perhaps a few Western nations would be the only ones capable and willing to mine the ocean bottom, a task that requires technology and capital. Thus, the nations not capable of mining the ocean bottom invented complex regulations to make sure that any mining that would take place would be under the auspices of an international body to be set up. This body would make sure that all nations share in the profits (the expenses and risks were to be left to the nations actually engaged in the operations). The profits would be handed out by the international body as received from the operating corporations. But the ocean bottom would be regarded as the property of all nations. Our diplomats, *mirabile dictu*, thought this a great idea, and we almost signed the document. After all, we were told, the areas are "the common heritage of mankind"; hence, everybody in Uganda, Yemen, or Czechoslovakia should participate in regulating the mining operations and share in the profits.

Nobody—at least nobody in the state department—seemed to ask: Why isn't the North American continent part of "the common heritage of mankind," so that the people of Uganda are entitled to its coal or copper no less than those of America? The answer is, of course, that America belongs to Americans, Russia to Russians, and China to the Chinese because they have effectively occupied these territories. But the oceans, so far, are not occupied by anyone, any more than the air is, or the space surrounding the globe.

By law and custom, that which is *res nullius* (belongs to no one) belongs to him who effectively takes possession of it. Thus, game in an unowned (public) forest belongs to the hunter who effectively catches or kills it—not to a nonhunter who claims it is the common heritage of mankind and that he is a coheir.

There are qualifications to the notion that property rights belong to the user of *res nullius*. The right of passage through the oceans belongs to all. It is nonexclusive. But surely, Switzerland, which is not located on any body of water and has no fleet, cannot claim a right to get some of the profit seafaring nations make. Yet, once labeled as part of the common heritage of mankind, the oceans would belong to the Swiss no less than to the English, and they could claim a share of the profit made by using them. Fish now caught in the ocean are owned and utilized by those who do the fishing. Should they give part of their catch to the Swiss or to all nonfishing nations?

Obviously, if the oceans are mined, the metals recovered in the areas not claimed by adjoining nations belong to those who do the mining. The abortive treaty of the sea was just a rather clumsy attempt—not clumsy enough, though, to allow our state department to understand what was happening—by faraway undeveloped nations to profit from the efforts of the more developed ones. But even the attempt would have been inconceivable without the U.N., which tried to get the treaty of the sea accepted.

Consider another case currently still active. Antarctica is one of the few land masses not claimed by any one nation. It too may hold metals, coal, oil, and other resources that at some future time could be mined. To avoid a destructive rivalry, and to make sure that no nation will act in ways destructive to the environment, the nations adjacent to Antarctica—the Soviet Union, the United States, Argentina, New Zealand, Australia, Chile, South Africa, et al.—negotiated a treaty to protect both the environment and one another's rights to future mining activities. It was one of the rare successful diplomatic negotiations. It produced equitable results and avoided strife. However, some countries, not located near Antarctica or ever having participated in the difficult and costly exploration of that continent, decided to put in a claim. Thus, a new conflict arose that could never have arisen except for the convenient forum offered by the U.N. and for the notions invented in and for it.

The claim by Malaysia et al. now is working its way through U.N. committees. It may well be supported by the General Assembly, which usually supports silly claims. It will get nowhere in the end since the U.N. cannot compel anyone to go out of Antarctica or submit to regulation or share profits. (Who knows, the

U.N. could try to finance a Malaysian expedition into that continent—good luck. It does not seem likely though.)

The Malaysian claim is of course a direct offspring of the "common heritage of mankind" concept, according to which anything not yet fully done, or possessed by any one nation, must be shared by all nations, regardless of interests, capacities, propinquities, etc. This concept, apart from being inconsistent with all legal customs and traditions, and totally impractical, is also, fortunately, unenforceable. Remarkably—or perhaps not so remarkably—the U.S. state department fell for it. Although there is no reason to believe that anything will come of it, it is an opportunity for mischief and the U.N. seized it and made the most of it.

JOHN P. CONRAD

Professor van den Haag finds mischief where I find embarrassment. His case against the Law of the Sea[1] can hardly please anyone other than the few American corporations interested in the money to be made out of Davy Jones's locker. Naturally, such adventurous entrepreneurs want to make the most they can out of their operations with the fewest possible responsibilities to others. What could be more attractive than a site in which there are no restrictions as to what can be done to the environment, no limits on the areas to be explored, and no obligations to any governmental agency other than the long arm of the Internal Revenue Service? True, there will be technical difficulties that few corporations will be equipped to surmount, but ingenuity, supported by adequate cash, can always be counted on to do the apparently impossible.

Unfortunately for pioneering entrepreneurs and for my opponent's case as well, the mineral wealth at the bottom of the sea will not be worth the effort for many years to come. What can be dredged up from the bottom of the ocean can be much more cheaply produced in mines more conveniently situated on the earth's surface. It will be many years, at least 10 and perhaps as many as

50, before the nodules of manganese and copper on the seabed can be profitably mined.[2]

Let us see what "mischief" the Law of the Sea would do to the Yankee entrepreneur, bearing in mind that the commercial aspects will be entirely theoretical for many years to come. Professor van den Haag's account of this United Nations project is a little cursory. I think most of our readers will want more information before making up their minds about this complex and multilateral treaty.

The long story began in 1967 when the General Assembly adopted a resolution introduced by the government of Malta calling for the reservation of the ocean floor for peaceful purposes and the use of its resources for common benefit of mankind.[3] There followed more resolutions by the General Assembly, which we won't need to include in this summary, and eventually the organization of a United Nations Conference on The Law of the Sea. Its first meeting was convened by the secretary-general on December 3, 1973, and annual sessions were held until December 10, 1982, when 119 nations signed the convention, and one, Fiji, immediately ratified it.[4]

Now for the mischief. The Law of the Sea contains 17 parts and nine annexes, governing the following concerns: the limits of national jurisdiction over ocean space, access to the seas, navigation, protection and preservation of the marine environment, exploitation of living resources and conservation, scientific research, seabed mining and other exploitation of nonliving resources, and the settlement of disputes.

The Law of the Sea incorporates the international law as it has been observed for generations with regard to the freedom of navigation on the high seas and rules of the road, making some significant changes. The traditional 12-mile limit for territorial jurisdiction is continued in the statute, but provision is also made to extend that limit to 200 miles as an "exclusive economic zone" for the benefit of coastal states wishing to regulate fisheries and other oceanic resources. Within this fairly broad span of ocean, any state with jurisdiction is free to claim exclusive fishing rights and the rights to exploit mineral and oil deposits. No country claiming this 200-mile jurisdiction may interfere with the freedom of navigation by vessels of any other state within these waters. The concept of the freedom of the seas is further abridged to allow for the enforcement of safety regulations and the prevention of traffic in illegal narcotics. Professor van den Haag does not enter any objection in his opening statement to any of these provisions. His fulminations are aimed at another target.

The real controversy over the Law of the Sea arose from the Reagan administration's opposition to the concept of the "common heritage of mankind" as applied to seabed mining.[5] Because of this provision, the president has steadfastly refused to refer this treaty to the Senate for ratification. The United States has chosen to support Yankee enterprise wherever it may go, regardless of opinion in the rest of the world. Thus, we oppose a complex but essentially fair system of regulation, control, and allocation of profits, which has been introduced so that the benefits of the ocean floor, over which no nation can claim sovereignty, may be equitably divided among the peoples living together on this globe. Nothing in the Law of the Sea will deprive the entrepreneur of the costs of his investment or a reasonable profit thereon.

The Law of the Sea provides that in the vast oceanic domain beyond any nation's 200-mile exclusive economic zone the United Nations shall establish an International Sea-Bed Authority, open to membership by all nations. In the familiar United Nations organizational pattern, the authority will have an assembly, comprising representatives of all member states and a council of 36 members,[6] elected by the members of the assembly.

The functions of the authority call for it to regulate the strictly commercial activities taking place on the seabed. It may also set up its own mining operations through a commercial unit to be called The Enterprise. The profits from The Enterprise will be disposed in accordance with rules to be established by the assembly.

The authority will establish rules for the qualification of seabed miners to engage in explorations and extraction of minerals. A fee of $250,000 will be paid by "pioneer" investors when applying for their qualification, and annual payments of $1,000,000 will be made during the period that the exclusive allocation of an area for exploration is in force. Profits over and above these fees, under the law as it now stands, will go to the investor.

Because any commercial enterprise will eventually run into situations in which disputes will arise with other enterprises, the law sets up an International Tribunal for the Law of the Sea with a specialized Sea-Bed Disputes Chamber with exclusive jurisdiction over all disputes involving the International Sea-Bed Areas. This tribunal and its specialized chambers are to have compulsory powers; parties submitting disputes to its judgment are bound to abide by the tribunal's findings.

So what is the American objection that Dr. van den Haag so sternly upholds? He doesn't like international bodies. He doesn't believe that American entrepreneurs should submit to regulation by an international body, probably including representatives from irresponsible Third World nations or, even worse, bureaucrats from Eastern Europe. He doesn't believe that mankind has a common heritage. He thinks that when nobody actually has title to a place, whatever is there to be found should be for the sole benefit of the first comer. Therefore, the United States should firmly reject the Law of the Sea.

A case that is not without precedent, of course. During the centuries when the New World was opened for colonization nobody had title to lands in the Americas that Europeans would recognize, so the Spanish, Portuguese, French, Dutch, and British moved in and the heritage of the native American population was transferred to conquistadors and colonists. The same thing happened to Africa and most of Asia. The precedent for taking over the riches of the ocean floor has a long history. Guns made possible the white nations' plunder of the other continents; technology enables us to take over the seabeds. It is a precedent that has not endeared Europeans and Americans to the rest of the world, and its unfairness is obvious to nearly everybody in the world outside of the Reagan administration and its most inflexibly conservative supporters. What looks like a good business opportunity for enterprising and advanced countries looks like unmitigated greed to the rest of the world. As an American I am embarrassed by the unpleasant impression we are conveying to the rest of the world—after all, most of the other advanced nations have accepted the Law of the Sea; even those that have not signed have not proclaimed, as the United States has done, that they will not ratify it. I am also puzzled by the behavior of our conservative political establishment. As a matter of good international politics, what economic or political gains to us can offset our unfriendly and high-handed conduct in this matter? It is significant that the United States is the only nation that has not only refused to ratify the Law of the Sea but has also declined to participate in the work of the Preparatory Commission to initiate the International Sea-Bed Authority. We are out of step with the rest of the world. Is it possible that we are right and everyone else is hopelessly wrong?

A Note on Antarctica

Professor van den Haag's account of the international situation as to Antarctica is uncharacteristically hazy. Let me recapitulate the basic treaty situation. To begin with, it is a complicated and still unsettled situation; there were seven nations that after World War II announced claims to portions of that unoccupied continent. These nations were the United Kingdom, Australia, New Zealand, Norway, France, Argentina, and Chile. Most of the activity was scientific; there has been no serious attempt to exploit whatever natural resources there may be on the continent.

In 1957 an international committee organized the International Geophysical Year (the IGY), which extended from July 1, 1957, to December 31, 1959. The purpose was to survey the whole planet and its environment in as systematic a way as was possible given the nature of the relevant sciences. No geophysicist myself, I have to take the word of those who should know that the "year" was a spectacular success.

The IGY took a special interest in Antarctic studies, and in addition to the seven nations actually claiming territory, five others, the United States, the USSR, Belgium, Japan, and South Africa, volunteered to place observation stations on Antarctic territory.

From all accounts, this cooperative endeavor succeeded beyond expectations. Much was learned, and a consensus was reached that the Antarctic should be protected from international conflict. A treaty was drafted, signed, and ratified by all 12 nations in 1961. It is a comprehensive set of agreements providing that the territory should not be used for other than peaceful purposes, that plans for development should be exchanged, and that a system of inspections should be established. There was provision for new nations to participate and the treaty was to be binding for 30 years. If Malaysia decides that it wishes to engage in Antarctic exploration and scientific activity, there is nothing to prevent it from becoming another treaty signatory. The exploration and activities to be undertaken will be at Malaysia's own expense—one wonders whether that nation will decide that that game is worth the cost. I am not clear as to what bothers my intransigent adversary so much. Surely there's enough room in that vast and glacial land mass for a Malaysian expedition.

Mischief or Lawlessness?

I suspect that only our most hidebound conservative readers will be disturbed by the mischief that my adversary has uncovered. For my part, I want the rule of law to be introduced not only to the high seas, where civilized nations have always observed it, but also to Davy Jones's locker. As scientists have repeatedly discovered in their observations of the heavens, the earth, and the watery deep, our planet is a fragile environment whose equilibrium seems to be unique in the universe. The survival of the human race depends on an international understanding and acceptance of the need to protect the planet and its resources.

Even the least advanced nations are coming to understand that the environment within their borders can and must be protected.

Likewise the sea. Unrestrained hunting can reduce the population of whales to extinction; unregulated fishing has already depleted the ocean's stock of some fishes to commercial unavailability. Except for offshore petroleum drilling, we have hardly begun to exploit the seabeds. When this process begins there must be international regulation, regardless of who gets what share of the profits. It does not become the United States, the richest nation in the world, a nation whose professions of faith in the rule of law have embellished our history for two centuries, now to insist that the sea needs no law—that lawlessness is good enough. There is the mischief: We tarnish our good name and the respect of mankind—for what? Perhaps Professor van den Haag will enlighten us further.

Notes

1. For a more complete account of the Law of the Sea than we can provide here, see *A Quiet Revolution: The United Nations Convention on the Law of the Sea* (New York: United Nations, 1984).
2. See "The Enterprise; Economic Viability of Deep-Sea-Bed Mining of Polymetallic Nodules," submitted by the Delegation of Australia to the Preparatory Commission for the International Sea-Bed Authority. Document LOS/PCN/SCN.2/WP.10, 14 January 1986. Note, however, that the volume of minerals on the ocean beds is not merely "suspected," as Dr. van den Haag puts the matter, but reliably estimated to be about 1.5 trillion tons in the Pacific Ocean alone.
3. This concept originated with President Johnson's warning in 1966 against "a new form of colonial competition among the maritime powers...a race to grab and hold the lead under the high seas.... We must ensure that the deep sea-beds and the ocean bottoms are, and remain, the legacy of all human beings."
4. As of this writing, 159 nations have now signed, and 26 have ratified. Sixty ratifications are required before the treaty can go into force.
5. Opposition to this basic concept seems to have originated with President Reagan. In 1970 President Nixon, no radical internationalist, proposed that all nations adopt a treaty under which they would renounce all national claims to resources of the sea beyond the continental shelf and agree to regard these as

the "common heritage of mankind." I do not claim that this phrase originated with President Nixon, but he certainly did not reject it.
6. Although the assembly would "elect" the council membership, eligibility would be constrained by rules. Four states would come from those nations that are the largest investors in seabed mining, 4 would come from major consumers of seabed minerals, 4 would be major land-based exporters of the same minerals, 6 would be from landlocked nations, and 18 would be chosen geographically, with at least one country from each region.

ERNEST VAN DEN HAAG

John Conrad believes that our failure to sign the Law of the Sea treaty will make mining the sea attractive to American corporations. Well, not attractive enough, so far, for any of them to mine the sea. Conrad, however, thinks that even the attempt to make an enterprise attractive to investors is wrong. I don't. If investing weren't attractive to capitalists we wouldn't have capitalism—which produces the highest standard of living (with the most leisure) the world has ever seen. Surely the United States does much better than any country where investing has been made as unattractive as John Conrad might wish—e.g., the socialist nations or the Third World, the countries, indeed, that have tried making mining the sea unprofitable.

Basically, as Conrad admits in his historical resumé of the rejected Law of the Sea treaty, the profits from the seabed mining would go, in part, to noninvestors, and the technology would be transferred by law to nations that did not invent it or pay for it. Conflicts would be decided and regulations issued by bodies elected by nations that do not invest or participate in the mining but want to profit from it. This is my objection. Conrad has not refuted it. (Other parts of the treaty were neither objectionable nor particularly needed.) In law whatever is *res nullius* (does not belong to anyone) can be used by anyone who cares to. Thus, game in an unowned forest belongs to whoever manages to hunt it, and a nonhunter is not entitled to the game the hunter kills. That is why the sea-lanes are free and the user nations don't have to pay

Switzerland or Tanzania to use them, or to catch fish in the open seas. Beyond territorial limits the sea (or the air, the birds, or the fish) belongs to the user, and no one has the right to exclude anyone else or to get a share of the profits.

Of course, treaties to make sure of conservation and to prevent conflicts are useful. But the Law of the Sea did something quite different by proclaiming the right of nonparticipant noninvestors (who, of course, take no risk) to profit from and regulate the activities of those who actually engaged in mining—because they utilize "the common heritage of mankind," a newly invented legal concept. With this reasoning a nation without airlines could claim some of the profits (and help impose regulations) of airlines using international air space, even when they do not use any national air space. Ghana could claim profits (if any) from, or a right to regulate, air or space activities outside Ghana.

If, as John Conrad asserts (without evidence), our repudiating the attempt to deprive us of the profits of our future enterprise looks like "unmitigated greed" to others, too bad for them. I suspect it looks like common sense to them. It does to me. Of course, common sense is unexpected and seems odd in the U.N. environment, which appears to have infected John Conrad beyond rehabilitation. Still, I shall not despair for him—at heart I am an optimist.

About Antarctica, I think the treaty John Conrad describes is useful. I thought I had said so. As Conrad says, it does not prevent nations such as Malaysia from getting involved. My objection was not against the treaty but against attempts, currently sponsored in the U.N. by Malaysia, to have the treaty set aside, and to generate a conflict by declaring Antarctica part of the "common heritage of mankind" and thus claiming that nations that either do not adjoin Antarctica or have not explored it are somehow entitled to sharing any potential benefits from it. Why should they? Nothing in what Mr. Conrad writes even addresses my objection.

Here the following from *The New York Times*, December 4, 1985, may be of interest:

UNITED NATIONS, N.Y., Dec. 3—Delegates from countries that administer Antarctica said today that they would boycott future debates on the future of the continent unless a group of developing countries abandons what the delegates described as a confrontational approach.

The decision was linked to the adoption Monday of three resolutions in the General Assembly that seek to undermine the authority of the Antarctica Treaty, an accord that gives 18 "consultative parties," including the United States and the Soviet Union, the right to determine how the continent is run.

The parties work together to ban military use of the continent, carry out scientific studies, control mineral exploration and prevent further territorial claims.

The resolutions Monday called for "international management and equitable sharing of the benefits" of Antarctica's minerals, expulsion of South Africa from the treaty organization that administers the continent and expansion of a United Nations study.

Since 1983, when Antarctica was first discussed in the General Assembly, both sides have worked out generally worded resolutions that could be unanimously accepted. This year, however, Malaysia, supported by several other nations that say they are nonaligned, introduced resolutions that try to reduce the control of the treaty members and eventually declare Antarctica the "common heritage of mankind."

Of course I do not disapprove of protecting the planet, as Mr. Conrad implies. I do object, though, to being robbed under the pretext of protection—a not uncommon practice in general and one the U.N. is trying to institutionalize.

JOHN P. CONRAD

There he goes again. The analogies gush out as though they are all that his argument needs. Surely their flimsiness will impress our readers, or at least those who are not dyed-in-the-wool ideologues. For the benefit of those who are unaccustomed to picking their way through Professor van den Haag's prose, allow me a paragraph or two to deal with the invalidity of an argument that, I am sorry to say, seems to be moot.

The proposed common heritage doctrine is meant to establish an interest for all nations in the minerals lying on the open seabed or in the natural resources of Antarctica. It is based on the existence of tangible objects situated in unclaimed parts of the planet. Whether one agrees with President Johnson, President Nixon, and me that the doctrine is reasonable, or with President Reagan and my opponent that it isn't, the object is to settle the disposition of this potential, unrealized, but tangible wealth.

Ocean liners and freighters plying the sea and airplanes hurtling through open space are obviously not exploiting tangible resources belonging to no one. The sea traversed by a ship, the air through which a jumbo jet ploughs its way are intact after the passage is complete. Our airlines have nothing to fear from Ghana, nor will Switzerland have a basis for claiming a share of the profits of Cunard. But once those nodules of manganese have been gathered, they are gone. Under the common heritage doctrine, those who gather them are entitled to a reasonable profit, but shares should be reserved for those nations that, through no fault of their own, are not situated geographically or technologically to participate in the harvest. Under the "firstest with the mostest" doctrine that Professor van den Haag advocates so strenuously, three or four wealthy countries—probably the United States, Japan, the United Kingdom, and the Soviet Union—will reap the entire profit. This seems fair enough to anyone who invokes the *res nullius* doctrine, laid down by Roman lawyers who long ago wanted to establish the rights of hunters in an open forest. It doesn't seem fair to nations that do not have the advantages of wealth and technology to exploit what riches there may be at the bottom of the sea or under those glaciers in Antarctica. As for the fish, most of the catch is well within the 200-mile limits allowed by the Law of the Sea treaty.

Nature has not been equitable in the distribution of natural resources. Lavish with America and Russia, she has been niggardly with many others. It does not seem at all unfair to me to seek an equitable distribution of the resources that no one owns rather than to reserve them for the benefit of nations that have a head start because they are rich.

But Professor van den Haag holds that the devil should take the hindmost. That doctrine will win no friends for the United States, but perhaps my stalwart opponent doesn't think we need friends.

As I said at the outset, the common heritage doctrine appears to be moot for the present. Ratification of the Law of the Sea treaty is proceeding very slowly, perhaps because of the implacable opposition of the Reagan administration, perhaps because the Soviet Union doesn't like it either.

As for the Malaysian aspiration for a piece of the action in Antarctica, that initiative is going nowhere, too. Inspired by Dr. van den Haag's derision of the very idea, I have checked with the United Nations Secretariat staff. My stoutly capitalist opponent will be pleased to learn that the United States and the Soviet Union stand shoulder to shoulder in opposition to any application of the common heritage doctrine to Antarctica. An entente like that is much too formidable for even those wily Malaysians to overcome.

CHAPTER 8

South Africa in an Unfriendly World

ERNEST VAN DEN HAAG

The U.N. was founded to keep the peace among nations. Its constitution makes it entirely clear that it was not to get involved in the domestic order of the constituent nations. Thus, bloody and inhuman dictatorships such as Stalin's could and did become members, as did the Western democracies. In one sense the U.N. has stuck to this idea. It has not criticized the Soviet Union.

But this policy has not been extended equally to all constituent nations. South Africa and Israel have been consistently accused of disturbing the peace; South Africa simply because the majority of nations did not like its domestic order and Israel because the majority did not like its successful defense against attack.

It is certainly true that three-quarters of the South African population—the blacks—are separated from the remaining quarter—the whites—and that this separation (apartheid) is used to oppress the blacks in various ways. They have no political rights and cannot vote except in reservations (Bantustans) where most of them do not live. In the past they could hold only menial jobs. Although job reservation (for whites) has gone, most of the blacks haven't received the education that would qualify them for better jobs. Indeed, education for blacks is much inferior to education for whites. So is their income.

Now it is true that the majority of blacks in the black-governed countries of Africa also have no political rights and are pushed around by dictators. Indeed, their education, jobs, and living standards are on the whole inferior to what is available to them in South Africa. But, understandably enough, this does not assuage the feeling of South African blacks about the shabby way in which the dominant white minority treats them.

What has all this to do with the U.N.? One might say nothing, or at least no more than oppression in Uganda, the Soviet Union, Kampuchea, or Vietnam does. But the majority of members of the U.N. now are from the "Third World." They do not mind dictatorships or oppression—unless it is of whites over blacks. Black oppression by blacks is OK and so is white oppression by whites. But not black oppression by whites.

The issue clearly is a domestic one. South Africa does not appear to have ambitions to conquer any neighboring nations. Nonetheless, the U.N. has repeatedly accused the South African government of endangering the peace and, using that as a pretext, has passed resolutions asking member states to harm South Africa as much as possible without actual military violence.

All this demonstrates that the U.N. not only is useless, it can also be harmful. For it clearly wishes to support violent revolution in South Africa unless the government is handed over to blacks, or, should that not work, invasion of South Africa by anyone who would be willing to replace the present government with a black one. Fortunately none of South Africa's neighbors is strong enough to risk such an invasion. Yet the U.N. is doing what it can to weaken South Africa's defensive strength, hoping that someone, sooner or later, will use military force to institute a black government. The U.N. in Africa is hardly a force for peace.

JOHN P. CONRAD

One of the saddest ironies in the history of internationalism is the place of that great South African man for all seasons, Field

Marshal Jan Christiaan Smuts. His terse memorandum on the organization and structure of the League of Nations made that precursor of the United Nations a practical reality.[1] He lived on to play a major role in the San Francisco conference on the United Nations in 1945 and was the author of the preamble of the Charter. That document contains noble language committing the member states "To reaffirm faith in fundamental human rights, in the dignity and worth of the human person, in the equal rights of men and women of nations large and small. . . ."

In 1946 Smuts, then the prime minister of the Union of South Africa, attended the General Assembly for the purpose of persuading that body that sovereignty over Southwest Africa (the former German colony, mandated to South Africa by the League of Nations, and now generally known as Namibia) should be transferred to South Africa. With international prestige of long standing as a soldier, statesman, and philosopher, he expected to accomplish his mission with ease. To his astonished discomfiture, before he could make his case, the Indian delegation fiercely attacked him on account of legislation newly passed by the South African parliament that discriminated against Indian residents. His response that South Africa was not the only nation that discriminated against certain minorities got him nowhere; only South Africa had legislated racial discrimination into the law of the land. His plea for the annexation of Southwest Africa was roundly defeated. He returned to Africa a bitterly disillusioned man, denounced in his country as responsible for exposing the nation to an "avalanche of condemnation." Not much later his government was turned out of office.[2]

It can be said that Dr. van den Haag has the distinguished authority of Field Marshal Smuts to support his argument that South Africa is not the only nation on that unhappy continent that engages in the oppression of its people. That was the argument that Smuts made to the General Assembly. It has two flaws. First, it is a *tu quoque* defense, never an acceptable means of exculpation. Second, while many other countries, particularly including India, which first raised the issue, have tolerated customs that de-

grade some classes of citizens, only South Africa has legislated racial discrimination. Moreover, in the passage of the Charter
preamble quoted above, the signatory members of the United Nations commit themselves to "the equal rights of men and women
of nations large and small."

The Republic of South Africa does not complicate the issue.
Apartheid is the law and it is vigorously enforced. That it violates
a fundamental principle of the Charter is not relevant to the maintenance of the ideology. The South African government is composed of practical men who ardently wish to maintain the *status
quo* if they can. They will make some concessions but only those
that will, they hope, placate the international opposition without
disturbing the foundation of oppressive discrimination.

Professor van den Haag's *tu quoque* argument will not wash
for him any better than it did for Field Marshal Smuts. To assert,
"You're another, who are you to complain about us?" is no defense at all. It is to be expected that representatives of African and
Asian nations would use the General Assembly to mobilize opposition to apartheid. But my peace-loving friend is woefully naive if
he really supposes that in this shrinking world the black, colored,
and Indian populations of South Africa would subside into docile
acceptance of their inferior condition if only the United Nations
would pay no attention to them. No self-respecting Indian or African politicians, however deplorable their conduct in the domestic
affairs of their nations, could remain silent about the racial oppression that would never end without the universal condemnation it
receives—not only in the United Nations but everywhere outside
of that unhappy republic.

Alas, the tragedy of South Africa is that everyone either urges
or resists change, but no one is looking for the difficult solutions.
After the inevitable deluge, peace and harmony will be a long time
in coming unless statesmanship of a high order is applied to the
reconstruction of the nation. That kind of leadership is not now
visible in any quarter.

The essay to which I am responding includes Israel as a nation
that has been subjected to iniquities at the hands of the United Na-

tions. No argument is offered to support this assertion, and I will defer comment on this agonizing subject until I learn what Dr. van den Haag has in mind.

Notes

1. See his *The League of Nations; A Practical Suggestion* (London: Hodder and Stoughton, 1918).
2. For a full account of Smuts's fall, see Bernard Friedman, *Smuts: A Reappraisal* (London: George Allen & Unwin, 1975), pp. 155–212.

ERNEST VAN DEN HAAG

I did not justify South Africa's domestic policies by saying that other African countries have worse ones. This *tu quoque* argument would not work, as Conrad points out. I did argue that:

1. Those who share the Conrad–U.N. view seem to be interested in South Africa's domestic order, but not in that—concededly worse—of other African countries, let alone the Soviet Union. We have a case of highly selective indignation and prosecution here, and I regret that Conrad endorses it.

2. I also pointed out—to a resounding silence by Conrad—that, contrary to various U.N. resolutions, South Africa does not endanger the peace. Hence, sanctions are not justified.

The General Assembly for nearly 10 years has refused to accept the credentials of the South African delegation, thus preventing it from speaking and voting. This, of course, is contrary to professed U.N. rules. It compares oddly with the easy accreditation of the Ukrainian and White Russian delegates—although even U.N. delegates know that neither state is independent, whereas South Africa, to the chagrin of the delegates, is. And what about the social conditions imposed by the Ukrainian/Soviet government?

If it weren't so sad the U.N. assembly would be funny. When it was young, Cordell Hull (Roosevelt's secretary of state) said about the U.N., "no balance of power, no spheres of influence, no alliances, none of the traditional forms of diplomacy will be necessary now that there is an international organization." For comment I yield to Abba Eban, former Israeli foreign minister and former ambassador to the U.N.: "This is a sure competitor in any contest for the most absurd utterance ever made since the invention of language."[1]

Note

1. See Abba Eban, Interest and conscience in diplomacy, XXIII *Society* 3 (April 1986), p. 19.

JOHN P. CONRAD

A reasonable defense of South Africa's racial policies is beyond the capabilities of that nation's most zealous apologists, so it is not surprising that Dr. van den Haag has had to struggle with the all too familiar strategy of pointing out all the other black kettles. Look at the Soviet Union, he says, look at those other African countries that are "concededly" worse than the last bastion of *legislated* racial oppression. As I pointed out in my earlier rebuttal, the official, legal status of apartheid is unique. It is also a violation of the Charter of the United Nations, a charter that a great South African, Jan Smuts, had a hand in drafting. No wonder South Africa is excluded from the General Assembly, no wonder it is the target of sanctions urged and partially implemented by the Security Council. This is a nation that has no legitimate claim to membership in the United Nations.

After the events of the last year in Soweto and Port Elizabeth, I am not sure what I will concede to my opponent's argument that if South Africa is bad, other nations are worse. With police in armored cars shooting schoolchildren and gassing unarmed crowds, the South African scene qualifies as among the ugliest on the international stage. Comparative barbarism is not a useful intellectual exercise, but anyone who observes what is going on in that wretched country must classify the situation now prevailing as first-degree barbarism.

The tragedy is that whatever happens and whenever, it will be a long time before a civilized polity can be restored. Many scores will have to be settled, many impossible obstacles to reconciliation will have to be surmounted. In the present climate of ferocious confrontation, no one can spare attention to the future reconstruction of a new and democratic regime committed to the economic, political, and social well-being of the whole country.

It is no longer true that the African nations are unconcerned about the rights of their citizens. The Organization of African Unity has been drafting its own declaration of human rights, to be presented for ratification at the next assembly of that body. In this connection, it is relevant to note that although everyone deplored Idi Amin and his murderous buffoonery for the duration of his regime, it was left to Tanzania, one of the most impoverished nations in the world, to destroy him. International society was pleased, but the Tanzanians have had little tangible reward for their service to civilization.

My "resounding silence" about my opponent's contention that South Africa does not endanger the peace need resound no longer. It is quite true that Pretoria presents no threat to any European or North American nation. For its neighboring countries, South Africa is a constant menace. Lesotho, Angola, and Mozambique have all been invaded; Zambia and Zimbabwe have been given to understand that their conduct toward South Africa must be circumspect. Malawi and Botswana know how careful they must be with a brutal and unscrupulous neighbor at their frontiers. For a professor comfortably situated in Manhattan, South African bellicosity is the least of his worries. For a citizen of a nation on the borders of Afrikanerdom, not only is the threat real, but from time to time it turns into terror.

My anti-Communist friend brings up once again the anomaly of the Ukrainian and Byelorussian membership in the United Nations. I will unreservedly agree that this is an absurdity. It should be remedied in the interest of tidiness and equity.

Professor van den Haag is selectively indulgent. Rules should be observed by all member states. The Ukraine and Byelorussia should not be members because they are not sovereign nations. South Africa should not be a member because it is in gross, chronic, and explicit violation of the Charter. All three nations should be blackballed until these disqualifications are remedied.

ERNEST VAN DEN HAAG

I still don't see why South Africa's claim to membership in the U.N. is less "legitimate" than that of the Soviet Union, the Ukraine, Cambodia, or any number of other nations whose domestic atrocities far exceed in quantity those of South Africa even though they are not always interracial. Anyone who believes that Stalin was better than Mr. Botha, or that Gorbachev is, has indeed a sense of morality that is altogether bizarre.

Incidentally, South Africa was never "excluded," as Conrad asserts, from the U.N. Assembly. The Assembly committee that is charged with accreditation simply refused to recognize the credentials of the South African delegates, which is, of course, illegal and improper by any standard, since the South African delegates are indeed the delegates of a government that rules its territory, even if we do not like the way it rules.

Unlike Conrad, I doubt that the successor to the present South African government is likely to be better. If the present South African government were overthrown, any black government that would take its place would infinitely worsen the fate of South African blacks. Wherefore I believe that the only thing that can be done to help them is gradual reforms that extend democracy to them.

JOHN P. CONRAD

I will be brief. Let us agree that neither the Ukraine nor Byelorussia nor Cambodia belongs in the United Nations any more than the Republic of South Africa. I will not pass judgment on the comparative morals of General Secretary Gorbachev and President Botha. The fine points of such a comparison may interest Professor van den Haag. I don't find any characteristics in either of them that I would like an American president to emulate.

As I write (in May 1986), the recent bombardment of Zambia, Botswana, and Zimbabwe by the South African air force—vigorously denounced by President Reagan and Secretary Shultz—establishes the threat to peace that the Botha government presents to its neighbors. South Africa wants peace only on its own rigid terms. It prefers its deserved isolation to the ordinary comity of nations.

Professor van den Haag resorts to an exhausted cliché, propounded at every opportunity by South African apologists, that the "fate" of South African blacks would "infinitely worsen" under any black government that might replace the present regime. It is hard to see how the plight of this unfortunate people could be worse—let alone "infinitely" worse—than the wretched condition of apartheid, universally deplored by all who have observed it. Comfortable professors, whether in Manhattan or California, should not presume to compare the present misery of South African black people with their probable condition in a democratic polity.

Nor does it make sense to complain, as Professor van den Haag does, that the United Nations acts against South African oppression but does nothing about the Soviet denial of human rights. There is some reason to believe that concerted action by the United Nations and the countries that compose it will bring about change in South Africa. A strategy for the improvement of conditions in Russia is beyond present political ingenuity. It is best to keep the Soviet Union in the United Nations, where it will be compelled to justify its brutal ways.

PART IV

CONCLUDING STATEMENTS

CHAPTER 9

Summing Up

JOHN P. CONRAD

The Case for the United Nations

Dr. van den Haag has done what he could with a bad brief. He has made an unconvincing case against the United Nations that consists of the following propositions:

1. The United Nations has not prevented war.
2. It costs too much.
3. It provides a forum for anti-American propaganda, particularly the Communist brand.
4. Its specialized agencies don't do anything that could not be done as well by private organizations. Some, especially UNESCO, are badly managed platforms for anti-American agenda.

Underlying these propositions is a fatalism that should repel our readers. Again and again he has emphasized his conviction that war is inevitable and efforts to prevent it are futile. Although war is "supremely undesirable," many undesirable events occur in human existence and must be accepted as the ineluctable fate of mankind. Anyone holding to this dark view of the future must believe that enlightened leaders can only act to delay the inevitable. Immediate national interests must be identified and policies formulated to advance these interests regardless of the long-term effects on other nations or on one's own. Foreign affairs should not be complicated with international organizations. Efforts to reconcile conflict should take second place to policies assuring that our own interests will always prevail.

The difference between us is the difference between a pessimist who sees history lurching toward catastrophe, far beyond the control of human minds or action, and an optimist of sorts, one who sees the dangers but believes that it is not beyond the wit of man to escape them—perhaps by the skin of our teeth. Nothing Dr. van den Haag has written in this debate offers a basis for hope. He can project the end of history. We must accept our fate like brave stoics.

I am stubborn. A vigorous effort to build a better world must be made, but I do not foresee perpetual harmony. Utopia is an impossible prospect. Conflicts will persist for as long as the minds of men and women can find reasons to differ with other men and women. Differences can and must be resolved without resort to arms. The United Nations provides a necessary arena for conflict resolution. The world must learn to use it effectively. The United States should lead the way.

I have dealt with Professor van den Haag's weak barrage of denunciations and unsupported assertions with specific refutations stemming from the central conviction that the United Nations is an indispensable agency for building peace. Now is the time to put the case for the United Nations into a perspective of affirmations.

I do not rest my case on the contention that the United Nations is a perfect organization that cannot be improved. That is not the case, and in what follows I shall address the imperfections as specifically as an outside observer can. This is an age when an international organization is a necessary support for peace. After 40 years, it is apparent that the nations of the world still don't know how to use it. With centuries of practice, the habits of traditional diplomacy die slowly.

We are drifting into a dangerous condition of international anarchy, which must be returned to the orderly processes of interdependence. The world we now have is a world of sorrows. We must understand how we arrived at this condition and what can be done to improve it.

What Kind of World Do We Have?

For four decades the great powers have managed to avoid a repetition of the slaughter and destruction of World Wars I and II. The credit for this respite from madness goes only marginally, if at all, to the United Nations. Everyone knows that the standoff between the two superpowers is the stalemate of dread, not the flowering of amity. Because each side is amply provided with nuclear missiles that can be delivered from the air, from the sea, or from carefully hardened silos, neither dares to threaten the other with warfare that would culminate in the certain ruin of both. One of the two foundations of the laws of nations, as proposed two centuries ago by Montesquieu, is thus observed as though a new natural law had been proclaimed: *above all, nations must do no irreparable harm to their enemies in time of war.*[1] Montesquieu also held that in time of peace, nations should do as much good for each other as their interests would allow. This rule has yet to apply in Soviet–American relations.

Both sides could do each other a great deal more good than they are now disposed to do. Both also know that in a war the harm one side could inflict on the other in a nuclear attack would almost certainly spread to its own territory and to the territory of nonbelligerents. The real interests of a nuclear power not bent on national suicide require restraint even if those interests are in seemingly irreconcilable conflict with those of the other superpower. It is a condition without precedent in the history of politics and war. The stockpiles of missiles grow, and so does the realization that they cannot be used. A violent confrontation between the superpowers has become a practical impossibility. Angry and insulting rhetoric—often on the floor of the General Assembly, and everywhere else that responsive audiences can be found—partially takes the place of warfare. Each side knows what it thinks of the other, even if both sides must restrain themselves from suiting action to the thought.

Confrontations need not be direct. Both powers supply arms to smaller nations engaged in their own nonnuclear conflicts; some of these conflicts become "proxy wars" between the superpowers. Both powers have directly involved themselves in wars that seem to affect their national interests—the United States in Vietnam, the Soviet Union in Afghanistan.

It is usually estimated that there have been 150 wars of varying destructiveness since V-J Day in 1945. Many observers, including my opponent, conclude that this is all that needs to be said. The United Nations was founded to prevent war. Over its lifetime many wars have not been prevented. Therefore, the United Nations is a failure and its futile existence should be brought to a merciful end.

This shortsighted perspective takes no account of the historical processes that have brought the world to its present state of affairs. Those who arrive at Dr. van den Haag's pessimistic outlook have surveyed the disorder in international relations and conclude that a truly international society cannot exist. The best we can hope for is security through a system of alliances among nations with common security interests, all heavily armed in readiness for an impossible war. Some American polemicists and politicians seem to be saying that the United States, as the world's most powerful nation, should go it alone, allowing those lesser nations who want our protection to receive it on our terms. Those who are not prepared to meet our terms are not trustworthy allies.

I am not a historicist; I do not believe that there are iron laws of history that bind mankind to an ineluctable fate. Nevertheless, we cannot understand the present or peer usefully into the future without knowing how we got into our present condition. With the broadest of brushes I shall sketch the patterns of international relations from early history to our perilous times. There is a progression from a world of many regions, with minimal contact with each other, to a world of European dominance, and now to a world in which dominance in the old sense has become impossible. It is a platitude to speak of the interdependence of the nations, but like so many platitudes, it is an expression of a reality. The more powerful the nation, the more difficult it is to recognize that interdependence imposes limits on the power that that nation can exert.

Propinquity and common cultures set the framework for relations between city-states and later between states. In the days of Thucydides, five centuries before Christ, the important interstate relations were conducted between the leagues of cities allied respectively to Athens and Sparta. In the offing were the Persians and the Egyptians, but relations with those empires were no longer significant. Hellenic forces had united to expel the Persian armies and fleet from Greece forever. The important conflicts were now contained within the small Grecian universe.

Readers of Thucydides's *History of the Peloponnesian Wars* would hardly know that there was a world outside of the eastern Mediterranean Sea. What mattered was the rivalry between the great cities of Attica and Lacedaemon. When the Persians threatened Hellenic security, Athenians and Spartans could achieve solidarity against a common danger. Once the Persian threat was repulsed, the rival powers built up their alliances in Greece (there was no question of affiliation with any "barbarian" power) and maneuvered for military, diplomatic, and commercial advantage. Eventually the Peloponnesian wars culminated in the ruin of the Hellenic world.

This regional pattern of interstate relations was natural during all the centuries when the world was divisible into regions and no nation had the military power to extend its dominance beyond the roughly defined borders of the region in which it was located. Alexander the Great could dominate Greece and the eastern Mediterranean, but his forays beyond the area of effective movement and communications were meaningless military adventures with no lasting implications for the expansion of Hellenic power.

Roman communications and the genius of Roman generals and proconsuls for organization made it possible to consolidate an empire far beyond the bounds of Alexander's achievement. The *Pax Romana* covered a vast area of Europe and the Middle East, but it was no more than the extension of a region of control, far from a worldwide political embrace. While the Roman legions were fending off the Goths and Visigoths, India and China had entirely separate cultures and histories of political and military control of which the Romans knew little and never attempted to challenge seriously.

The fall of the Roman Empire was the end of a system that had maintained order throughout Europe, the Near East, and northern Africa. For many centuries, nothing took its place in Europe. There were orderly regional systems in the Islamic crescent extending from Persia to Morocco, in southern Asia, and in the Orient. The gradual development of nation-states in Europe restored a semblance of regular order, out of which there emerged a system of European interstate relations, and, much later, with the development of overseas empires, a Eurocentric world.

It was only in the eighteenth century that technology and communications made possible European imperialism on the scale that seemed so durable until the end of World War II. A Eurocentric world consolidated commerce and politics into one system. It was fractured in World War I, put back together by the treaties that ended that conflict, and smashed forever by World War II.[2]

The Eurocentric world revolved around the interests of a few nations on the continent of Europe. Powers like the United States, the British dominions, and Japan conducted their foreign relations on European terms. The colonial possessions had no foreign relations, no matter how populous or rich. They were the property of European powers or, in the case of the Philippines, of the United States.

The vast nation of China could do as it pleased with its internal affairs so long as the interests of the Great Powers—the British and French empires, the United States, Germany, and Japan— were not affected. Each of these imperial powers arranged "extraterritorial" concessions within which the Chinese government's writ could not run. The legitimacy and the authority of the weak Nanking government were always under credible challenge from local warlords, and eventually from the Communist party, because of the European intrusion in Chinese commerce and politics.

Eurocentrism was oppressive, often violent, degrading to non-European humanity, a drag on the free trade of the world economy, and a vast geopolitical distortion. As Dr. van den Haag never tires of insisting, it was not without its benefits to the subject populations. Colonized peoples gained cohesion and a sense of national identity, usually in opposition to their foreign masters. Institutions for the administration of political and economic affairs were introduced, though seldom with any participation by representatives of the subject peoples. Codes of justice, courts, and police were imposed and to a surprising extent have survived the departure of the colonial powers. Preliterate peoples were provided with some education, though hardly as much as would have been requisite if decolonization had been a serious intention of the imperial powers.

It was a system that had to end. The British wound up their empire with negotiations that were mostly amicable, and the same was true of most of the French sub-Sahara possessions.[3] The Dutch, the Belgians, and the Portuguese vacated their colonies grudgingly, bitterly, under great international pressure and relentless rebellion from the subject populations.

The legacy of colonialism is the Third World, a "world" of generally impoverished nations, resentful of their colonial past, sure that their poor condition can be traced to exploitation by their former overlords. A few have emerged from their subordination to relative prosperity—in the case of those Islamic nations fortunate enough to enjoy a patrimony of oil, to a condition of splendid affluence. Most of the Third World is heavily in debt, largely unavoidable, and dependent on the export of raw materials to fluctuating markets. Precarious governments maintain such control as they can with heavy-handed police and their armed forces in reserve for action in domestic uprisings.

These Third World nations compose the majority of the United Nations General Assembly. They have transformed institutional operations of the United Nations beyond all recognition from the relatively small and fairly orderly assemblies of its early days when the courtesies of international discourse were for the most part observed and the main problem facing the organization was the deadlock between the United States and the USSR. Now we have a United Nations that is annually preoccupied with the grievances—real and imagined—of the nations of the Third World. The insistent demand for remedies is accompanied by rhetorical denunciations of the old colonial powers, with special attention to the United States as the richest power in the First World.

The three worlds into which our planet is now divided are disparate and conflicting. Eurocentrism survives in the First World, communism persists by dint of military force in the Second, and poverty and postcolonial resentments haunt the Third. That is the kind of world we have, and every September its glaring hostilities are given raucous voice in the General Assembly. Unfortunately, these deliberations take place in New York where every stentorian note of anti-American and anti-Western rhetoric is amplified by the press and television in America's dominant communications center.

The imprudent sentiments of Third World leaders touch every raw nerve of the substantial number of isolationist survivors in this country. One would think that America's future was in grave jeopardy because of the presence of these contentious guests on our soil. A careful account of votes is kept, and nations that do not toe the American line are put on notice that American aid may be withheld. If recent American missions to the United Nations have attempted the logrolling and horse-trading and resolution of issues by face-saving compromises that go on as a matter of course in our Congress and state legislatures, nothing is said about such procedures in reports of our delegates' participation in the Security Council or the General Assembly. Ours is a posture of intimidation. We can count on willy-nilly compliance by nations that have no other choice; we must also expect lasting resentment. Friendship is never engendered by coercion.

Third World Illusions and American Disillusion

The United Nations was born at the end of a long and destructive war. There was a consensus of hindsight that it had been a just war that could have been prevented. American statesmen unanimously agreed that the creation of a multilateral organization such as the United Nations would serve to block the rise of another Hitler and suppress the predatory violations of the sovereignty of weaker nations by military adventurers.

Nothing would do but that the United Nations should find a home in the New World, far away from the incessant conflicts of the Old World. The new organization came into being in a warm and protective glow of American power, prosperity, and altruism. In those early years conflict between the United States and the Soviet Union was not foreseen as unmanageable—at least by American leaders. No one glimpsed the nuclear stalemate that terrifies the world while at the same time keeping the uneasy peace.

For years the United States could count on its dominance of United Nations proceedings. It was more than an instrument of American foreign policy; it was the stage on which American foreign policy was conducted. Debates in the General Assembly, resolutions in the Security Council, and the deployment of peace-keeping forces were front-page news. The secretary-general occupied an office equivalent in stature to the chiefs of great states.

The United Nations no longer is the summit where great things happen and great men are in office. As Linda Fasulo, a historian of the United Nations, has noted, "twenty or thirty years ago, most major U.S. newspapers and magazines maintained full-time correspondents at the U.N. Today only the *New York Times* has one—a presence that is perhaps explained by the fact that for nine years during the 1950s the *Times's* present executive editor...covered the U.N. beat."[4] Because of this inattention by the media, public understanding of the United Nations has lapsed into confusion and the advocates of American isolation have eagerly filled the information gap. Disillusion was enhanced by the anti-American antics of inexperienced delegates from new Third World nations who supposed—and to some extent still suppose—that their manhood and the independence of the nations they represent has been demonstrated by standing in opposition to American positions.

In spite of the confusion and lack of information, the American people still seem to be supportive of the United Nations. A

Roper poll conducted in 1983 found that about 60% of the respondents thought that "the UN should be given more power to reduce the danger of superpower confrontation, enhance human rights, and conserve natural resources. In addition, over 50% believe[d] the UN should play a greater role in helping poor countries develop."[5] A probing poll of 1769 persons, conducted by the League of Women Voters in 1977, found that only 32% of the respondents thought the U.N. was doing a good job, but only 13% wanted the United States to withdraw. The League's analyst summarized the significance of the findings.

> What seems to be happening is that people's expectations have become more realistic. Fewer Americans expect the United Nations to solve all the world's complex problems. People are ready to back the United Nations on the more modest grounds that it serves as a necessary forum for communication among nations.... The down to earth assessments...come both from those who give the United Nations a "poor job" rating and those who give it a favorable evaluation.[6]

Although support for the United Nations in the American public has declined since the first Gallup poll was taken in 1951, showing that 75% of the respondents favored American membership, the 1977 Roper poll showed 70% still in favor of our participation, and in 1983 52% believed that participation should be either increased or maintained at its present level.

Reviewing the data collected by four different polling agencies over the lifetime of the United Nations, Paul D. Martin, a Columbia University political scientist, comments:

> There has certainly been a drastic decrease in support for the UN, particuarly since the early 1970s, but there has been a slight upward trend since 1976.... But it is also clear that the UN will have to get its house in order if there is to be any change in the American public's perception of how the United Nations does its job....
>
> If the United States chooses to disengage or withdraw from the UN, disagreeable subjects will not disappear. This country will merely deny itself an opportunity to present its point of view on issues of concern to the world community, thus... blocking lines of communication and eliminating the possibility of a constructive US

role in international efforts to relieve tensions. The responses of the
American public in poll after poll show an instinctive understanding
that this country cannot afford to pursue such a defensive, ostrich-
like policy.[7]

That nineteenth-century British realist, Lord Palmerston, laid
it down that "Great Britain has no permanent friends, only permanent interests." The Third World nations emerged from colonialism with a most imperfect understanding of where their permanent
interest lay. It may be argued that the USSR, living under the illusion that the laws of history lead relentlessly to world socialism,
also misunderstands its permanent interests. These illusions distort
international relations and discourse in the United Nations. It is
too much to hope that membership and participation in the United
Nations will suffice to dissolve illusions, but this is the arena in
which the unreality of conflict-oriented foreign policy can be exposed in day-to-day interaction.

The Meaning of Sovereignty

Invoking the sixteenth-century shade of Jean Bodin, a French
political philosopher, my opponent has from the first contended
that sovereignty "is what makes war possible and ultimately
likely."[8] Because the United Nations assumes the equal sovereignty of each of its members, and because for the dozens of new
nations that have been admitted, membership in the United Nations is the proof positive of sovereignty, some observations must
be made about this elusive and ambiguous term.

Bodin had very little to say about the significance of sovereignty in international relations. His *Six Books of the Commonwealth* contain one brief chapter on the keeping of treaties and the
making of alliances.[9] His ideas about sovereignty were intended
to justify the legitimacy, power, and authority of princes by the di-
vine right which entitled them to their royal position. As for international relations, Bodin advised his princely readers to keep the
faith "sacred and inviolable in all cases where no injustice is con-
templated. . . . Wise princes should never bind themselves by oath

to other princes to do anything forbidden by natural law, or the law of nations.''[10] The unlimited sovereignty of the prince in his own lands was limited by treaties in which he voluntarily engaged his honor and good faith.

And so it is, *mutatis mutandis*, in modern times. Governments limit their freedom of action by voluntarily engaging in treaties. When Kaiser Wilhelm dismissed as a "scrap of paper" the engagement of his Reich to observe the neutrality of Belgium, he outraged international opinion. Nations make and ratify treaties that define and limit sovereignty in some specific field of international conduct.

The Charter of the United Nations is a multilateral treaty that neither creates a world government nor renders meaningless the concept of sovereignty. It does create certain limits on the freedom of any nation's action with respect to other nations. That many nations have violated their commitments under the Charter does not invalidate that document. Its principles are still the way to peace. Whenever a nation agrees to limit its sovereignty in the interest of a peaceful resolution of all its conflicts, it has committed itself to peace. The argument that sovereignty, the manifestation of the nation-state's authority, is the cause of war collapses when we consider the ample history of warfare during the last 40 years.

The traditional wars up to and including World War II concerned sovereignty. The United Nations was formed to prevent that kind of violence. The Italian invasion of Ethiopia, the Japanese conquest of Manchuria, the successive invasions of Poland, France, and Russia by Nazi Germany, and the Russian invasion of Finland were predatory violations of the sovereignty of states. Sovereignty in each case meant the sovereign right of the powerful invader to loot the territory of a weaker neighbor. It also meant international anarchy.

Any reading of the Charter clearly indicates that the draftsmen had the prevention of that kind of war, the most destructive of all, as their primary objective. Wars of national liberation, revolutionary wars, and retaliatory strikes against terrorism were not on the agenda. These kinds of conflict had not surfaced as problems for resolution by the statesmen of those times. To this day, there is no unanimity about what should be done about them, within or without the United Nations. What is clear is that sovereignty is not the question in most modern conflicts. The exceptions test the rule.

The Soviet Union has conducted three major invasions: In Hungary in 1956, in Czechoslovakia in 1968, and in Afghanistan in 1979. In each case the justification presented to the world by Russian spokesmen was that the survival of legitimate governments to which the USSR was allied required "fraternal" interventions. Although these invasions were condemned from virtually all sides, no serious action was taken by the United Nations or any of its individual member-states. The actions of the Red Army in each case demonstrated that the sovereignty claimed by each of the governments of these countries was fictitious. The overwhelming power of the USSR made it possible to do as it pleased. A flimsy justification was all that was necessary. The contempt that this claim received when presented to the world did not reverse the Soviet action. Regardless of the United Nations, world opinion, or any possible combination of powers, nothing could be done.[11]

The Israeli incursion into Lebanon was an act of self-defense against terrorism, the wisdom of which is open to considerable question, but which under the terms of the Charter appears to be justifiable. Certainly there was no intention by the Israeli government to conquer and annex Lebanon—no politician or military man in his right mind would attempt to gain permanent control of that anarchic land. All that was intended was the destruction of a base for terrorists. There is no real sovereignty in Lebanon that Israel could violate. If there were, the incursion might not have been necessary.

In Angola a precarious regime is maintained with the support of a Cuban expeditionary force, apparently invited by a government that was initially fearful of South African invasion and now of a revolution cautiously sponsored by the United States. Here we have another chaotic territory vacated by an incompetent colonial power and kept in a disorderly condition by many conflicting interests. The Angolan government has technical sovereignty but little else. It does have the sovereign right to invite Cuba to send support, and it is reasonable to suppose that neither the Castro government nor its sponsors in Moscow expect that there will be a permanent Cuban presence in Africa. Nevertheless, a regime that must rely on foreign troops for survival cannot be counted as possessing true sovereignty. Here is another proxy conflict between the First and Second Worlds, with a Third World nation waiting to be born. It may be a long wait.

Miserable wars are under way between Iran and Iraq, between Ethiopia and its neighbors over territory in long-standing dispute, in East Timor, where Indonesia seeks to impose its rule on an unwilling population, and in the old Spanish Sahara, where Morocco and the indigenous "Polisario" are in an interminable dispute over the right of succession to the colonial regime. No one knows what to do about any of these out-of-the-way conflicts. The efforts of the United Nations have led to no significant abatement of combat, but no one has suggested promising alternative interventions. Does anyone care enough to make a proposal?

Is the United Nations merely an exercise in futility, as my opponent glibly argues? My answer should be obvious to anyone who has read this far. The United Nations is the indispensable institution for the maintenance of peace, if peace is the world's objective. Unfortunately, there are some nations that do not exhibit a desire for peace in their actions. The world would not be more peaceful without the United Nations, and indeed would probably be more dangerous. Its failures are the failures of the powers that now dominate it, not the failure of the institution itself. To dissolve it would be a disaster for the safety and prosperity of a world that will be dangerous for many decades to come.

The dangers come not from the preservation of the idea of sovereignty but rather from the desperation of poverty and the cynicism arising from the failing ideology of Marxism-Leninism. These are dangers against which the United Nations can offer protection in the long term, if it is used as it was intended. There really is no acceptable alternative. The United States would retreat into Fortress America only at great risk to our own prosperity and the values of freedom and altruism that have adorned the best moments of our history.

Estrangement and the Superpowers

In a thorough tour of the American diplomatic horizon, 12 American foreign policy experts, sponsored by the Carnegie Endowment for International Peace, considered the increasing isolation of the United States under the arresting title *Estrangement*.[12] A convincing case is made that during the last 40 years, the foreign policy of the United States—forged by both Democrats and Republicans—has led to the estrangement of our country, not only from the various nonaligned nations, but also from public opinion in many countries that are our natural friends and allies.

These experts do not make the point explicitly, but the same could be said about Soviet foreign policy. The grand strategy of the Kremlin seems to have been to enlist the support of the Muslim nations by military assistance and diplomatic support, to take advantage of the alienation of the former colonies in Africa by a vociferous alignment against South African apartheid, and to furnish military assistance to anti-American movements in the major trouble spots. In this way, America would at least be placed on a diplomatic defensive, and with luck geopolitical advantages would be gained by the USSR.

Neither strategy is working well. Muslim nations are uneasy, to say the least, with the atheism explicit in Marxism-Leninism. The brutal Russian occupation of Afghanistan, a Muslim nation, is even more unacceptable. As for Africa, the Kremlin has resolutely refused to engage in any economic assistance on the score that the relief of African poverty is the responsibility of the old colonial powers. It has become clear that all African governments can expect hollow but resounding words about South Africa and the evils of imperialism, some African governments can expect some guns, but no African government can expect more substantial assistance from Moscow.

The USSR is even more estranged than the United States. The only foreign friends on whom the Kremlin can rely are the governing officers of its tributary satellites in Eastern Europe, Cuba, and Vietnam. The architect of this virtually bankrupt policy was Andrei Gromyko, an expert survivor, a man who can impress his adversaries by the length of his experience and his elephantine memory for persons and events. As a manager of foreign policy his successes have been negligible. The few that he can claim are evaporating. Estrangement is a problem for the Russians, and at a time when the Russian economic fortunes are at a low ebb with few signs of early improvement. Whether the Russians in power care about their almost universal unpopularity is not clear. It is their problem, but I will suggest that it is our opportunity.

In his contribution to *Estrangement*, Richard Ullman argues that "an exaggerated perception of the Soviet threat has run like a red thread through post-1945 American foreign policy."[13] Our preoccupation with that perceived threat from Moscow has affected virtually all of our international relationsihps. It has led to our estrangement in three ways. First, our military expenditures, which have soared since the outset of the Reagan administration, squeeze out resources that might have been available for economic development in the Third World. As Ullman points out, "it is painfully obvious that if even a small fraction of the world's military expenditures were to be converted for development purposes, the effect would be significant."[14]

The United States has never come close to matching the other Western nations in economic assistance as a percentage of gross national product. Since 1981 the emphasis has been on linking our assistance to our anti-Soviet strategy by emphasizing aid to such countries as Israel, Egypt, El Salvador, and the Philippines. It may be said that beggars cannot be choosers, but rejected beggars cannot be expected to be friends. It is particularly tactless for a wealthy northern nation to tell the desperate African supplicant that for his nation's own good it must solve its own problems by relying on the free market. African realists must conclude that nothing is to be expected from either the West or the East, and that, so far as the North is concerned, poverty is the African lot forever and ever. From that conclusion it is hardly a step at all to decide that there is nothing to choose between American and Russian foreign policies. So far as possible a desperate nation should play off the one against the other.

The second cause of estrangement in Ullman's view is the increasing tendency toward restrictions on foreign trade. These restrictions bear heavily on the Third World, and they are troublesome and divisive among the rich northern nations. The enormous political and economic difficulties in the management of fair and free trade are not easy to resolve. When the United States is the largest market of all, a market on which most of the rest of the world must rely for prosperity, the restrictions that we place on lumber from Canada, textiles from the Orient, and agricultural products from Europe and Australia do not enhance our worldwide reputation for fairness or commitment to the principles of free trade.

The third source of estrangement lies in our increasing scorn for multilateralism. During the Reagan administration particularly, international cooperation has received short shrift. We have departed from UNESCO, we have refused to have anything to do with the Law of the Sea, we have rejected the jurisdiction of the International Court of Justice, and our support for the Contadora nations' negotiations to end Central American strife has been at the most nominal—if that.

A rich nation with vanishing sympathy for the poor, a nation professing a commitment to free enterprise and free trade that sets up restrictions on the flow of trade, and a nation that will scarcely give lip service to international cooperation—is it any wonder that we are estranged, not only from nonaligned countries but from some of our traditional friends? Add to these general causes our insistence—until recently—on "constructive engagement" in our policy toward South Africa, and estrangement can become outright hostility. I hasten to add that the complete isolation of South

Africa is not likely to improve an intolerable situation. But a realistic foreign policy must take account of the standing reactions of African nations to American positions that are seen as diametrically contrary to their interests.

Our dilemma in the Middle East is a persisting source of the estrangement of the Islamic nations. Few Americans question the right of Israel to exist or the obligation of the United States to extend it the support it must have if it is to survive in an ocean of Arab hostility. We will continue to do what we should and must, but at a cost to us in the hostility of many Arab nations and billions of dollars of economic aid to Egypt, to Jordan, and eventually to a few others who need us more than they hate Israel.

These subventions will produce docility as long as they continue, but we cannot expect loyalty or even gratitude. Leaders of the Arab masses committed to fundamentalist Islam are not inclined to accept the conditions implied by American grants of assistance. A government accepting aid in these circumstances has assured its economic survival and at the same time created the conditions for political instability. How long can such a government forestall its upheaval?

Ullman points out that the costs of estrangement are bearable and the consequences are "serious, but neither urgent or potentially catastrophic."[15] We are in no danger of military attack, no Americans will go hungry, no needed raw materials will become unavailable because of our estrangement. We will hear that we are to blame for woes everywhere, and a strong case will be made that we could have prevented at least some of these woes. But our hides can be thickened. We can go it alone, knowing that the rest of the world needs us more than we need it.

I do not like this prospect. It is inconsistent with American values and traditions. I doubt that the American people will tolerate the prospect of avoidable famines, oppression, revolutions, and counterrevolutions in the rest of the world. I doubt that most Americans want the world to see us as greedy plutocrats, indifferent to the real suffering of less fortunate people. I vote for a return to a revitalized United Nations, shorn of unrealistic expectations and committed to the promotion of the ways of peace.

What Is to Be Done?

Whether it is realistic to suppose that American preoccupation with Russian behavior can be attenuated in the prevailing neoconservative miasma is more than doubtful. A liberal like myself can foresee a distant world in which Russian and American interests will coincide in more matters than the prevention of nuclear war, but the road map to that world has not yet been drawn. When it is achieved the world's miseries will not be instantly relieved, but problems will become soluble that now resist any kind of solution.

For the present, a moratorium on official denunciations both in Washington and in Moscow, even when denunciation is richly deserved, would be a beginning. Invitations to the Russians to work with us on initiatives in troubled regions of the world would cost us little, and might get an occasional positive response.

But the overriding objective should be a renaissance of the United Nations, no longer a "dangerous place," as Ambassador Moynihan saw it, but a place in which avenues to peace are designed and paved. Instead of constantly proclaiming our unwavering opposition to communism—which should not waver—we should use the forums of the United Nations to present programs and initiatives that will make communism less attractive to poor and despairing nations. America should be seen as the hope of the world, as the "shining city on the hill," to borrow President Reagan's evocative phrase. The world should not regard America as an inaccessible vision but rather as a model for practical emulation. Our performance in the United Nations can begin to make this dissolution of estrangement a realistic prospect.

America must change, but so must the United Nations. The bureaucratic paper mill on Manhattan's East River needs a thorough renovation. More is written, translated, and published in six different languages than anyone can be expected to read. Resolutions are passed that will be ignored by everyone except the sponsors.[16] Discipline in the flood of verbiage will improve the organization's reputation for good sense.

In my preparation for this debate, I heard many suggestions, some of them good, some of them naive, but all reflecting some unease about the present state of affairs. I shall disregard the scurrilous nonsense uttered by uninformed and unreflective critics; I am concerned with the positive reconstruction of an essential organ of international order. Here are my proposals:

1. The United Nations budget should be under firm control. At present, its expenditures are authorized by the General Assembly, most of whose members contribute less than 1% of the budget. The Kassebaum Amendment requires that the United States contribution must be reduced to 20% unless a system of weighted voting on budget matters is adopted. Another way of introducing accountability would be to submit the secretary-general's budget for review by a special finance committee composed of representatives of those nations that contribute more than a certain percentage of the United Nations revenue. There are doubtless other possible methods for removing those nations making minimum contributions to the United Nations revenue from the power to authorize expenditures that they will not have to defend to their constituents.

2. The United Nations is entirely too dependent on the 25% American contribution. Far better that our share should be gradually reduced, perhaps to no more than 10%. The contributions of some other nations would have to be scaled upward.[17] The feasibility of increased assessments for the more affluent nations is obvious. The total budget of the United Nations would not maintain the United States Department of Defense for a single day.

3. The secretary-general should be limited to one term, thereby eliminating for good and all the influence of elective politics on the conduct of his office and increasing his freedom of action.

4. The secretary-general should be authorized to take initiatives in conflicts or disputes that, in his opinion, might endanger the peace. His actions should be subject to the approval of the Security Council.

5. All specialized agencies should be under the general supervision of the secretary-general; their budgets should be reviewed by him before submission to the agency councils. In 1977 the

General Assembly took a wobbly step in this direction. Resolution 32/197 established the office of Director-General for Development and International Economic Cooperation, which is charged with providing "effective leadership to the various components of the United Nations system...and in exercising overall coordination...to ensure a multidisciplinary approach to the problems of development on a system wide basis" and "ensuring, within the United Nations, the coherence, coordination and efficient management of all activities in the economic and social fields financed by the regular budget or by extra-budgetary sources." The toothlessness of this measure as far as the specialized agencies are concerned is readily apparent, and my informants tell me that the director-general has had little effect on them, although he has had considerable impact on the United Nations itself. As the United Nations witticism has it, "those who can, do; those who can't, coordinate." An infusion of more authority over agencies using the name and reputation of the United Nations is obviously needed.

6. Directors of specialized agencies should be limited to one term for the same reasons that this limit should be applied to the office of the secretary-general.

7. The General Assembly should authorize a review of the United Nations policies in organizing and maintaining specialized agencies. It is possible that some could be merged to good effect, as for example the Food and Agricultural Organization, the International Fund for Agricultural Development, and the United Nations Conference on Trade Development.

8. While the international civil service of the United Nations has been subjected to unfair derogation, the rules need an overhaul. Merit cannot be the sole criterion for holding an office, nor can seniority or national origin. But there must be better ways of weeding out incompetents, whatever their nationality. I liked the position of the permanent representative of Singapore, who told me that he has been instructed never to recommend a Singapore national for employment—Singaporeans desiring United Nations jobs are on their own. This policy should be general.

That's a beginning. There will be more studies of the management and personnel practices of the United Nations during the coming year as the effect of the money crisis continues to be felt. It is unfortunate that it requires a crisis to renovate a system, but out of this crisis the United Nations should emerge as a stronger and more respected organization.

Many of the criticisms of the United Nations are exaggerations for an effect intended by American polemicists hostile to the very existence of the United Nations. Most of the many people I have interviewed in various United Nations facilities have been well qualified, hard working experts in their particular fields. They do not deserve the detractions and ridicule showered on them by think-tank occupants who don't know what they are talking about. My recommendations for a review of the organization and rules governing the international civil service are meant to assure that the majority of competent people are not damaged by the presence of the useless few.

The constitutional and administrative changes I have proposed, and others that may be advanced by persons more intimately familiar with the United Nations, are surely needed, and no doubt some of them will be put into effect. Their value depends on a renewal of the use of the United Nations by a world that is drifting into international anarchy in an age when an international system is needed as never before.

What Is Peace?

There is an old Quaker saying, the origin of which I have never traced, that is apposite to any answer to this question: *There is no way to peace. Peace is the way.* Peace is not the mere absence of war; if that were all, we would have to resign ourselves, as my adversary complacently does, to the inevitability of eventual war.

Peace must be the active pursuit of conditions that remove the causes of war. If nations stagnate in hopeless poverty, aware, as they must be in a shrinking world, of affluence elsewhere, eventually there will be conflict and warfare. To engage in a purposeful rational campaign to raise such nations from their miseries is to pursue peace.

A campaign to collect funds for the relief of famine in Ethiopia may be necessary to prevent the atrocity of starvation. The measures required to prevent the periodic recurrence of famine call for more than fund-raising. Practical research under many disciplines, the introduction of new technology, and education of the people are all urgently required if we are not to be called on for an endless succession of campaigns for famine relief. Ways must be found to mollify the suspicious Ethiopian government so that its cooperation may be obtained for a process that will take many years to complete. It is unrealistic to expect that this task can be undertaken by a Western government acting alone, or that the Soviet government has the expertise, the will, or the material and technical resources to do what has to be done for its client state. A coordinated program under United Nations auspices is needed. The example of Ethiopia is only one of the many thrusts toward peace that will make peace possible for destitute nations. I cannot resist a repetition of the obvious: If we were not wasting so much money on munitions, if we were not preparing so avidly for war, we could prepare more easily and more effectively for peace.

The Preamble of the United Nations Charter is explicit on the organization's purposes. Beyond the maintenance of international peace and security, the nations are "to cooperate in solving international problems of an economic, social, cultural or humanitarian character, and in promoting respect for human rights and fundamental freedoms for all."

To the embarrassment of the nations of the First World, the "Group of 77," the coalition of Third World nations, has been outspoken in demanding that the United Nations should be as vigorous as possible in promoting cooperation toward these ends. It irritates conservatives that the Third World appears to consider the solution of its economic problems as a more important objective than an unambiguous resistance to communism.

Fortunately, the international community contains wise and resourceful personages who recognize that there are other objectives beyond the dismantling of Communist influence that the world must achieve. In 1978 an Independent Commission on International Development Issues was formed under the chairmanship of Willy Brandt, the former chancellor of West Germany. The commission's report was published in 1980, to some applause for its high-minded altruism, and with little apparent practical effect. A particular sticking point was the inclusion in its "emergency program" of a proposal for "a large scale transfer of resources to developing countries."[18] While the commission noted that the underutilization of industrial plant in the affluent North could be remedied by production of capital goods for the South, this suggestion fell on resistant ears in the major northern countries. The report documented in stark detail the increasing economic and agricultural adversities of the African countries and other nations falling into the "least-developed" class. Much discussion followed within the United Nations community, leading to the appointment under General Assembly auspices of an *Ad Hoc* Committee on the Critical Economic Situation in Africa.

The committee submitted its findings and recommendations in a report to the General Assembly in May 1986.[19] The heart of the report is a "United Nations Program of Action for African Economic Recovery and Development 1986–1990." The program calls for an investment of 128. billion dollars over these five years, of which the African nations would commit themselves to provide 82.5 billion dollars (64.4% of the total cost). The general objective is the creation of conditions that will make possible economic growth. A great deal of emphasis is placed on the achievement of self-sufficiency by African countries through "South–South cooperation." The program necessarily requires a lot of assistance from the non-African "international community," especially through easing the financial constraints imposed by the enormous indebtedness with which most of these countries are burdened, as well as with substantial subventions under the coordination of the secretary-general.

As I write, it is far too early to predict success for this urgently necessary undertaking. At a time when severe budgetary constraints restrict appropriations for foreign aid in most countries, there will be considerable difficulty in raising the 45.6 billion dollars the program calls for from the developed international community. Whether it is realistic to expect the enormous investment specified for the African nations must be in serious doubt for the present. The program itself is impressively practical; there is little of the sonorous rhetoric that clutters up so many United Nations documents. It is an example of an initiative that would not have been possible without the General Assembly's interest. It remains to be seen how well the global community can carry it out.

Because of the horrifying violations of human rights in so many countries on such large scales and over so many years, this is an age when as never before men of goodwill must be concerned about the limits that sovereign states must place on their power to restrict political dissidents and to punish criminals. From the beginning, in its Charter, the United Nations has been called on to define these limits and to take such steps as may be possible to assure that limits are observed. Its success has been sadly deficient. Reports of human rights violations are made to the General Assembly, resolutions are passed calling on nations that are in violation to end practices that are often abominable—with little more effect than publicity. The recalcitrance of South Africa and the Soviet Union[20] in the face of innumerable justified resolutions are only two of many examples.

My opponent objects on theoretical grounds to the concept of natural rights, but this is an age when these rights, by whatever word we refer to them, must be reinforced by world public opinion. We build for peace by vigorous international support for the rights to life, freedom, and information.[21]

Despite the present shortcomings of UNESCO management, the attainment of the objectives of that agency are essential to the goal of peace. Educated people can be misled, as Hitler and Mussolini convincingly demonstrated, but freedom and the improvement of the human condition do not take place in countries where the population gropes in the night of ignorance. Science should not be the prerogative of a few rich countries. Its benefits and opportunities should be available throughout the world. A strong program to promote education and to increase engagement in and understanding of science is the pursuit of peace.

The sound and fury in the General Assembly and the ponderous resolutions of the Security Council are inescapable elements of the United Nations procedures. Even when it is most outrageous—as for example in the debate over the Zionism-is-racism resolution—the steamy eloquence of anti-Western delegates is harmless, if offensive to the thin-skinned. It is in the power of the Security Council to do a great deal of good. Once the United States and the Soviet Union find more common ground than that on which they now stand, the stabilization of most of the world's most serious trouble spots can be expected. Nevertheless, as one manager in the United Nations Development Fund remarked to me, the General Assembly and the Security Council are much less important activities of the United Nations than his agency and many others that are charged with building peace rather than preventing war.

These sentiments were more authoritatively expressed in October 1985 by the late Olof Palme, then prime minister of Sweden, when he addressed the General Assembly at the commemoration of the 40th anniversary of the United Nations:

> A child in Africa learns to read in a UNESCO-financed school. A farmer in Asia receives a sack of seed labelled FAO or WFP. UNDP, with its technical projects, touches almost every developing country in the world. Refugees in all continents are protected by the activities of the High Commissioner for Refugees. Women fighting for equality and dignity are encouraged by discussions in United Nations fora such as the recent Nairobi Conference.... If, as we sincerely hope, the initiative taken by WHO and UNICEF to immunize the children in the world against serious infectious disease by 1990 is crowned with success, innumerable families will think of the United Nations as a benefactor.
>
> Many of the people who have such direct experience of what the United Nations stands for may have scant knowledge of the intricacies of great power politics and the workings of United Nations organs. But they instinctively feel that the United Nations is essential...to their well-being, perhaps to their survival. It can be hoped that they will form, over time, a much needed United Nations con-

stituency, that they will make their voices heard, claiming a say, demanding that power politics, high over their heads, do not jeopardize their lives....

There is simply no alternative to international cooperation. Only through joint endeavours can we hope to move from common fear to common security.[22]

In the beginning, the United States was the dominant nation in the councils of the United Nations. The devastated European powers and those developing countries that were members looked to us for leadership. The USSR and its satellites were inept in their participation and unable to muster support for blocking many of our initiatives.

All that has changed. Not much happens that we don't want to happen, but our initiatives have been infrequent and unimportant. Our peevish complaints of our beneficiaries' ingratitude and our demands for support for our positions are inconsistent with the leadership in the international community to which we are entitled. In short, the United States is not *using* the United Nations.

There are far too many Americans who are willing to drift back to the isolationism that constituted our foreign policy throughout most of our lucky history. Dr. van den Haag's conviction of the inevitability of war suggests that in his mind a reversion to an age of innocence and isolation would be the desirable route to peace. We are no longer in a position to pull up the drawbridge and huddle in Fortress America. The world is too small, and our own need for interdependence is too great. We have to share in the building of peace.

The absence of war will be cause enough for rejoicing. In building a peaceful world in which the fear of war has been replaced by the active pursuit of peace there will always be problems and conflicts. None of them will be beyond peaceful resolution. As desperate want is erased from the long list of our concerns, as human rights become generally respected, as ignorance is relieved, a general peace can be expected from which the human race will not wish to retreat. Let the United Nations flourish toward this end!

Notes

1. See Chapter 1, p. 32.
2. For an extended review of this historical sweep, see Hedley Bull and Adam Watson, eds., *The Expansion of International Society* (Oxford: Clarendon Press, 1984), especially pp. 425–435.
3. But not of North Africa or Indochina, of course. The First World paid a heavy price for French obstinacy. The unfortunate inhabitants of the former French colonies of Indochina are still paying.
4. Linda M. Fasulo, "Covering the U.N.," *The Interdependent* 12 (3) (May–June 1986), p. 1.
5. "Directions for the UN: US Public Opinion on the United Nations," results of the 1983 Roper poll commissioned by the United Nations Association of the United States of America (background paper prepared by UNA-USA, September 1983).
6. "Public Opinion on the UN: What Pollsters Forget to Ask," *Bulletin of the League of Women Voters Education Fund* (July 1977).
7. Paul D. Martin, "US Public Opinion and the UN," in *The US, the UN and the Management of Global Change*, ed. Toby Trister Gati (New York: New York University Press, 1983), pp. 300–301.
8. See Part I, p. 21.
9. Jean Bodin, *Six Books of the Commonwealth*, abr. and trans. M. J. Tooley (Oxford: Basil Blackwell, no date), pp. 174–180.
10. Ibid., p. 178.
11. The presence of Soviet troops on the territory of its Eastern European "allies" obviously limits the sovereignty of each of these nations, none of which can conduct either foreign or domestic policy that deviates from Soviet ideology. It has been a long time since the last Western intervention in the affairs of West Germany, which is still occupied by the Allied powers.
12. Sanford J. Ungar, ed., *Estrangement: America and the World* (New York and Oxford: Oxford University Press, 1985).
13. Ibid., p. 289.
14. Ibid., p. 299.
15. Ibid., p. 284.
16. Not that parliamentary loquacity is unique to the United Nations, as any casual reader of the *Congressional Record*, or, in England, of the *Hansard* record of the debates in the House of Commons, will be well aware.
17. In his speech at the 40th anniversary celebration of the United Nations, the late Olof Palme, then prime minister of Sweden, remarked, "A more even distribution of the assessed contributions would better reflect the fact that this Organization is the instrument of all nations and make it less dependent on contributions from any single member state. In that case, the rest of us would have to shoulder a somewhat greater responsibility." Statement of Prime

Minister Olof Palme, October 21, 1945 (Permanent Mission of Sweden to the United Nations, photocopy).

18. *North-South: A Program for Survival*, the report of the Independent Commission on International Development Issues under the chairmanship of Willy Brandt (Cambridge, Massachusetts: M.I.T. Press, 1980), pp. 276–282.

19. Report of the *Ad Hoc* Committee on the Critical Economic Situation in Africa, May 27–31, 1986 (Document A/S-13/AC.1/L3. May 31, 1986).

20. See "Report on the situation of human rights in Afghanistan," prepared by the special rapporteur, Mr. Felix Ermacora, in accordance with Commission on Human Rights resolution 1984/55. (Economic and Social Council, Commission on Human Rights, Document E/N.4/1985/21, February 19, 1985).

21. It is encouraging to note that President Reagan has reversed his earlier position that human rights are not the business of American foreign policy. For an assessment, see Tamar Jacoby, "The Reagan Turnaround on Human Rights," *Foreign Affairs* 64(5) (Summer 1986), p. 1066.

22. Palme, note 11.

CHAPTER 10

In Conclusion

ERNEST VAN DEN HAAG

The time has come to summarize what I have to say about the U.N., what it is and does, and what it was supposed to be and do. Can it be useful? Has it been? Has it been harmful? Has the world benefited? Has the United States? Has it had any effect? What will the U.N. future be like, and what, if anything, can we do about it?

The United States participated in the last two world wars and, when peace was reestablished, pushed for an international organization meant to prevent war in the future. The League of Nations (which ultimately the Senate refused to let President Wilson join) was born with high hopes after the First World War, the U.N. (which the United States joined) after the Second. We fathered both, and they developed numerous subsidiary agencies.

The League of Nations disappeared with the Second World War, leaving no mourners, but it was revived as the U.N. at the end of it. One might say it was reborn with a vengeance, for the U.N. is a far more elaborate organization, with a far more complex and numerous bureaucracy and many more subsidiary agencies. Can it do better than the League of Nations? Has it done so? Above all, is it likely to prevent wars, major or minor, by means direct or indirect?

Unfortunately, the answer to all these questions must be negative. The U.N., as was the League of Nations, is an international organization. It consists of far too many bureaucrats and of the member states, meeting periodically and voting on resolutions, enforceable only if the member states are willing to be bound by them—i.e., not enforceable, except if the power of the supporting member states is used against the member states that do not comply. But each state, or group of states, always has been free, and sometimes able, to enforce its will on another. Thus, the U.N. offers nothing new, other than the label. This goes as well for the many activities supporters like to credit the U.N. with: helping to remedy or prevent epidemics here, illiteracy or slavery somewhere else; sending neutral troops to prevent the troops of two consenting enemy states from going at each other; watching the weather; or helping agricultural production, giving advice, lending money, sponsoring treaties, etc., etc. All this was being done privately or by concerned governments, or groups of governments, long before the U.N. was invented. Only the label is new and, for better or for worse, the bloated bureaucracy. Attempts to enforce U.N. resolutions may include anything from economic sanctions to war. None of this is new either, or less dangerous, or more effective or smooth under the U.N. label than under any other label—no different from, say, the Allies versus the Axis before and during the Second World War, or the Western powers (including Japan) versus the Eastern powers currently.

Somehow most of the people who put their faith in the U.N. confuse this international organization—a collection of all the nations that meet together regularly in New York to make speeches at one another and to pass forgettable resolutions—with a supranational one. A supranational organization would have authority over the member nations (as the federal government of the United States has over the states) and the power to enforce its authority. That would mean that the nations would give up the right to go to war against one another—they occasionally have pretended to give up this right, but only in theory—and, consequently, their separate national military forces, which no longer would be needed if nations actually renounced war as a means of settling conflicts. Disarmament would ultimately make it possible for the supranational organization to run the world with a small police force, sufficient if there are no other military forces. But would-be conquerors won't give up the forces needed for conquest; nor will those fearful of being conquered give up the forces they need for defense.

Obviously a renunciation of war cannot be taken seriously if each nation keeps the military forces that are useful only for war. There is no chance for actual renunciation, and, contrary to opinions often heard, I cannot see wherein the U.N. is a way station to it.

Although a supernational organization in principle may prevent war (the way the Roman Empire did through the *Pax Romana*, the peace it enforced by monopolizing military might), a supernational authority that would monopolize military power would have some serious drawbacks. The world would be run by a centralized bureaucracy meant to prevent serious conflicts among the nations without interfering in their domestic affairs. It is hard to see how this would be done. Harder still to see how conflicts—no longer called wars, but instead revolutions—would be prevented. Further, if revolutions were prevented, the domestic order of many nations might well be totally frozen, whether that order be just or unjust, democratic or dictatorial, equitable or oppressive. Actually, revolutions and civil and guerrilla wars—such as have been endemic for years in Colombia and El Salvador—would take the place of international wars, to little advantage. But there is no danger that we will have a supernational order: China, the Soviet Union, Japan, the European nations, and the United States are not likely to volunteer in any foreseeable future to renounce their sovereignty and to be governed by a supernational authority. It is hard to see even who would select it and how. Conquest may do the job as it did for Rome. But, fortunately, that threat too is remote. So is anything resembling a supernational authority.

Thus, we are reduced to international organizations, which, by definition, are impotent. They consist of just those nations and alliances among which they are supposed to keep the peace, without having independent means of doing so. There is no reason why nations hostile to one another will be less hostile, or less inclined to violence, if they are given the collective name "U.N."

Could the various agencies of the U.N. be useful, then, in reducing the hostility of the various nations to one another and in replacing violence with negotiations? And could they accomplish things in the common interest that would not be accomplished otherwise? Not really. Most of the agencies have served simply as arenas for the pursuit of the hostility of the nations and blocks of nations toward one another, as was predictable.

Even agencies that have straightforward and universally accepted goals have been perverted. Labor unions, employers, and governments were to work out international labor problems in the International Labor Agency (a leftover from the League of Nations). But the agency mainly served the Soviet government. Its "unions" are actually government agencies. Thus, the Soviet employer, union, and government representatives were actually all government representatives. The Marxist and pro-Marxist Third World nations were no better. Together they dominated the labor agency. The United States, under pressure by its own quite independent labor unions, left the agency. We returned only after some of the worst anticapitalist and pro-Soviet extravagances were corrected. Still, the usefulness of the agency is doubtful and the cost excessive relative to the accomplishment.

Most of its agencies, as does the U.N. itself, spend money with abandon. A quarter of this money comes from the United States (actually much more does, if contributions for many special projects are counted). Thus, the U.N. spent $70 million to build a conference hall in Addis Ababa, while throughout Ethiopia, the country of which Addis Ababa is the capital, people died of hunger. (Communist governments seem to have a talent for creating famines that kill many of the peasants whom these governments dislike. What hapened in Ethiopia happened on a grander scale in the Soviet Union before.)

Not only is our money wasted, it is also used to harm us. Since the nations hostile, on ideological or other grounds, to the United States do not have the power to harm us materially, they use our money to try to harm us through propaganda. They are fairly successful in this, and we have been exceedingly and, I think, excessively patient. They have done so for years while the

United States continues to pay the bill and would leave a U.N. agency, such as UNESCO, only after a decennium of abuse.

The U.N. is used as a vehicle to abuse not only the United States with its own money; our money is used as well to abuse allies such as Israel. Thus, resolutions are passed according to which Zionism is racism, such as the Nazis displayed. In every one of the U.N. agencies, Third World and Eastern countries pushed resolutions—often totally irrelevant to the agencies' task—abusing Israel and attempting to isolate it. Similar resolutions are sponsored against dictatorships lacking leftist symbols by those armed with them.

Actually, the U.N. itself is a racist organization using its energies to make a pariah of South Africa. In that country a white minority oppresses a black majority. Despite that oppression, the black majority has a higher standard of living and more effective rights and liberties than the black majority has in most black-run African states. Indeed, South African racism is in the process of being slowly dismantled. Never mind. What the Third World nations resent is not dictatorship and oppression. Most of these nations have both, in far more flagrant form than in South Africa. What is resented is that the dictatorship is by whites over blacks, and not by blacks over other blacks. This certainly seems to be racism at its worst. What is wrong is dictatorship and oppression—regardless of the race of the oppressor and the oppressed. Yet in the U.N. not an eyebrow is raised when Soviet delegates excoriate South Africa—which never had a Gulag and does not prevent anyone from leaving, or persecute churches. Nor when Middle Eastern dictatorships, such as Syria, excoriate Israel for oppressing Arabs, who, in fact, are far less oppressed in Israel than in Syria.

On the whole, the organization, always ineffective, has become harmful. The problem for us is not whether, but when to leave, and in what manner. We should try not to upset too much the deluded idealists such as Professor Conrad, of which there are many in our own universities and in other liberal hangouts.

As I am writing, a great furor is made about Kurt Waldheim, the retired secretary-general of the U.N., who, using his former position as a springboard, became president of Austria. Waldheim is accused of having been a war criminal, of taking an active part in Nazi atrocities while serving in the German army during World War II. The evidence for this is questionable. However, there seems little doubt that Waldheim—despite his denial—was aware of these atrocities and, without committing any himself, passively tolerated them and cooperated in the bureaucratic organizations that backed them up. It would have taken a courage that few can be expected to have to oppose these atrocities from within the German army in which Waldheim was an officer. Such opposition would have been futile. Still, if Waldheim ever tried to help the persecuted, or to prevent the death of innocent hostages, or to help a single person, it is a well-kept secret. Unfortunately, not many of us are in a position to cast the first stone at Waldheim. Still, he was dishonest by pretending that he was deaf and dumb and never knew anything while he served as part of the command of the German army in Greece and Yugoslavia. The Austrians decided they want him as president. They are entitled to him. As for the U.N., it probably deserved that loathsome opportunist as secretary-general. After all, the organization has many member governments—a majority—known for committing atrocities, though, with the exception of the Soviet Union, on a smaller scale than the Nazis.

What is the outlook for peace and prosperity that the U.N. was to help bring about? The outlook is better without the U.N. But even with the U.N. I am fairly optimistic. Neither of the superpowers is interested in a major conflict. The Soviet Union will continue to try to expand its power wherever it finds an opportunity, but it does not wish to risk a major war, which would endanger the power of its ruling *nomenklatura*. We certainly don't either. The superpowers each want to be strong enough to prevent tempting the other to fight. Both seem likely to succeed in the foreseeable future. Small wars and invasions will be with us. As I pointed out, as long as there are major sovereign powers, war is going to be as certain as death is. But just as one may say of a healthy individual that his death is certain but not imminent, so we can say of the state of international relations that war is certain but not imminent.

The U.N.? It is quite irrelevant to war and peace, important only to public relations. It will probably survive until the next world war in its bloated, expensive, and useless way, whether or not we participate, and it will try to inflict what harm it can on the United States and its allies. But it will play no serious role in foreign policy, being on the whole a media spectacle, of as much importance to international relations as football or Sumo wrestling. In time, I hope that even our state department will understand this. I am an optimist.

Charter of the United Nations

WE THE PEOPLES OF THE UNITED NATIONS DETERMINED
to save succeeding generations from the scourge of war,
which twice in our lifetime has brought untold sorrow
to mankind, and
to reaffirm faith in fundamental human rights, in the
dignity and worth of the human person, in the equal
rights of men and women and of nations large and small,
and
to establish conditions under which justice and respect
for the obligations arising from treaties and other
sources of international law can be maintained,
and
to promote social progress and better standards of life
in larger freedom,
AND FOR THESE ENDS
to practice tolerance and live together in peace with
one another as good neighbors, and
to unite our strength to maintain international peace
and security, and
to ensure, by the acceptance of principles and the
institution of methods, that armed force shall not be
used, save in the common interest, and
to employ international machinery for the promotion
of the economic and social advancement of all peoples,
HAVE RESOLVED TO COMBINE OUR EFFORTS TO ACCOMPLISH
THESE AIMS
Accordingly, our respective Governments, through
representatives assembled in the city of San Francisco,
who have exhibited their full powers found to be in
good and due form, have agreed to the present Charter

of the United Nations and do hereby establish an
international organization to be known as the United Nations.

Chapter I
PURPOSES AND PRINCIPLES

Article 1
The Purposes of the United Nations are:

1. To maintain international peace and security, and to that end: to take effective collective measures for the prevention and removal of threats to the peace, and for the suppression of acts of aggression or other breaches of the peace, and to bring about by peaceful means, and in conformity with the principles of justice and international law, adjustment or settlement of international disputes or situations which might lead to a breach of the peace;

2. To develop friendly relations among nations based on respect for the principle of equal rights and self-determination of peoples, and to take other appropriate measures to strengthen universal peace;

3. To achieve international co-operation in solving international problems of an economic, social, cultural, or humanitarian character, and in promoting and encouraging respect for human rights and for fundamental freedoms for all without distinction as to race, sex, language, or religion; and

4. To be a centre for harmonizing the actions of nations in the attainment of these common ends.

Article 2
The Organization and its Members, in pursuit of the Purposes stated in Article 1, shall act in accordance with the following Principles.

1. The Organization is based on the principle of the sovereign equality of all its Members.

2. All Members, in order to ensure to all of them the rights and benefits resulting from membership, shall fulfil in good faith the obligations assumed by them in accordance with the present Charter.

3. All Members shall settle their international disputes by peaceful means in such a manner that international peace and security, and justice, are not endangered.

4. All Members shall refrain in their international relations from the threat or use of force against the territorial integrity or political independence of any state, or in any other manner inconsistent with the Purposes of the United Nations.

5. All Members shall give the United Nations every assistance in any action it takes in accordance with the present Charter, and shall refrain from giving assistance to any state against which the United Nations is taking preventive or enforcement action.

6. The Organization shall ensure that states which are not Members of the United Nations act in accordance with these Principles so far as may be necessary for the maintenance of international peace and security.

7. Nothing contained in the present Charter shall authorize the United Nations to intervene in matters which are essentially within the domestic jurisdiction of any state or shall require the Members to submit such matters to settlement under the present Charter; but this principle shall not prejudice the application of enforcement measures under Chapter VII.

Chapter II

MEMBERSHIP

Article 3

The original Members of the United Nations shall be the states which, having participated in the United Nations Conference on International Organization at San Francisco, or having previously signed the Declaration by United Nations of 1 January 1942, sign the present Charter and ratify it in accordance with Article 110.

Article 4

1. Membership in the United Nations is open to all other peace-loving states which accept the obligations contained in the present Charter and, in the judgment of the Organization, are able and willing to carry out these obligations.

2. The admission of any such state to membership in the United Nations will be effected by a decision of the General Assembly upon the recommendation of the Security Council.

Article 5

A Member of the United Nations against which preventive or enforcement action has been taken by the Security Council may be suspended from the exercise of the rights and privileges of membership by the General Assembly upon the recommendation of the Security Council. The exercise of these rights and privileges may be restored by the Security Council.

Article 6

A Member of the United Nations which has persistently violated the Principles contained in the present Charter may be expelled from the Organization by the General Assembly upon the recommendation of the Security Council.

Chapter III

ORGANS

Article 7

1. There are established as the principal organs of the United Nations: a General Assembly, a Security Council, an Economic and Social Council, a Trusteeship Council, an International Court of Justice, and a Secretariat.

2. Such subsidiary organs as may be found necessary may be established in accordance with the present Charter.

Article 8

The United Nations shall place no restrictions on the eligibility of men and women to participate in any capacity and under conditions of equality in its principal and subsidiary organs.

Chapter IV

THE GENERAL ASSEMBLY

Composition

Article 9

1. The General Assembly shall consist of all the Members of the United Nations.

2. Each Member shall have not more than five representatives in the General Assembly.

Functions and Powers

Article 10

The General Assembly may discuss any questions or any matters within the scope of the present Charter or relating to the powers and functions of any organs provided for in the present Charter, and, except as provided in Article 12, may make recommendations to the Members of the United Nations or to the Security Council or to both on any such questions or matters.

Article 11

1. The General Assembly may consider the general principles of co-operation in the maintenance of international peace and security, including the principles governing disarmament and the regulation of armaments, and may make recommendations with regard to such principles to the Members or to the Security Council or to both.

2. The General Assembly may discuss any questions relating to the maintenance of international peace and security brought before it by any Member of the United Nations, or by the Security Council, or by a state which is not a Member of the United Nations in accordance with Article 35, paragraph 2, and, except as provided in Article 12, may make recommendations with regard to any such questions to the state or states concerned or to the Security Council or to both. Any such question on which action is necessary shall be referred to the Security Council by the General Assembly either before or after discussion.

3. The General Assembly may call the attention of the Security Council to situations which are likely to endanger international peace and security.

4. The powers of the General Assembly set forth in this Article shall not limit the general scope of Article 10.

Article 12

1. While the Security Council is exercising in respect of any dispute or situation the functions assigned to it in the present Charter, the General Assembly shall not make any recommendation with regard to that dispute or situation unless the Security Council so requests.

2. The Secretary-General, with the consent of the Security Council, shall notify the General Assembly at each session of any matters relative to the maintenance of international peace and security which are being dealt with by the Security Council and shall similarly notify the General Assembly, or the Members of the United Nations if the General Assembly is not in session, immediately the Security Council ceases to deal with such matters.

Article 13

1. The General Assembly shall initiate studies and make recommendations for the purpose of:

a. promoting international co-operation in the political field and encouraging the progressive development of international law and its codification;

b. promoting international co-operation in the economic, social, cultural, educational, and health fields, and assisting in the realization of human rights and fundamental freedoms for all without distinction as to race, sex, language, or religion.

2. The further responsibilities, functions and powers of the General Assembly with respect to matters mentioned in paragraph 1(b) above are set forth in Chapters IX and X.

Article 14

Subject to the provisions of Article 12, the General Assembly may recommend measures for the peaceful adjustment of any situation, regardless of origin, which it deems likely to impair the general welfare or friendly relations among nations, including situations resulting from a violation of the provisions of the present Charter setting forth the Purposes and Principles of the United Nations.

Article 15

1. The General Assembly shall receive and consider annual and special reports from the Security Council; these reports shall include an account of the measures that the Security Council has decided upon or taken to maintain international peace and security.

2. The General Assembly shall receive and consider reports from the other organs of the United Nations.

Article 16

The General Assembly shall perform such functions with respect to the international trusteeship system as are assigned to it under Chapters XII and XIII, including the approval of the trusteeship agreements for areas not designated as strategic.

Article 17

1. The General Assembly shall consider and approve the budget of the Organization.

2. The expenses of the Organization shall be borne by the Members as apportioned by the General Assembly.

3. The General Assembly shall consider and approve any financial and budgetary arrangements with specialized agencies referred to in Article 57 and shall examine the administrative budgets of such specialized agencies with a view to making recommendations to the agencies concerned.

Voting

Article 18

1. Each member of the General Assembly shall have one vote.

2. Decisions of the General Assembly on important questions shall be made by a two-thirds majority of the members present and voting. These questions shall include: recommendations with respect to the maintenance of international peace and security, the election of the non-permanent members of the Security Council, the election of the members of the Economic and Social Council, the election of members of the Trusteeship Council in accordance with paragraph 1(c) of Article 86, the admission of new Members to the United Nations, the suspension of the rights and privileges of membership, the expulsion of Members, questions relating to the operation of the trusteeship system, and budgetary questions.

3. Decisions on other questions, including the determination of additional categories of questions to be decided by a two-thirds majority, shall be made by a majority of the members present and voting.

Article 19

A Member of the United Nations which is in arrears in the payment of its financial contributions to the Organization shall have no vote in the General Assembly if the amount of its arrears equals or exceeds the amount of the contributions due from it for the preceding two full years. The General Assembly may, nevertheless, permit such a Member to vote if it is satisfied that the failure to pay is due to conditions beyond the control of the Member.

Procedure

Article 20

The General Assembly shall meet in regular annual sessions and in such special sessions as occasion may require. Special sessions shall be convoked by the Secretary-General at the request of the Security Council or of a majority of the Members of the United Nations.

Article 21

The General Assembly shall adopt its own rules of procedure. It shall elect its President for each session.

Article 22

The General Assembly may establish such subsidiary organs as it deems necessary for the performance of its functions.

Chapter V
THE SECURITY COUNCIL

Composition
Article 23

1. The Security Council shall consist of fifteen Members of the United Nations. The Republic of China, France, the Union of Soviet Socialist Republics, the United Kingdom of Great Britain and Northern Ireland, and the United States of America shall be permanent members of the Security Council. The General Assembly shall elect ten other Members of the United Nations to be non-permanent members of the Security Council, due regard being specially paid, in the first instance to the contribution of Members of the United Nations to the maintenance of international peace and security and to the other purposes of the Organization, and also to equitable geographical distribution.

2. The non-permanent members of the Security Council shall be elected for a term of two years. In the first election of the non-permanent members after the increase of the membership of the Security Council from eleven to fifteen, two of the four additional members shall be chosen for a term of one year. A retiring member shall not be eligible for immediate re-election.

3. Each member of the Security Council shall have one representative.

Functions and Powers
Article 24

1. In order to ensure prompt and effective action by the United Nations, its Members confer on the Security Council primary responsibility for the maintenance of international peace and security, and agree that in carrying out its duties under this responsibility the Security Council acts on their behalf.

2. In discharging these duties the Security Council shall act in accordance with the Purposes and Principles of the United Nations. The specific powers granted to the Security Council for the discharge of these duties are laid down in Chapters VI, VII, VIII, and XII.

3. The Security Council shall submit annual and, when necessary, special reports to the General Assembly for its consideration.

Article 25

The Members of the United Nations agree to accept and carry out the decisions of the Security Council in accordance with the present Charter.

Article 26

In order to promote the establishment and maintenance of international peace and security with the least diversion for armaments of the world's human and economic resources, the Security Council shall be responsible for formulating, with the assistance of the Military Staff Committee referred to in Article 47, plans to be submitted to the Members of the United Nations for the establishment of a system for the regulation of armaments.

Voting

Article 27

1. Each member of the Security Council shall have one vote.

2. Decisions of the Security Council on procedural matters shall be made by an affirmative vote of nine members.

3. Decisions of the Security Council on all other matters shall be made by an affirmative vote of nine members including the concurring votes of the permanent members; provided that, in decisions under Chapter VI, and under paragraph 3 of Article 52, a party to a dispute shall abstain from voting.

Procedure

Article 28

1. The Security Council shall be so organized as to be able to function continuously. Each member of the Security Council shall for this purpose be represented at all times at the seat of the Organization.

2. The Security Council shall hold periodic meetings at which each of its members may, if it so desires, be represented by a member of the government or by some other specially designated representative.

3. The Security Council may hold meetings at such places other than the seat of the Organization as in its judgment will best facilitate its work.

Article 29

The Security Council may establish such subsidiary organs as it deems necessary for the performance of its functions.

Article 30

The Security Council shall adopt its own rules of procedure, including the method of selecting its President.

Article 31

Any Member of the United Nations which is not a member of the Security Council may participate, without vote, in the discussion of any question brought before the Security Council whenever the latter considers that the interests of that Member are specially affected.

Article 32

Any Member of the United Nations which is not a member of the Security Council or any state which is not a Member of the United Nations, if it is a party to a dispute under consideration by the Security Council, shall be invited to participate, without vote, in the discussion relating to the dispute. The Security Council shall lay down such conditions as it deems just for the participation of a state which is not a Member of the United Nations.

Chapter VI
PACIFIC SETTLEMENT OF DISPUTES

Article 33

1. The parties to any dispute, the continuance of which is likely to endanger the maintenance of international peace and security, shall, first of all, seek a solution by negotiation, enquiry, mediation, conciliation, arbitration, judicial settlement, resort to regional agencies or arrangements, or other peaceful means of their own choice.

2. The Security Council shall, when it deems necessary, call upon the parties to settle their dispute by such means.

Article 34

The Security Council may investigate any dispute, or any situation which might lead to international friction or give rise to a dispute, in order to determine whether the continuance of the dispute or situation is likely to endanger the maintenance of international peace and security.

Article 35

1. Any Member of the United Nations may bring any dispute, or any situation of the nature referred to in Article 34, to the attention of the Security Council or of the General Assembly.

2. A state which is not a Member of the United Nations may bring to the attention of the Security Council or of the General Assembly any dispute to which it is a party if it accepts in advance, for the purposes of the dispute, the obligations of pacific settlement provided in the present Charter.

3. The proceedings of the General Assembly in respect of matters brought to its attention under this Article will be subject to the provisions of Articles 11 and 12.

Article 36

1. The Security Council may, at any stage of a dispute of the nature referred to in Article 33 or of a situation of like nature, recommend appropriate procedures or methods of adjustment.

2. The Security Council should take into consideration any procedures for the settlement of the dispute which have already been adopted by the parties.

3. In making recommendations under this Article the Security Council should also take into consideration that legal disputes should as a general rule be referred by the parties to the International Court of Justice in accordance with the provisions of the Statute of the Court.

Article 37

1. Should the parties to a dispute of the nature referred to in Article 33 fail to settle it by the means indicated in that Article, they shall refer it to the Security Council.

2. If the Security Council deems that the continuance of the dispute is in fact likely to endanger the maintenance of international peace and security, it shall decide whether to take action under Article 36 or to recommend such terms of settlement as it may consider appropriate.

Article 38

Without prejudice to the provisions of Articles 33 to 37, the Security Council may, if all the parties to any dispute so request, make recommendations to the parties with a view to a pacific settlement of the dispute.

Chapter VII

ACTION WITH RESPECT TO THREATS TO THE PEACE, BREACHES OF THE PEACE, AND ACTS OF AGGRESSION

Article 39

The Security Council shall determine the existence of any threat to the peace, breach of the peace, or act of aggression and shall make recommendations, or decide what measures shall be taken in accordance with Articles 41 and 42, to maintain or restore international peace and security.

Article 40

In order to prevent an aggravation of the situation, the Security Council may, before making the recommendations or deciding upon the measures provided for in Article 39, call upon the parties concerned to comply with such provisional measures as it deems necessary or desirable. Such provisional measures shall be without prejudice to the rights, claims, or position of the parties concerned. The Security Council shall duly take account of failure to comply with such provisional measures.

Article 41

The Security Council may decide what measures not involving the use of armed force are to be employed to give effect to its decisions, and it may call upon Members of the United Nations to apply such measures. These may include complete or partial interruption of economic relations and of rail, sea, air, postal, telegraphic, radio, and other means of communication, and the severance of diplomatic relations.

Article 42

Should the Security Council consider that measures provided for in Article 41 would be inadequate or have proved to be inadequate, it may take such action by air, sea, or land forces as may be necessary to maintain or restore international peace and security. Such action may include demonstrations, blockade, and other operations by air, sea, or land forces of Members of the United Nations.

Article 43

1. All Members of the United Nations, in order to contribute to the maintenance of international peace and security, undertake to make available to the Security Council, on its call and in accordance with a special agreement or agreements, armed forces, assistance, and facilities, including rights of passage, necessary for the purpose of maintaining international peace and security.

2. Such agreement or agreements shall govern the numbers and types of forces, their degree of readiness and general location, and the nature of the facilities and assistance to be provided.

3. The agreement or agreements shall be negotiated as soon as possible on the initiative of the Security Council. They shall be concluded between the Security Council and Members or between the Security Council and groups of Members and shall be subject to ratification by the signatory states in accordance with their respective constitutional processes.

Article 44

When the Security Council has decided to use force it shall, before calling upon a Member not represented on it to provide armed forces in fulfilment of the obligations assumed under Article 43, invite that Member, if the Member so desires, to participate in the decisions of the Security Council concerning the employment of contingents of that Member's armed forces.

Article 45

In order to enable the United Nations to take urgent military measures, Members shall hold immediately available national air-force contingents for combined international enforcement action. The strength and degree of readiness of these contingents and plans for their combined action shall be determined, within the limits laid down in the special agreement or agreements referred to in Article 43, by the Security Council with the assistance of the Military Staff Committee.

Article 46

Plans for the application of armed force shall be made by the Security Council with the assistance of the Military Staff Committee.

Article 47

1. There shall be established a Military Staff Committee to advise and assist the Security Council on all questions relating to the Security Council's military requirements for the maintenance of international peace and security, the employment and command of forces placed at its disposal, the regulation of armaments, and possible disarmament.

2. The Military Staff Committee shall consist of the Chiefs of Staff of the permanent members of the Security Council or their representatives. Any Member of the United Nations not permanently represented on the Committee shall be invited by the Committee to be associated with it when the efficient discharge of the Committee's responsibilities requires the participation of that Member in its work.

3. The Military Staff Committee shall be responsible under the Security

Council for the strategic direction of any armed forces placed at the disposal of the Security Council. Questions relating to the command of such forces shall be worked out subsequently.

4. The Military Staff Committee, with the authorization of the Security Council and after consultation with appropriate regional agencies, may establish regional sub-committees.

Article 48

1. The action required to carry out the decisions of the Security Council for the maintenance of international peace and security shall be taken by all the Members of the United Nations or by some of them, as the Security Council may determine.

2. Such decisions shall be carried out by the Members of the United Nations directly and through their action in the appropriate international agencies of which they are members.

Article 49

The Members of the United Nations shall join in affording mutual assistance in carrying out the measures decided upon by the Security Council.

Article 50

If preventive or enforcement measures against any state are taken by the Security Council, any other state, whether a Member of the United Nations or not, which finds itself confronted with special economic problems arising from the carrying out of those measures shall have the right to consult the Security Council with regard to a solution of those problems.

Article 51

Nothing in the present Charter shall impair the inherent right of individual or collective self-defence if an armed attack occurs against a Member of the United Nations, until the Security Council has taken measures necessary to maintain international peace and security. Measures taken by Members in the exercise of this right of self-defence shall be immediately reported to the Security Council and shall not in any way affect the authority and responsibility of the Security Council under the present Charter to take at any time such action as it deems necessary in order to maintain or restore international peace and security.

Chapter VIII

REGIONAL ARRANGEMENTS

Article 52

1. Nothing in the present Charter precludes the existence of regional arrangements or agencies for dealing with such matters relating to the maintenance of international peace and security as are appropriate for regional action, provided that such arrangements or agencies and their activities are consistent with the Purposes and Principles of the United Nations.

2. The Members of the United Nations entering into such arrangements or constituting such agencies shall make every effort to achieve pacific settlement of local disputes through such regional arrangements or by such regional agencies before referring them to the Security Council.

3. The Security Council shall encourage the development of pacific settlement of local disputes through such regional arrangements or by such regional agencies either on the initiative of the states concerned or by reference from the Security Council.

4. This Article in no way impairs the application of Articles 34 and 35.

Article 53

1. The Security Council shall, where appropriate, utilize such regional arrangements or agencies for enforcement action under its authority. But no enforcement action shall be taken under regional arrangements or by regional agencies without the authorization of the Security Council, with the exception of measures against any enemy state, as defined in paragraph 2 of this Article, provided for pursuant to Article 107 or in regional arrangements directed against renewal of aggressive policy on the part of any such state, until such time as the Organization may, on request of the Governments concerned, be charged with the responsibility for preventing further aggression by such a state.

2. The term enemy state as used in paragraph 1 of this Article applies to any state which during the Second World War has been an enemy of any signatory of the present Charter.

Article 54

The Security Council shall at all times be kept fully informed of activities undertaken or in contemplation under regional arrangements or by regional agencies for the maintenance of international peace and security.

Chapter IX

INTERNATIONAL ECONOMIC AND SOCIAL CO-OPERATION

Article 55

With a view to the creation of conditions of stability and well-being which are necessary for peaceful and friendly relations among nations based on respect for the principle of equal rights and self-determination of peoples, the United Nations shall promote:

a. higher standards of living, full employment, and conditions of economic and social progress and development;

b. solutions of international economic, social, health, and related problems; and international cultural and educational co-operation; and

c. universal respect for, and observance of, human rights and fundamental freedoms for all without distinction as to race, sex, language, or religion.

Article 56

All Members pledge themselves to take joint and separate action in cooperation with the Organization for the achievement of the purposes set forth in Article 55.

Article 57

1. The various specialized agencies, established by intergovernmental agreement and having wide international responsibilities, as defined in their basic instruments, in economic, social, cultural, educational, health, and related fields, shall be brought into relationship with the United Nations in accordance with the provisions of Article 63.

2. Such agencies thus brought into relationship with the United Nations are hereinafter referred to as specialized agencies.

Article 58

The Organization shall make recommendations for the co-ordination of the policies and activities of the specialized agencies.

Article 59

The Organization shall, where appropriate, initiate negotiations among the states concerned for the creation of any new specialized agencies required for the accomplishment of the purposes set forth in Article 55.

Article 60

Responsibility for the discharge of the functions of the Organization set forth in this Chapter shall be vested in the General Assembly and, under the authority of the General Assembly, in the Economic and Social Council, which shall have for this purpose the powers set forth in Chapter X.

Chapter X
THE ECONOMIC AND SOCIAL COUNCIL

Composition

Article 61

1. The Economic and Social Council shall consist of fifty-four Members of the United Nations elected by the General Assembly.

2. Subject to the provisions of paragraph 3, eighteen members of the Economic and Social Council shall be elected each year for a term of three years. A retiring member shall be eligible for immediate re-election.

3. At the first election after the increase in the membership of the Economic and Social Council from twenty-seven to fifty-four members, in addition to the members elected in place of the nine members whose term of office expires at the end of that year, twenty-seven additional members shall be elected. Of these twenty-seven additional members, the term of office of nine members so elected shall expire at the end of one year, and of nine other members at the end of two years, in accordance with arrangements made by the General Assembly.

4. Each member of the Economic and Social Council shall have one representative.

Functions and Powers

Article 62

1. The Economic and Social Council may make or initiate studies and reports with respect to international economic, social, cultural, educational, health, and related matters and may make recommendations with respect to any such matters to the General Assembly, to the Members of the United Nations, and to the specialized agencies concerned.

2. It may make recommendations for the purpose of promoting respect for, and observance of, human rights and fundamental freedoms for all.

3. It may prepare draft conventions for submission to the General Assembly, with respect to matters falling within its competence.

4. It may call, in accordance with the rules prescribed by the United Nations, international conferences on matters falling within its competence.

Article 63

1. The Economic and Social Council may enter into agreements with any of the agencies referred to in Article 57, defining the terms on which the agency concerned shall be brought into relationship with the United Nations. Such agreements shall be subject to approval by the General Assembly.

2. It may co-ordinate the activities of the specialized agencies through consultation with and recommendations to such agencies and through recommendations to the General Assembly and to the Members of the United Nations.

Article 64

1. The Economic and Social Council may take appropriate steps to obtain regular reports from the specialized agencies. It may make arrangements with the Members of the United Nations and with the specialized agencies to obtain reports on the steps taken to give effect to its own recommendations and to recommendations on matters falling within its competence made by the General Assembly.

2. It may communicate its observations on these reports to the General Assembly.

Article 65

The Economic and Social Council may furnish information to the Security Council and shall assist the Security Council upon its request.

Article 66

1. The Economic and Social Council shall perform such functions as fall within its competence in connexion with the carrying out of the recommendations of the General Assembly.

2. It may, with the approval of the General Assembly, perform services at the request of Members of the United Nations and at the request of specialized agencies.

3. It shall perform such other functions as are specified elsewhere in the present Charter or as may be assigned to it by the General Assembly.

Voting

Article 67

1. Each member of the Economic and Social Council shall have one vote.
2. Decisions of the Economic and Social Council shall be made by a majority of the members present and voting.

Procedure

Article 68

The Economic and Social Council shall set up commissions in economic and social fields and for the promotion of human rights, and such other commissions as may be required for the performance of its functions.

Article 69

The Economic and Social Council shall invite any Member of the United Nations to participate, without vote, in its deliberations on any matter of particular concern to that Member.

Article 70

The Economic and Social Council may make arrangements for representatives of the specialized agencies to participate, without vote, in its deliberations and in those of the commissions established by it, and for its representatives to participate in the deliberations of the specialized agencies.

Article 71

The Economic and Social Council may make suitable arrangements for consultation with non-governmental organizations which are concerned with matters within its competence. Such arrangements may be made with international organizations and, where appropriate, with national organizations after consultation with the Member of the United Nations concerned.

Article 72

1. The Economic and Social Council shall adopt its own rules of procedure, including the method of selecting its President.
2. The Economic and Social Council shall meet as required in accordance with its rules, which shall include provision for the convening of meetings on the request of a majority of its members.

Chapter XI

DECLARATION REGARDING NON-SELF-GOVERNING
TERRITORIES

Article 73

Members of the United Nations which have or assume responsibilities for the administration of territories whose peoples have not yet attained a full measure of self-government recognize the principle that the interests of the inhabitants of these territories are paramount, and accept as a sacred trust the obligation to promote to the utmost, within the system of international peace and security established by the present Charter, the well-being of the inhabitants of these territories, and, to this end:

a. to ensure, with due respect for the culture of the peoples concerned, their political, economic, social and educational advancement, their just treatment, and their protection against abuses;

b. to develop self-government, to take due account of the political aspirations of the peoples, and to assist them in the progressive development of their free political institutions, according to the particular circumstances of each territory and its peoples and their varying stages of advancement;

c. to further international peace and security;

d. to promote constructive measures of development, to encourage research, and to co-operate with one another and, when and where appropriate, with specialized international bodies with a view to the practical achievement of the social, economic, and scientific purposes set forth in this Article; and

e. to transmit regularly to the Secretary-General for information purposes, subject to such limitation as security and constitutional considerations may require, statistical and other information of a technical nature relating to economic, social, and educational conditions in the territories for which they are respectively responsible other than those territories to which Chapters XII and XIII apply.

Article 74

Members of the United Nations also agree that their policy in respect of the territories to which this Chapter applies, no less than in respect of their metropolitan areas, must be based on the general principle of good-neighbourliness, due account being taken of the interests and well-being of the rest of the world, in social, economic, and commercial matters.

Chapter XII

INTERNATIONAL TRUSTEESHIP SYSTEM

Article 75

The United Nations shall establish under its authority an international trusteeship system for the administration and supervision of such territories as may be placed thereunder by subsequent individual agreements. These territories are hereinafter referred to as trust territories.

Article 76

The basic objectives of the trusteeship system, in accordance with the Purposes of the United Nations laid down in Article 1 of the present Charter, shall be:

a. to further international peace and security;

b. to promote the political, economic, social, and educational advancement of the inhabitants of the trust territories, and their progressive development towards self-government or independence as may be appropriate to the particular circumstances of each territory and its peoples and the freely expressed wishes of the peoples concerned, and as may be provided by the terms of each trusteeship agreement;

c. to encourage respect for human rights and for fundamental freedoms for all without distinction as to race, sex, language, or religion, and to encourage recognition of the interdependence of the peoples of the world; and

d. to ensure equal treatment in social, economic, and commercial matters for all members of the United Nations and their nationals, and also equal treatment for the latter in the administration of justice, without prejudice to the attainment of the foregoing objectives and subject to the provisions of Article 80.

Article 77

1. The trusteeship system shall apply to such territories in the following categories as may be placed hereunder by means of trusteeship agreements:

a. territories now held under mandate;

b. territories which may be detached from enemy states as a result of the Second World War; and

c. territories voluntarily placed under the system by states responsible for their administration.

2. It will be a matter for subsequent agreement as to which territories in the foregoing categories will be brought under the trusteeship system and upon what terms.

Article 78

The trusteeship system shall not apply to territories which have become Members of the United Nations, relationship among which shall be based on respect for the principle of sovereign equality.

Article 79

The terms of trusteeship for each territory to be placed under the trusteeship system, including any alteration or amendment, shall be agreed upon by the states directly concerned, including the mandatory power in the case of territories held under mandate by a Member of the United Nations, and shall be approved as provided for in Articles 83 and 85.

Article 80

1. Except as may be agreed upon in individual trusteeship agreements, made under Articles 77, 79, and 81, placing each territory under the trusteeship system, and until such agreements have been concluded, nothing in this Chapter shall be construed in or of itself to alter in any manner the rights whatsoever of any states or any peoples or the terms of existing international instruments to which Members of the United Nations may respectively be parties.

2. Paragraph 1 of this Article shall not be interpreted as giving grounds for delay or postponement of the negotiation and conclusion of agreements for placing mandated and other territories under the trusteeship system as provided for in Article 77.

Article 81

The trusteeship agreement shall in each case include the terms under which the trust territory will be administered and designate the authority which will exercise the administration of the trust territory. Such authority, hereinafter called the administring authority, may be one or more states of the Organization itself.

Article 82

There may be designated, in any trusteeship agreement, a strategic area or areas which may include part or all of the trust territory to which the agreement applies, without prejudice to any special agreement or agreements made under Article 43.

Article 83

1. All functions of the United Nations relating to strategic areas, including the approval of the terms of the trusteeship agreements and of their alteration or amendment, shall be exercised by the Security Council.

2. The basic objectives set forth in Article 76 shall be applicable to the people of each strategic area.

3. The Security Council shall, subject to the provision of the trusteeship agreements and without prejudice to security considerations, avail itself of the assistance of the Trusteeship Council to perform those functions of the United Nations under the trusteeship system relating to political, economic, social, and educational matters in the strategic areas.

Article 84

It shall be the duty of the administering authority to ensure that the trust territory shall play its part in the maintenance of international peace and security. To this end the administering authority may make use of volunteer forces, facilities, and assistance from the trust territory in carrying out the obligations towards the Security Council undertaken in this regard by the administering authority, as well as for local defence and the maintenance of law and order within the trust territory.

Article 85

1. The functions of the United Nations with regard to trusteeship agreements for all areas not designated as strategic, including the approval of the terms of the trusteeship agreements and of their alteration or amendment, shall be exercised by the General Assembly.

2. The Trusteeship Council, operating under the authority of the General Assembly, shall assist the General Assembly in carrying out these functions.

Chapter XIII
THE TRUSTEESHIP COUNCIL

Composition

Article 86

1. The Trusteeship Council shall consist of the following Members of the United Nations:

a. those Members administering trust territories;

b. such of those Members mentioned by name in Article 23 as are not administering trust territories; and

c. as many other Members elected for three-year terms by the General Assembly as may be necessary to ensure that the total number of members of the Trusteeship Council is equally divided between those Members of the United Nations which administer trust territories and those which do not.

2. Each member of the Trusteeship Council shall designate one specially qualified person to represent it therein.

Functions and Powers

Article 87

The General Assembly and, under its authority, the Trusteeship Council, in carrying out their functions, may:

a. consider reports submitted by the administering authority;

b. accept petitions and examine them in consultation with the administering authority;

c. provide for periodic visits to the respective trust territories at times agreed upon with the administering authority; and

d. take these and other actions in conformity with the terms of the trusteeship agreements.

Article 88

The Trusteeship Council shall formulate a questionnaire on the political, economic, social, and educational advancement of the inhabitants of each trust territory, and the administering authority for each trust territory within the competence of the General Assembly shall make an annual report to the General Assembly upon the basis of such questionnaire.

Voting

Article 89

1. Each member of the Trusteeship Council shall have one vote.

2. Decisions of the Trusteeship Council shall be made by a majority of the members present and voting.

Procedure

Article 90

1. The Trusteeship Council shall adopt its own rules of procedure, including the method of selecting its President.

2. The Trusteeship Council shall meet as required in accordance with its rules, which shall include provision for the convening of meetings on the request of a majority of its members.

Article 91

The Trusteeship Council shall, when appropriate, avail itself of the assistance of the Economic and Social Council and of the specialized agencies in regard to matters with which they are respectively concerned.

Chapter XIV
THE INTERNATIONAL COURT OF JUSTICE

Article 92

The International Court of Justice shall be the principal judicial organ of the United Nations. It shall function in accordance with the annexed Statute, which is based upon the Statute of the Permanent Court of International Justice and forms an integral part of the present Charter.

Article 93

1. All Members of the United Nations are *ipso facto* parties to the Statute of the International Court of Justice.

2. A state which is not a Member of the United Nations may become a party to the Statute of the International Court of Justice on conditions to be determined in each case by the General Assembly upon the recommendation of the Security Council.

Article 94

1. Each Member of the United Nations undertakes to comply with the decision of the International Court of Justice in any case to which it is a party.

2. If any party to a case fails to perform the obligations incumbent upon it under a judgment rendered by the Court, the other party may have recourse to the Security Council, which may, if it deems necessary, make recommendations or decide upon measures to be taken to give effect to the judgment.

Article 95

Nothing in the present Charter shall prevent Members of the United Nations from entrusting the solution of their differences to other tribunals by virtue of agreements already in existence or which may be concluded in the future.

Article 96

1. The General Assembly or the Security Council may request the International Court of Justice to give an advisory opinion on any legal question.

2. Other organs of the United Nations and specialized agencies, which may at any time be so authorized by the General Assembly, may also request advisory opinions of the Court on legal questions arising within the scope of their activities.

Chapter XV
THE SECRETARIAT

Article 97

The Secretariat shall comprise a Secretary-General and such staff as the Organization may require. The Secretary-General shall be appointed by the General Assembly upon the recommendation of the Security Council. He shall be the chief administrative officer of the Organization.

Article 98

The Secretary-General shall act in that capacity in all meetings of the General Assembly, of the Security Council, of the Economic and Social Council, and of the Trusteeship Council, and shall perform such other functions as are entrusted to him by these organs. The Secretary-General shall make an annual report to the General Assembly on the work of the Organization.

Article 99

The Secretary-General may bring to the attention of the Security Council any matter which in his opinion may threaten the maintenance of international peace and security.

Article 100

1. In the performance of their duties the Secretary-General and the staff shall not seek or receive instructions from any government or from any other authority external to the Organization. They shall refrain from any action which might reflect on their position as international officials responsible only to the Organization.

2. Each Member of the United Nations undertakes to respect the exclusively international character of the responsibilities of the Secretary-General and the staff and not to seek to influence them in the discharge of their responsibilities.

Article 101

1. The staff shall be appointed by the Secretary-General under regulations established by the General Assembly.

2. Appropriate staffs shall be permanently assigned to the Economic and Social Council, the Trusteeship Council, and, as required, to other organs of the United Nations. These staffs shall form a part of the Secretariat.

3. The paramount consideration in the employment of the staff and in the determination of the conditions of service shall be the necessity of securing the highest standards of efficiency, competence, and integrity. Due regard shall be paid to the importance of recruiting the staff on as wide a geographical basis as possible.

Chapter XVI

MISCELLANEOUS PROVISIONS

Article 102

1. Every treaty and every international agreement entered into by any Member of the United Nations after the present Charter comes into force shall as soon as possible be registered with the Secretariat and published by it.

2. No party to any such treaty or international agreement which has not been registered in accordance with the provisions of paragraph 1 of this Article may invoke that treaty or agreement before any organ of the United Nations.

Article 103

In the event of a conflict between the obligations of the Members of the United Nations under the present Charter and their obligations under any other international agreement, their obligations under the present Charter shall prevail.

Article 104

The Organization shall enjoy in the territory of each of its Members such legal capacity as may be necessary for the exercise of its functions and the fulfilment of its purposes.

Article 105

1. The Organization shall enjoy in the territory of each of its Members such privileges and immunities as are necessary for the fulfilment of its purposes.

2. Representatives of the Members of the United Nations and officials of the Organization shall similarly enjoy such privileges and immunities as are necessary for the independent exercise of their functions in connexion with the Organization.

3. The General Assembly may make recommendations with a view to determining the details of the application of paragraphs 1 and 2 of this Article or may propose conventions to the Members of the United Nations for this purpose.

Chapter XVII

TRANSITIONAL SECURITY ARRANGEMENTS

Article 106

Pending the coming into force of such special agreements referred to in Article 43 as in the opinion of the Security Council enable it to begin the exercise of its responsibilities under Article 42, the parties to the Four-Nation Declaration, signed at Moscow, 30 October 1943, and France, shall, in accordance with the provisions of paragraph 5 of that Declaration, consult with one another and as occasion requires with other Members of the United Nations with a view to such joint action on behalf of the Organization as may be necessary for the purpose of maintaining international peace and security.

Article 107

Nothing in the present Charter shall invalidate or preclude action, in relation to any state which during the Second World War has been an enemy of any signatory to the present Charter, taken or authorized as a result of that war by the Governments having responsibility for such action.

Chapter XVIII

AMENDMENTS

Article 108

Amendments to the present Charter shall come into force for all Members of the United Nations when they have been adopted by a vote of two thirds of the members of the General Assembly and ratified in accordance with their respective constitutional processes by two thirds of the Members of the United Nations, including all the permanent members of the Security Council.

Article 109

1. A General Conference of the Members of the United Nations for the purpose of reviewing the present Charter may be held at a date and place to be fixed by a two-thirds vote of the members of the General Assembly and by a vote of any nine members of the Security Council. Each Member of the United Nations shall have one vote in the conference.

2. Any alteration of the present Charter recommended by a two-thirds vote of the conference shall take effect when ratified in accordance with their respective constitutional processes by two thirds of the Members of the United Nations including all the permanent members of the Security Council.

3. If such a conference has not been held before the tenth annual session of the General Assembly following the coming into force of the present Charter, the proposal to call such a conference shall be placed on the agenda of that session of the General Assembly, and the conference shall be held if so decided by a majority vote of the members of the General Assembly and by a vote of any seven members of the Security Council.

Chapter XIX

RATIFICATION AND SIGNATURE

Article 110

1. The present Charter shall be ratified by the signatory states in accordance with their respective constitutional processes.

2. The ratifications shall be deposited with the Government of the United States of America, which shall notify all the signatory states of each deposit as well as the Secretary-General of the Organization when he has been appointed.

3. The present Charter shall come into force upon the deposit of ratifications by the Republic of China, France, the Union of Soviet Socialist Republics, the United Kingdom of Great Britain and Northern Ireland, and the United States of America, and by a majority of the other signatory states. A protocol of the ratifications deposited shall thereupon be drawn up by the Government of the United States of America which shall communicate copies thereof to all the signatory states.

4. The states signatory to the present Charter which ratify it after it has come into force will become original Members of the United Nations on the date of the deposit of their respective ratifications.

Article 111

The present Charter, of which the Chinese, French, Russian, English, and Spanish texts are equally authentic, shall remain deposited in the archives of the

Government of the United States of America. Duly certified copies thereof shall be transmitted by that Government to the Governments of the other signatory states.

IN FAITH WHEREOF the representatives of the Governments of the United Nations have signed the present Charter.

DONE at the city of San Francisco the twenty-sixth day of June, one thousand nine hundred and forty-five.

Statute of the International Court of Justice

Article 1
The International Court of Justice established by the Charter of the United Nations as the principal judicial organ of the United Nations shall be constituted and shall function in accordance with the provisions of the present Statute.

Chapter I
ORGANIZATION OF THE COURT

Article 2
The Court shall be composed of a body of independent judges, elected regardless of their nationality from among persons of high moral character, who possess the qualifications required in their respective countries for appointment to the highest judicial offices, or are jurisconsults of recognized competence in international law.

Article 3
1. The Court shall consist of fifteen members, no two of whom may be nationals of the same state.

2. A person who for the purposes of membership in the Court could be regarded as a national of more than one state shall be deemed to be a national of the one in which he ordinarily exercises civil and political rights.

Article 4
1. The members of the Court shall be elected by the General Assembly and by the Security Council from a list of persons nominated by the national groups in the Permanent Court of Arbitration, in accordance with the following provisions.

2. In the case of Members of the United Nations not represented in the Permanent Court of Arbitration, candidates shall be nominated by national groups appointed for this purpose by their governments under the same conditions as those prescribed for members of the Permanent Court of Arbitration by Article

44 of the Convention of The Hague of 1907 for the pacific settlement of international disputes.

3. The conditions under which a state which is a party to the present Statute but is not a Member of the United Nations may participate in electing the members of the Court shall, in the absence of a special agreement, be laid down by the General Assembly upon recommendation of the Security Council.

Article 5

1. At least three months before the date of the election, the Secretary-General of the United Nations shall address a written request to the members of the Permanent Court of Arbitration belonging to the states which are parties to the present Statute, and to the members of the national groups appointed under Article 4, paragraph 2, inviting them to undertake, within a given time, by national groups, the nomination of persons in a position to accept the duties of a member of the Court.

2. No group may nominate more than four persons, not more than two of whom shall be of their own nationality. In no case may the number of candidates nominated by a group be more than double the number of seats to be filled.

Article 6

Before making these nominations, each national group is recommended to consult its highest court of justice, its legal faculties and schools of law, and its national academies and national sections of international academies devoted to the study of law.

Article 7

1. The Secretary-General shall prepare a list in alphabetical order of all the persons thus nominated. Save as provided in Article 12, paragraph 2, these shall be the only persons eligible.

2. The Secretary-General shall submit this list to the General Assembly and to the Security Council.

Article 8

The General Assembly and the Security Council shall proceed independently of one another to elect the members of the Court.

Article 9

At every election, the electors shall bear in mind not only that the persons to be elected should individually possess the qualifications required, but also that in the body as a whole the representation of the main forms of civilization and of the principal legal systems of the world should be assured.

Article 10

1. Those candidates who obtain an absolute majority of votes in the General Assembly and in the Security Council shall be considered as elected.

2. Any vote of the Security Council, whether for the election of judges or for the appointment of members of the conference envisaged in Article 12, shall

be taken without any distinction between permanent and non-permanent members of the Security Council.

3. In the event of more than one national of the same state obtaining an absolute majority of the votes both of the General Assembly and of the Security Council, the eldest of these only shall be considered as elected.

Article 11

If, after the first meeting held for the purpose of the election, one or more seats remain to be filled, a second and, if necessary, a third meeting shall take place.

Article 12

1. If, after the third meeting, one or more seats still remain unfilled, a joint conference consisting of six members, three appointed by the General Assembly and three by the Security Council, may be formed at any time at the request of either the General Assembly or the Security Council, for the purpose of choosing by the vote of an absolute majority one name for each seat still vacant, to submit to the General Assembly and the Security Council for their respective acceptance.

2. If the joint conference is unanimously agreed upon any person who fulfils the required conditions, he may be included in its list, even though he was not included in the list of nominations referred to in Article 7.

3. If the joint conference is satisfied that it will not be successful in procuring an election, those members of the Court who have already been elected shall, within a period to be fixed by the Security Council, proceed to fill the vacant seats by selection from among those candidates who have obtained votes either in the General Assembly or in the Security Council.

4. In the event of an equality of votes among the judges, the eldest judge shall have a casting vote.

Article 13

1. The members of the Court shall be elected for nine years and may be reelected; provided, however, that of the judges elected at the first election, the terms of five judges shall expire at the end of three years and the terms of five more judges shall expire at the end of six years.

2. The judges whose terms are to expire at the end of the above-mentioned initial periods of three and six years shall be chosen by lot to be drawn by the Secretary-General immediately after the first election has been completed.

3. The members of the Court shall continue to discharge their duties until their places have been filled. Though replaced, they shall finish any cases which they may have begun.

4. In the case of the resignation of a member of the Court, the resignation shall be addressed to the President of the Court for transmission to the Secretary-General. This last notification makes the place vacant.

Article 14

Vacancies shall be filled by the same method as that laid down for the first election, subject to the following provision: the Secretary-General shall, within one month of the occurrence of the vacancy, proceed to issue the invitations provided for in Article 5, and the date of the election shall be fixed by the Security Council.

Article 15

A member of the Court elected to replace a member whose term of office has not expired shall hold office for the remainder of his predecessor's term.

Article 16

1. No member of the Court may exercise any political or administrative function, or engage in any other occupation of a professional nature.

2. Any doubt on this point shall be settled by the decision of the Court.

Article 17

1. No member of the Court may act as agent, counsel, or advocate in any case.

2. No member may participate in the decision of any case in which he has previously taken part as agent, counsel, or advocate for one of the parties, or as a member of a national or international court, or of a commission of enquiry, or in any other capacity.

3. Any doubt on this point shall be settled by the decision of the Court.

Article 18

1. No member of the Court can be dismissed unless, in the unanimous opinion of the other members, he has ceased to fulfil the required conditions.

2. Formal notification thereof shall be made to the Secretary-General by the Registrar.

3. This notification makes the place vacant.

Article 19

The members of the Court, when engaged on the business of the Court, shall enjoy diplomatic privileges and immunities.

Article 20

Every member of the Court shall, before taking up his duties, make a solemn declaration in open court that he will exercise his powers impartially and conscientiously.

Article 21

1. The Court shall elect its President and Vice-President for three years; they may be re-elected.

2. The Court shall appoint its Registrar and may provide for the appointment of such other officers as may be necessary.

Article 22

1. The seat of the Court shall be established at The Hague. This, however, shall not prevent the Court from sitting and exercising its functions elsewhere whenever the Court considers it desirable.

2. The President and the Registrar shall reside at the seat of the Court.

Article 23

1. The Court shall remain permanently in session, except during the judicial vacations, the dates and duration of which shall be fixed by the Court.

2. Members of the Court are entitled to periodic leave, the dates and duration of which shall be fixed by the Court, having in mind the distance between The Hague and the home of each judge.

3. Members of the Court shall be bound, unless they are on leave or prevented from attending by illness or other serious reasons duly explained to the President, to hold themselves permanently at the disposal of the Court.

Article 24

1. If, for some special reason, a member of the Court considers that he should not take part in the decision of a particular case, he shall so inform the President.

2. If the President considers that for some special reason one of the members of the Court should not sit in a particular case, he shall give him notice accordingly.

3. If in any such case the member of the Court and the President disagree, the matter shall be settled by the decision of the Court.

Article 25

1. The full Court shall sit except when it is expressly provided otherwise in the present Statute.

2. Subject to the condition that the number of judges available to constitute the Court is not thereby reduced below eleven, the Rules of the Court may provide for allowing one or more judges, according to circumstances and in rotation, to be dispensed from sitting.

3. A quorum of nine judges shall suffice to constitute the Court.

Article 26

1. The Court may from time to time form one or more chambers, composed of three or more judges as the Court may determine, for dealing with particular categories of cases; for example, labour cases and cases relating to transit and communications.

2. The Court may at any time form a chamber for dealing with a particular case. The number of judges to constitute such a chamber shall be determined by the Court with the approval of the parties.

3. Cases shall be heard and determined by the chambers provided for in this article if the parties so request.

Article 27

A judgment given by any of the chambers provided for in Articles 26 and 29 shall be considered as rendered by the Court.

Article 28

The chambers provided for in Articles 26 and 29 may, with the consent of the parties, sit and exercise their functions elsewhere than at The Hague.

Article 29

With a view to the speedy dispatch of business, the Court shall form annually a chamber composed of five judges which, at the request of the parties, may hear and determine cases by summary procedure. In addition, two judges shall be selected for the purpose of replacing judges who find it impossible to sit.

Article 30

1. The Court shall frame rules for carrying out its functions. In particular, it shall lay down rules of procedure.

2. The Rules of the Court may provide for assessors to sit with the Court or with any of its chambers, without the right to vote.

Article 31

1. Judges of the nationality of each of the parties shall retain their right to sit in the case before the Court.

2. If the Court includes upon the Bench a judge of the nationality of one of the parties, any other party may choose a person to sit as judge. Such person shall be chosen preferably from among those persons who have been nominated as candidates as provided in Articles 4 and 5.

3. If the Court includes upon the Bench no judge of the nationality of the parties, each of these parties may proceed to choose a judge as provided in paragraph 2 of this Article.

4. The provision of this Article shall apply to the case of Articles 26 and 29. In such cases, the President shall request one or, if necessary, two of the members of the Court forming the chamber to give place to the members of the Court of the nationality of the parties concerned, and, failing such, or if they are unable to be present, to the judges specially chosen by the parties.

5. Should there be several parties in the same interest, they shall, for the purpose of the preceding provisions, be reckoned as one party only. Any doubt upon this point shall be settled by the decision of the Court.

6. Judges chosen as laid down in paragraphs 2, 3 and 4 of this Article shall fulfil the conditions required by Articles 2, 17 (paragraph 2), 20, and 24 of the present Statute. They shall take part in the decision on terms of complete equality with their colleagues.

Article 32

1. Each member of the Court shall receive an annual salary.

2. The President shall receive a special annual allowance.

3. The Vice-President shall receive a special allowance for every day on which he acts as President.

4. The judges chosen under Article 31, other than members of the Court, shall receive compensation for each day on which they exercise their functions.

5. These salaries, allowances, and compensation shall be fixed by the General Assembly. They may not be decreased during the term of office.

6. The salary of the Registrar shall be fixed by the General Assembly on the proposal of the Court.

7. Regulations made by the General Assembly shall fix the conditions under which retirement pensions may be given to members of the Court and to the Registrar, and the conditions under which members of the Court and the Registrar shall have their travelling expenses refunded.

8. The above salaries, allowances, and compensation shall be free of all taxation.

Article 33

The expenses of the Court shall be borne by the United Nations in such a manner as shall be decided by the General Assembly.

Chapter II
COMPETENCE OF THE COURT

Article 34

1. Only states may be parties in cases before the Court.

2. The Court, subject to and in conformity with its Rules, may request of public international organizations information relevant to cases before it, and shall receive such information presented by such organizations on their own initiative.

3. Whenever the construction of the constituent instrument of a public international organization or of an international convention adopted thereunder is in question in a case before the Court, the Registrar shall so notify the public international organization concerned and shall communicate to it copies of all the written proceedings.

Article 35

1. The Court shall be open to the states parties to the present Statute.

2. The conditions under which the Court shall be open to other states shall, subject to the special provisions contained in treaties in force, be laid down by the Security Council, but in no case shall such conditions place the parties in a position of inequality before the Court.

3. When a state which is not a Member of the United Nations is a party to a case, the Court shall fix the amount which that party is to contribute towards the expenses of the Court. This provision shall not apply if such state is bearing a share of the expenses of the Court.

Article 36

1. The jurisdiction of the Court comprises all cases which the parties refer to it and all matters specially provided for in the Charter of the United Nations or in treaties and conventions in force.

2. The states parties to the present Statute may at any time declare that they recognize as compulsory *ipso facto* and without special agreement, in relation to any other state accepting the same obligation, the jurisdiction of the Court in all legal disputes concerning:

a. the interpretation of a treaty;

b. any question of international law;

c. the existence of any fact which, if established, would constitute a breach of an international obligation;

d. the nature or extent of the reparation to be made for the breach of an international obligation.

3. The declarations referred to above may be made unconditionally or on condition of reciprocity on the part of several or certain states, or for a certain time.

4. Such declarations shall be deposited with the Secretary-General of the United Nations, who shall transmit copies thereof to the parties to the Statute and to the Registrar of the Court.

5. Declarations made under Article 36 of the Statute of the Permanent Court of International Justice and which are still in force shall be deemed, as between the parties to the present Statute, to be acceptances of the compulsory jurisdiction of the International Court of Justice for the period which they still have to run and in accordance with their terms.

6. In the event of a dispute as to whether the Court has jurisdiction, the matter shall be settled by the decision of the Court.

Article 37

Whenever a treaty or convention in force provides for reference of a matter to a tribunal to have been instituted by the League of Nations, or to the Permanent Court of International Justice, the matter shall, as between the parties to the present Statute, be referred to the International Court of Justice.

Article 38

1. The Court, whose function is to decide in accordance with international law such disputes as are submitted to it, shall apply:

a. international conventions, whether general or particular, establishing rules expressly recognized by the contesting states;

b. international custom, as evidence of a general practice accepted as law;

c. the general principles of law recognized by civilized nations;

d. subject to the provisions of Article 59, judicial decisions and the teachings of the most highly qualified publicists of the various nations, as subsidiary means for the determination of rules of law.

2. This provision shall not prejudice the power of the Court to decide a case *ex aequo et bono*, if the parties agree thereto.

Chapter III

PROCEDURE

Article 39

1. The official languages of the Court shall be French and English. If the parties agree that the case shall be conducted in French, the judgment shall be de-

livered in French. If the parties agree that the case shall be conducted in English, the judgment shall be delivered in English.

2. In the absence of an agreement as to which language shall be employed, each party may, in the pleadings, use the language which it prefers; the decision of the Court shall be given in French and English. In this case the Court shall at the same time determine which of the two texts shall be considered as authoritative.

3. The Court shall, at the request of any party, authorize a language other than French or English to be used by that party.

Article 40

1. Cases are brought before the Court, as the case may be, either by the notification of the special agreement or by a written application addressed to the Registrar. In either case the subject of the dispute and the parties shall be indicated.

2. The Registrar shall forthwith communicate the application to all concerned.

3. He shall also notify the Members of the United Nations through the Secretary-General, and also any other states entitled to appear before the Court.

Article 41

1. The Court shall have the power to indicate, if it considers that circumstances so require, any provisional measures which ought to be taken to preserve the respective rights of either party.

2. Pending the final decision, notice of the measures suggested shall forthwith be given to the parties and to the Security Council.

Article 42

1. The parties shall be represented by agents.

2. They may have the assistance of counsel or advocates before the Court.

3. The agents, counsel, and advocates of parties before the Court shall enjoy the privileges and immunities necessary to the independent exercise of their duties.

Article 43

1. The procedure shall consist of two parts: written and oral.

2. The written proceedings shall consist of the communication to the Court and to the parties of memorials, counter-memorials and, if necessary, replies; also all papers and documents in support.

3. These communications shall be made through the Registrar, in the order and within the time fixed by the Court.

4. A certified copy of every document produced by one party shall be communicated to the other party.

5. The oral proceedings shall consist of the hearing by the Court of witnesses, experts, agents, counsel, and advocates.

Article 44

1. For the service of all notices upon persons other than the agents, counsel, and advocates, the Court shall apply direct to the government of the state upon whose territory the notice has to be served.

2. The same provision shall apply whenever steps are to be taken to procure evidence on the spot.

Article 45

The hearing shall be under the control of the President or, if he is unable to preside, of the Vice-President; if neither is able to preside, the senior judge present shall preside.

Article 46

The hearing in Court shall be public, unless the Court shall decide otherwise, or unless the parties demand that the public be not admitted.

Article 47

1. Minutes shall be made at each hearing and signed by the Registrar and the President.

2. These minutes alone shall be authentic.

Article 48

The Court shall make orders for the conduct of the case, shall decide the form and time in which each party must conclude its arguments, and make all arrangements connected with the taking of evidence.

Article 49

The Court may, even before the hearing begins, call upon the agents to produce any document or to supply any explanations. Formal note shall be taken of any refusal.

Article 50

The Court may, at any time, entrust any individual, body, bureau, commission, or other organization that it may select, with the task of carrying out an enquiry or giving an expert opinion.

Article 51

During the hearing any relevant questions are to be put to the witnesses and experts under the conditions laid down by the Court in the rules of procedure referred to in Article 30.

Article 52

After the Court has received the proofs and evidence within the time specified for the purpose, it may refuse to accept any further oral or written evidence that one party may desire to present unless the other side consents.

Article 53

1. Whenever one of the parties does not appear before the Court, or fails to defend its case, the other party may call upon the Court to decide in favour of its claim.

2. The Court must, before doing so, satisfy itself, not only that it has jurisdiction in accordance with Articles 36 and 37, but also that the claim is well founded in fact and law.

Article 54

1. When, subject to the control of the Court, the agents, counsel, and advo-

cates have completed their presentation of the case, the President shall declare the hearing closed.

2. The Court shall withdraw to consider the judgment.

3. The deliberations of the Court shall take place in private and remain secret.

Article 55

1. All questions shall be decided by a majority of the judges present.

2. In the event of an equality of votes, the President or the judge who acts in his place shall have a casting vote.

Article 56

1. The judgment shall state the reasons on which it is based.

2. It shall contain the names of the judges who have taken part in the decision.

Article 57

If the judgment does not represent in whole or in part the unanimous opinion of the judges, any judge shall be entitled to deliver a separate opinion.

Article 58

The judgment shall be signed by the President and by the Registrar. It shall be read in open court, due notice having been given to the agents.

Article 59

The decision of the Court has no binding force except between the parties and in respect of that particular case.

Article 60

The judgment is final and without appeal. In the event of dispute as to the meaning or scope of the judgment, the Court shall construe it upon the request of any party.

Article 61

1. An application for revision of a judgment may be made only when it is based upon the discovery of some fact of such a nature as to be a decisive factor, which fact was, when the judgment was given, unknown to the Court and also to the party claiming revision, always provided that such ignorance was not due to negligence.

2. The proceedings for revision shall be opened by a judgment of the Court expressly recording the existence of the new fact, recognizing that it has such a character as to lay the case open to revision, and declaring the application admissible on this ground.

3. The Court may require previous compliance with the terms of the judgment before it admits proceedings in revision.

4. The application for revision must be made at latest within six months of the discovery of the new fact.

5. No application for revision may be made after the lapse of ten years from the date of the judgment.

Article 62

1. Should a state consider that it has an interest of a legal nature which may
be affected by the decision in the case, it may submit a request to the Court to be
permitted to intervene.

2. It shall be for the Court to decide upon this request.

Article 63

1. Whenever the construction of a convention to which states other than
those concerned in the case are parties is in question, the Registrar shall notify all
such states forthwith.

2. Every state so notified has the right to intervene in the proceedings; but
if it uses this right, the construction given by the judgment will be equally binding upon it.

Article 64

Unless otherwise decided by the Court, each party shall bear its own costs.

Chapter IV

ADVISORY OPINIONS

Article 65

1. The Court may give an advisory opinion on any legal question at the request of whatever body may be authorized by or in accordance with the Charter
of the United Nations to make such a request.

2. Questions upon which the advisory opinion of the Court is asked shall be
laid before the Court by means of a written request containing an exact statement
of the question upon which an opinion is required, and accompanied by all documents likely to throw light upon the question.

Article 66

1. The Registrar shall forthwith give notice of the request for an advisory
opinion to all states entitled to appear before the Court.

2. The Registrar shall also, by means of a special and direct communication,
notify any state entitled to appear before the Court or international organization
considered by the Court, or, should it not be sitting, by the President, as likely
to be able to furnish information on the question, that the Court will be prepared
to receive, within a time limit to be fixed by the President, written statements, or
to hear, at a public sitting to be held for the purpose, oral statements relating to
the question.

3. Should any such state entitled to appear before the Court have failed to
receive the special communication referred to in paragraph 2 of this Article, such
state may express a desire to submit a written statement or to be heard; and the
Court will decide.

4. States and organizations having presented written or oral statements or
both shall be permitted to comment on the statements made by other states or or-

ganizations in the form, to the extent, and within the time limits which the Court, or, should it not be sitting, the President, shall decide in each particular case. Accordingly, the Registrar shall in due time communicate any such written statements to states and organizations having submitted similar statements.

Article 67

The Court shall deliver its advisory opinions in open court, notice having been given to the Secretary-General and to the representatives of Members of the United Nations, of other states and of international organizations immediately concerned.

Article 68

In the exercise of its advisory functions the Court shall further be guided by the provisions of the present Statute which apply in contentious cases to the extent to which it recognizes them to be applicable.

Chapter V

AMENDMENT

Article 69

Amendments to the present Statute shall be effected by the same procedure as is provided by the Charter of the United Nations for amendments to that Charter, subject however to any provisions which the General Assembly upon recommendation of the Security Council may adopt concerning the participation of states which are parties to the present Statute but are not Members of the United Nations.

Article 70

The Court shall have power to propose such amendments to the present Statute as it may deem necessary, through written communications to the Secretary-General, for consideration in conformity with the provisions of Article 69.

Index*

*n signifies Notes.